W9-AAN-168

Learning PHP Design Patterns

William Sanders

O'REILLY®

Beijing · Cambridge · Farnham · Köln · Sebastopol · Tokyo

Learning PHP Design Patterns

by William Sanders

Copyright © 2013 William B. Sanders. All rights reserved.

Printed in the United States of America.

Published by O'Reilly Media, Inc., 1005 Gravenstein Highway North, Sebastopol, CA 95472.

O'Reilly books may be purchased for educational, business, or sales promotional use. Online editions are also available for most titles (*http://my.safaribooksonline.com*). For more information, contact our corporate/institutional sales department: 800-998-9938 or *corporate@oreilly.com*.

Editors: Maria Gulick and Rachel Roumeliotis
Production Editor: Melanie Yarbrough
Copyeditor: Jasmine Kwityn

Proofreader: Becca Freed
Indexer: Fred Brown
Cover Designer: Karen Montgomery
Interior Designer: David Futato
Illustrator: Rebecca Demarest

February 2013: First Edition

Revision History for the First Edition:

2013-02-08   First release

See *http://oreilly.com/catalog/errata.csp?isbn=9781449344917* for release details.

Nutshell Handbook, the Nutshell Handbook logo, and the O'Reilly logo are registered trademarks of O'Reilly Media, Inc. *Learning PHP Design Patterns*, the cover image of an Alaska plaice, and related trade dress are trademarks of O'Reilly Media, Inc.

Many of the designations used by manufacturers and sellers to distinguish their products are claimed as trademarks. Where those designations appear in this book, and O'Reilly Media, Inc., was aware of a trademark claim, the designations have been printed in caps or initial caps.

While every precaution has been taken in the preparation of this book, the publisher and author assume no responsibility for errors or omissions, or for damages resulting from the use of the information contained herein.

ISBN: 978-1-449-34491-7

[LSI]

In memory of my father, William B. Sanders (1917–2012).

Table of Contents

Part V.   MySQL and PHP Design Patterns

Preface

As PHP expands to become the server-side program of choice among a significant portion of programmers, professional techniques and programming structures need to be incorporated. *Design patterns*, a concept borrowed from *The Timeless Way of Building* by Christopher Alexander (Oxford University Press), refers to *a general reusable solution to a commonly occurring problem within a given context*. In everyday development work, PHP programmers encounter "commonly occurring problems" in a software development context, and the use of PHP design patterns is a set of solutions to "commonly occurring" PHP programming problems. Pure and simple, PHP design patterns are tools used to deal with the reality of professional software development.

They are not libraries or templates but rather more general structures that can be used to solve problems. I like to think of design patterns in the same way as I do the loop structure. The loop is used when some kind of iteration is required. True, there are other ways to deal with iteration, but a loop is a flexible tool that saves time in the development process. (Besides, it's a lot neater than writing the same line of code 10,000 times!)

Further, I do not feel constrained by design patterns as "canned solutions" any more than a loop is a "canned solution" to iteration. Besides, I can use the loop structure in a variety of ways in PHP ranging from `for` to `while` statements and everything in between. Likewise, design patterns can be implemented in more than one way depending on the exact nature of the problem being solved.

The most important reason for incorporating design patterns, though, is that they provide solutions to complex problems. As one's programs become larger, they almost necessarily become more complex. In an object-oriented programming (OOP) environment, such complexity is reduced somewhat, as you are dealing with encapsulated modules, whereas in sequential or procedural programming, any changes can bring the program crashing down like a house of cards. Design patterns bring not only solutions to general programming problems, but they also allow changes to be made in large complex programs by providing loose coupling between objects. So when a change is made, instead of having to start programming all over from scratch, you can just add the necessary changes and everything keeps chugging along—even in large, complex programs.

Further, design patterns are meant for reuse. After all, programmers reuse the same algorithms all the time. Why not use larger structures as well? On the one hand, frameworks and templates serve to make reuse practical, but they are often too specific. That's where reuse of design-patterned PHP programs comes in, especially in the case of large, complex programs. Because making changes is easy with design patterns, reuse for specific problems of the same kind is easy as well. Reducing developmental time and resources saves money and better serves your clients. They get well-structured programs that do what the clients want, they're easy for the developers to change (customers always want change!), and they have strong foundations that are not as likely to fail.

Audience

At some point, all good programmers realize that they need to get out of a sequential and procedural programming rut. The next logical step is object-oriented programming, and moving into OOP requires a shift in perspective: instead of seeing programming as a series of statements, it must be seen as an interaction and communication between objects. Beyond OOP lie design patterns, where OOP principles are recast into patterns of reusable code. There you will find the tools of professional programmers. Because design patterns for programming were developed in cooperation between academics and businesses, the concepts both transcend single problems while at the same time possessing business-like practicality. Learning PHP design patterns is for professional programmers who want to optimize their own time in development and redevelopment and provide their clients with high-quality code.

In no small measure, this book is for those who felt a certain delight when programming was new to them. This is for the developer who thought nothing of working on a program all night long just because it was interesting, staggering off to bed, only to start on another program as soon as he woke up. When programming is new and every day promises a new discovery or a bug that challenges the developer to a fight to the death, and you must use your mind in complex and exciting ways, the experience can be Zen-like. If you've had that experience, you'll know what I mean. It cannot be spelled out or explained analytically. (I can't even explain it to myself, and I have no idea why I enjoy the kinds of challenges and rewards found in programming.)

Design patterns reintroduce mental challenges, and this book is *not* for someone who is new either to PHP or to programming. If you're learning PHP for the first time, take a look at Robin Nixon's book, *Learning PHP, MySQL, JavaScript, and CSS, 2nd Edition* (O'Reilly) before tackling PHP design patterns. Likewise, this book (or any decent book on design patterns) does not promise that you'll master design patterns quickly and easily. This kind of learning is a journey, and the wisest counsel is to learn to enjoy the journey. It takes time and mental effort.

Assumptions This Book Makes

This book assumes that you know how to program in PHP and want to take your programming skills to the next couple of levels. In fact, it assumes that you're a pretty good PHP programmer and you've used MySQL and know how to develop HTML pages and use CSS. It also assumes that you understand that learning PHP design patterns is not going to happen in a lazy afternoon. Learning design patterns is akin to a gradual metamorphosis.

Contents of This Book

This book is organized into five parts.

Part I is an OOP refresher/introduction:

> Chapter 1 introduces object-oriented programming (OOP) and how to more easily handle complex programming problems with modularization.

> Chapter 2 discusses basic concepts in OOP such as abstraction, encapsulation, inheritance, and polymorphism, as well as the PHP structures that implement these concepts.

> Chapter 3 moves on to examine the basic concepts in design patterns, their categorization, and how specific patterns are selected to handle specific problems.

> Chapter 4 introduces Unified Modeling Language (UML) and explains how it will be employed in this book.

Part II covers creational design patterns:

> Chapter 5 examines the Factory Method, which has a creational purpose and a class scope. Examples include dynamically creating pages that display graphics, body text, and header text.

> Chapter 6 shows how to use the Prototype pattern, which has a creational purpose and an object scope. The Prototype pattern is used when a single object is created as a prototype and then cloned to economically create further instances.

Part III explains structural design patterns:

> Chapter 7 illustrates how to use the Adapter pattern in both class and object scopes. Examples show how to take an existing structure and make changes that allow the developer to add new functionality.

> Chapter 8 explains how an existing object can be changed without disrupting a larger program using the Decorator pattern. You'll see how to decorate male and female dating objects with different preferences in a dating site.

Part IV looks at behavioral design patterns:

Chapter 9 shows how to use the Template Method pattern—one of the easiest design patterns to both create and use. In addition, you will see how the famous Hollywood Principle operates in design pattern programming. As a final feature of the chapter, two different patterns are combined to solve a single problem.

Chapter 10 presents the State design pattern along with how to use statecharts to map state processes and changes.

Part V introduces four more behavioral design patterns used in conjunction with MySQL:

Chapter 11 provides the Universal connection class and the Proxy design pattern for adding security to usernames and passwords stored in a MySQL database.

Chapter 12 explains how the Strategy design pattern is significantly different from the State pattern even though they have identical class diagrams. A survey example illustrates how the Strategy pattern can be used with different MySQL requests.

Chapter 13 has multiple examples of how the Chain of Responsibility pattern can be used, ranging from a Help Desk to automatically responding to a date timer to display (in conjunction with the Factory Method pattern) images and text.

Chapter 14 is the first to explore how to use the PHP built-in design pattern interfaces. The Observer design pattern can use interfaces from the Standard PHP Library. Another example uses the Observer design pattern with hand-built interfaces to make a simple content management system (CMS) with PHP and MySQL.

Conventions Used in This Book

The following typographical conventions are used in this book:

Italic

Indicates new terms, URLs, email addresses, filenames, and file extensions.

`Constant width`

Used for program listings, as well as within paragraphs to refer to program elements such as variable or function names, databases, data types, environment variables, statements, and keywords.

`Constant width bold`

Shows commands or other text that should be typed literally by the user.

`Constant width italic`

Shows text that should be replaced with user-supplied values or by values determined by context.

This icon signifies a tip, suggestion, or general note.

This icon indicates a warning or caution.

Using Code Examples

This book is here to help you get your job done. In general, if this book includes code examples, you may use the code in your programs and documentation. You do not need to contact us for permission unless you're reproducing a significant portion of the code. For example, writing a program that uses several chunks of code from this book does not require permission. Selling or distributing a CD-ROM of examples from O'Reilly books does require permission. Answering a question by citing this book and quoting example code does not require permission. Incorporating a significant amount of example code from this book into your product's documentation does require permission.

We appreciate, but do not require, attribution. An attribution usually includes the title, author, publisher, and ISBN. For example: "*Learning PHP Design Patterns* by William Sanders (O'Reilly). Copyright 2013 William B. Sanders, 978-1-449-34491-7."

If you feel your use of code examples falls outside fair use or the permission given above, feel free to contact us at *permissions@oreilly.com*.

Safari® Books Online

Safari Books Online (*www.safaribooksonline.com*) is an on-demand digital library that delivers expert content in both book and video form from the world's leading authors in technology and business.

Technology professionals, software developers, web designers, and business and creative professionals use Safari Books Online as their primary resource for research, problem solving, learning, and certification training.

Safari Books Online offers a range of product mixes and pricing programs for organizations, government agencies, and individuals. Subscribers have access to thousands of books, training videos, and prepublication manuscripts in one fully searchable database from publishers like O'Reilly Media, Prentice Hall Professional, Addison-Wesley Professional, Microsoft Press, Sams, Que, Peachpit Press, Focal Press, Cisco Press, John Wiley & Sons, Syngress, Morgan Kaufmann, IBM Redbooks, Packt, Adobe Press, FT Press, Apress, Manning, New Riders, McGraw-Hill, Jones & Bartlett, Course

Technology, and dozens more. For more information about Safari Books Online, please visit us online.

How to Contact Us

Please address comments and questions concerning this book to the publisher:

O'Reilly Media, Inc.
1005 Gravenstein Highway North
Sebastopol, CA 95472
800-998-9938 (in the United States or Canada)
707-829-0515 (international or local)
707-829-0104 (fax)

We have a web page for this book, where we list errata, examples, and any additional information. You can access this page at *http://oreil.ly/php_design_patterns*.

To comment or ask technical questions about this book, send email to *bookquestions@oreilly.com*.

For more information about our books, courses, conferences, and news, see our website at *http://www.oreilly.com*.

Find us on Facebook: *http://facebook.com/oreilly*

Follow us on Twitter: *http://twitter.com/oreillymedia*

Watch us on YouTube: *http://www.youtube.com/oreillymedia*

Acknowledgments

I want to thank everyone who helped out in one way or another. My colleagues at the University of Hartford's Multimedia Web Design and Development program were always helpful when I posed a query of one type or another. Professor John Gray, the department chair, was encouraging and helpful as always. Dr. Brian Dorn, my office next-door neighbor, who caught the bulk of my queries, was obliging, knowledgeable, and patient.

I was fortunate enough to meet Michael Bourque of the Boston PHP group at the inaugural Northeast PHP Conference, and appreciate his encouragement for this project. I look forward to working with Michael and the Boston PHP group more in exploring advanced PHP programming.

O'Reilly Media provided three capable technical reviewers. Robin Nixon, author of *Learning PHP, MySQL & JavaScript, 2nd Edition* (O'Reilly) offered corrections, suggestions, and several insights into PHP to make the code better in many different ways.

Aaron Saray, author of *Professional PHP Design Patterns* (Wrox) was incredibly detailed and generous in his suggestions. He has a wonderful editor's eye for even the slightest flaw. Aaron and I take very different approaches to design patterns, but such differences provide a wider view for PHP developers interested in design patterns. Finally, Dmitry Sheiko acted as a passionate technical reviewer and has his own blog (*http://bit.ly/UGYah7*) where his take on PHP design patterns can be found.

Senior Editor Rachel Roumeliotis at O'Reilly Media put all of the many parts together and moved the project along. Maria Gulick, another capable O'Reilly editor, took care of the bits and pieces as the project went through revisions. Copyeditor Jasmine Kwityn found and corrected details I did not know existed—in this galaxy or any other. The whole process was initiated by Margot Maley Hutchison at Waterside Productions, and I am grateful to her as ever.

My wife Delia was more understanding than most spouses since she recently had published a book of her own and knew the process. Our Greater Swiss Mountain Dog, WillDe, could care less about writing processes. As long as he got his treats, he'd go along with anything.

PART I

Easing into the Fundamentals of Design Patterns

All compromise is based on give and take, but there can be no give and take on fundamentals. Any compromise on mere fundamentals is a surrender. For it is all give and no take.

—Mahatma Gandhi

People talk fundamentals and superlatives and then make some changes of detail.

—Oliver Wendell Holmes, Jr.

An unfortunate thing about this world is that the good habits are much easier to give up than the bad ones.

—W. Somerset Maugham

Programming Habits

For years after I started programming regularly, I developed certain habits that changed from sequential to procedural programming and just cruised along on a combination of those two for years. This was due in part to the explorations of different languages. My first was Fortran II in college, then on to Basic, FORTH, PostScript, and then into assembly and machine language. I was more interested in learning about different languages than I was in good programming. Then with the Internet came Java, JavaScript, PHP, C#, and ActionScript 3.0, among others. Most of these languages were based (in part) on the kinds of structures found in C++. These were different languages, but I maintained the same old habits.

Quite by accident, I was introduced to *state machines* by Dr. Jonathan Kaye. Instead of thinking in terms of flow of control, he showed me how to think in terms of different states. Following state machines, I discovered the State design pattern and then *Design Patterns: Elements of Reusable Object-Oriented Software* by Erich Gamma, Richard Helm, Ralph Johnson, and John Vlissides (Addison-Wesley). The examples in *Design Patterns* were all written in SmallTalk or C++. Knowing no SmallTalk and very little C++, I was forced to concentrate on the conceptual materials. Oddly, that was one of the best things that could have happened because I was not stuck with examples in any particular language. When it came to PHP, it wasn't a matter of translating from Small-Talk to PHP but applying object-oriented programming (OOP) and design pattern concepts directly to PHP.

Slowly but surely, my programming habits began to change. By adding a little OOP here and there and incorporating a design pattern now and again, in time, I didn't want to program any other way. According to psychologists, a habit is formed over a period of 66 days on average, but in my case, the change took longer and it was more gradual. It was a very busy development period for me, and when the choice was between getting a project done for a customer and using OOP and design patterns, time pressures always won out. However, more and more OOP was creeping in my habitual coding practices, and before I knew it, my customers were getting solid OOP and design pattern-developed applications. The four chapters in this first section are designed to get you started on the OOP path:

- PHP and Object-Oriented Programming
- Basic Concepts in OOP
- Basic Design Pattern Concepts
- Using UMLs with Design Patterns

Focus on Substance, Not Style

Most of the good programmers I know have a certain style that points to professional programming habits. By and large, when you encounter good OOP programming, you'll see a certain way of doing everything from naming variables to commenting code. Variable names are clear, and comments in the code tell the story of the code so that other programmers know how to connect to their own modules. In this book, the comments in the code have been kept to a minimum because that job is done by the book's text. Further, I have often found that putting in too many comments get in the way of clearly seeing the structure of the code. So, with the goal of being able to see and sense objects as complete entities, the code is not fractionalized by long-winded comments.

(In programs not written for books, I subscribe to the idea that substantive commenting is essential.)

For some reason, PHP seems to be plagued by bad examples of design patterns. By bad, I'm not talking about dumb examples. I'm referring to design patterns written with missing parts. For example, a Strategy pattern written without a Context participant is a bad example. It is simply inaccurate. The same is true for any pattern that has missing parts. It's like writing a loop that has no termination condition. The Strategy pattern requires a Context just like a loop structure requires a termination condition.

In order to keep the focus as accurate as possible, I've used the original source of the design patterns discussed in this book: *Design Patterns: Elements of Reusable Object-Oriented Software* (Prentice Hall). Further, the Uniform Modeling Language (UML) is the one used in *Design Patterns*. Newer versions of the UML (UML2) have come along since then, but for learning PHP design patterns, and for understanding ones not discussed in this book, learning to use the original will help if you want to learn additional patterns from the original source.

CHAPTER 1

PHP and Object-Oriented Programming

*All the forces in the world are not so powerful as
an idea whose time has come.*

—Victor Hugo

*Do not pray for tasks equal to your powers. Pray
for powers equal to your tasks.*

—Phillips Brooks

*Immense power is acquired by assuring yourself in
your secret reveries that you were born to
control affairs.*

—Andrew Carnegie

*Ignorance is the curse of God; knowledge is the
wing wherewith we fly to heaven.*

—William Shakespeare

Entering into Intermediate and Advanced Programming

When we first learn to read, the stories, vocabularies, and words tend to be small and
simple. Dealing with small and simple stories requires small and simple tools. However,
when we are more advanced and introduced to the works of William Shakespeare, we
need a more complex, larger, and more sophisticated toolset. If a kindergarten teacher
handed her brood *Hamlet*, chances are the kids wouldn't understand it, but if they are
given an incremental set of reading tools over the years, by the time they reach high
school, they can read, understand, and appreciate *Hamlet*. This book is for developers
who are ready to read the PHP version of *Hamlet*.

To get what you need from this book, you need to begin with an understanding of and
experience with PHP. Other books in this series, *Learning PHP 5* by David Sklar and
Learning PHP, MySQL, and JavaScript, 2nd Edition, by Robin Nixon (O'Reilly) are good

places to start if you have no PHP experience. Of course, you may have learned PHP from any number of other books, courses, or online tutorials. What matters is that you know how to program in PHP. Further, we're going to be dealing with PHP 5 and nothing earlier, like the last version of PHP 4 (PHP 4.4.9). That's because just about everything we need for object-oriented programming (OOP) wasn't implemented until PHP 5.

Why Object-Oriented Programming?

Although OOP has been around for more than 40 years, it was not until the last 15 years or so that it's become more and more important. In large measure, this is due to the influence of Java, which includes built-in OOP structures. Newer languages associated with the Internet, such as JavaScript, ActionScript 3.0, and PHP 5, also have incorporated OOP in style or structure. In 1998, *JavaScript Objects* by Alexander Nakhimovsky and Tom Myers (Wrox), two Colgate University professors, showed that OOP could be incorporated into JavaScript. So OOP is nothing new, even for those whose main programming has been in the realm of Internet languages, and we can even say that it is a "tried and proven" method of programming in most languages designed to give instructions to computers.

Spending some time understanding OOP is important because understanding design patterns relies on understanding OOP. So while you may have substantial experience programming in PHP 5, if you do not have OOP experience, spend some time in Part I.

Making Problem Solving Easier

Computer programs are designed to solve human problems. A process called *dynamic programming* is a technique for breaking down larger problems into smaller ones. The plan is to solve each smaller problem and then put everything back together into a single, larger solution. Take, for example, planning a trip to Timbuktu. (It doesn't sound like a complex problem, but see if you can find a flight from your town to Timbuktu on an online travel site.) Let's break it down:

1. Does Timbuktu (aka Tombouctou or Timbuctu) exist? (Yes./No.) Answer = Yes.

2. Does Timbuktu have an airport? (Yes./No.) Answer = Yes, Airport Identifier = TOM.

3. Are there flights into TOM? (Yes./No.) Answer = Maybe. Flights are available from both Bamako and Mopti, but Islamist rebels took control of Timbuktu as of July 1, 2012, and flights have been canceled until further notice.

4. Are hostile rebels in control of Timbuktu now? (Yes./No.) If answer = Yes, there are no flights. If answer = No, there may be flights.

5. If flights are available, is Timbuktu safe for tourism or business? (Yes./No.) Answer = No.

6. Are visas from my country into Mali (country where Timbuktu is located) available? (Yes./No.) Answer = Yes.

7. Are vaccinations required? (Yes./No.) Answer = Yes.

As you can see, getting to and from Timbuktu is a complex issue, but the list of simple questions can all be answered by *yes* or *no*. Lots more questions would be included in the list, but each can be answered in a binary fashion. The "maybe" answer means that more questions need to be asked to get a yes/no answer.

Modularization

The process of decomposing a problem into small subproblems is the process of *modularization*. Just like the complexities of getting from your home to Timbuktu can be modularized into a set of yes/no steps, any other complex problem also can be modularized. Figure 1-1 illustrates this process.

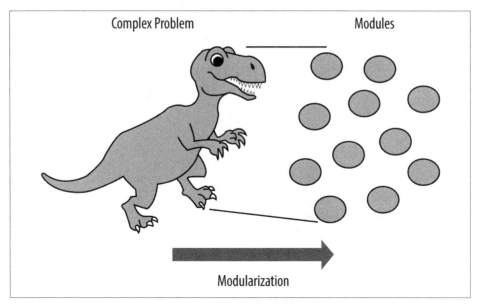

Figure 1-1. Even the most complex problem can be broken into modules

In looking at modularization, you may be thinking that it doesn't look too difficult. You'd be absolutely right. The more complex the problem, the more it makes sense to modularize it. So, the initial reasoning in OOP programming, far from being complex, simplifies the complex. Even the most daunting programming problem can be solved by this divide-and-conquer strategy.

Classes and Objects

Once a problem is modularized, what are you going to do with the modules? As you saw, breaking down a complex problem can transform it into many simple subproblems, but you need a way to organize the modules and work with them in relation to each other to handle the larger problem being solved. One way to look at a module is as a collection of related functions. In programming, these modules are called *classes*.

A class itself is made up of parts called properties and methods. The *properties* are different types of data objects like numbers, strings, nulls, and Booleans. Generally, the data are stored as abstract data types known as variables, constants, and arrays. *Methods*, on the other hand, are functions that operate on the data.

Single Responsibility Principle

One way to think of a class is as a collection of objects with common characteristics. The "commonness" of characteristics does not mean that they are the same, but instead they deal with the common problem assigned to the module—the class. Keeping in mind that the purpose of a module is to solve some aspect of a more complex problem, we arrive at one of the first principles of object-oriented programming: the single responsibility principle, which states that a class should have only a single responsibility.

It's not that a class cannot have multiple responsibilities, but keep in mind that we broke down a complex problem into simple modules so that we'd have several easy-to-solve problems. By limiting a class to a single responsibility, we not only remind ourselves of why we modularized the problem, but we also have an easier way of organizing the modules. Let's look at a class with a single responsibility. Suppose you're making a website for a client, and because the site is to be viewed by different devices ranging from desktops to tablets to smartphones, you want to have some way of determining what type of device and which browser is used to view your web page. With PHP, it's easy to write a class that provides that information using the built-in array $_SERVER and the related element, HTTP_USER_AGENT. The TellAll class in the following listing demonstrates a class with a single responsibility—to provide information about the user agent viewing the PHP page:

```php
<?php
//Saved as TellAll.php

class TellAll
{
    private $userAgent;

    public function __construct()
      {
        $this->userAgent=$_SERVER['HTTP_USER_AGENT'];
        echo $this->userAgent;
      }
```

```
    }

    $tellAll=new TellAll();

    ?>
```

Loading this class through a Safari browser on an iMac displays the following:

```
Mozilla/5.0 (Macintosh; Intel Mac OS X 10_7_4) AppleWebKit/ 534.57.2 (KHTML,
like Gecko) Version/5.1.7 Safari/534.57.2
```

When tested on an iPad using an Opera Mini browser, the results are different:

```
Opera/9.80 (iPad; Opera Mini/7.0.2/28.2051;U;en) Presto/2.8.119 Version/11.10
```

The class represents a module of a more complex operation, of which the class is only a single part. Like a good class in OOP, it has a single responsibility—finding information about the user agent.

Constructor Functions in PHP

A unique feature of PHP classes is the use of the __construct() statement as a *constructor function*. Most computer languages use the name of the class as the constructor function name; however, using the __construct() statement removes all doubt as to the function's purpose.

The constructor function in a class automatically launches as soon as the class is instantiated. In the TellAll class, the results are immediately printed to the screen, whether you want them there or not. For demonstration purposes, that's fine, but as a module, other modules may simply want to use the information about the device and/ or the browser. So, as you will see, not all classes include a constructor function.

The Client as a Requester Class

In the TellAll class, I included a little trigger at the bottom to launch the class. With the exception of the Client class, self-launching is not recommended. In your experience with PHP, you most likely launched a PHP program from HTML using a form tag something like the following:

```
<form action="dataMonster.php" method="post">
```

So, you're familiar with launching a PHP file from an external source. Similarly, PHP files containing classes should be used by other modules (classes) and not self-launched.

As we get more into design patterns, you'll find a class named Client keeps appearing. The Client has different roles in the larger project, but the primary one is to make requests from the classes that make up the design pattern. Here, the Client is shown in relation to a revised version of the TellAll class. This new class used by the Client is different in several ways from TellAll that are more useful to an overall project and reusable in other projects. The MobileSniffer class begins with the same user agent information, but the class makes it available in more useful ways with its properties and methods. Using a Unified Modeling Language (UML) diagram you can see that the Client instantiates (dashed arrow) the MobileSniffer. Figure 1-2 illustrates a simple class diagram of the two classes.

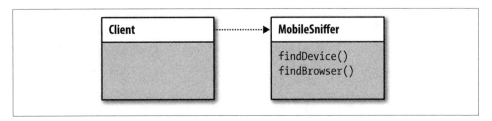

Figure 1-2. Client class instantiates MobileSniffer class and can use its properties and methods

Had a Client class instantiated automatically, the Client would have fewer options for how to use the MobileSniffer information. Take a look at the following listing to see how to create the class:

```php
<?php
//User agent as property of object
class MobileSniffer
{
    private $userAgent;
    private $device;
    private $browser;
    private $deviceLength;
    private $browserLength;

    public function __construct()
      {
        $this->userAgent=$_SERVER['HTTP_USER_AGENT'];
        $this->userAgent=strtolower($this->userAgent);

        $this->device=array('iphone','ipad','android','silk','blackberry',
          'touch');
        $this->browser= array('firefox','chrome','opera','msie','safari',
        'blackberry','trident');
        $this->deviceLength=count($this->device);
        $this->browserLength=count($this->browser);
      }
    public function findDevice()
    {
        for($uaSniff=0;$uaSniff < $this->deviceLength;$uaSniff ++)
        {
            if(strstr($this->userAgent,$this->device[$uaSniff]))
            {
```

```
                return $this->device[$uaSniff];
            }
        }
    }

    public function findBrowser()
    {
        for($uaSniff=0;$uaSniff < $this->browserLength;$uaSniff ++)
        {
            if(strstr($this->userAgent,$this->browser[$uaSniff]))
            {
                return $this->browser[$uaSniff];
            }
        }
    }
}

?>
```

Embedding Error Reporting in the *php.ini* File

I work in a university environment where the system administrators often are students (with varying levels of knowledge and competence), still honing their craft. Often, they'll forget to set the *php.ini* file to report errors. As a result, I got into the habit of adding the following lines to the beginning of my code:

```
ini_set("display_errors","1");
ERROR_REPORTING(E_ALL);
```

For some, such added lines of code are annoying, but I include them in the Client class to provide a reminder of how important error reporting is in developing applications where feedback is essential. Learning OOP and design patterns relies heavily on such feedback.

In order to use the MobileSniffer, the Client instantiates the class and uses its methods as shown in the following listing:

```
<?php
ini_set("display_errors","1");
ERROR_REPORTING(E_ALL);
include_once('MobileSniffer.php');
class Client
{
    private $mobSniff;
    public function __construct()
    {
        $this->mobSniff=new MobileSniffer();
        echo "Device = " . $this->mobSniff->findDevice() . "<br/>";
        echo "Browser = " . $this->mobSniff->findBrowser() . "<br/>";
```

```
    }
}

$trigger=new Client();
?>
```

Using the Client class provides a way to make the MobileSniffer class more useful. The MobileSniffer does not have to launch itself, and using a return statement, any class that calls MobileSniffer just gets the data. The Client can then use that data in any way it wants. In this case, the Client formats the data to output it to the screen, as you can see in Figure 1-3.

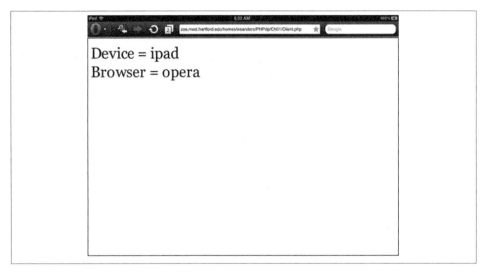

Figure 1-3. The Client uses the MobileSniffer's data to send to the screen

We could have formatted the data in the MobileSniffer class, but then it would not have been as flexible or useful. By allowing the Client to use the data in the most general way, it could do any number of things with it. For example, instead of formatting the data for screen output, it could have used the data to call a CSS file that formats for the particular device and/or browser. Had the data been preformatted in the MobileSniff er class, using it for identifying a CSS file would require stripping away the unneeded formatting. Keep in mind that one of the most important features of design patterns is reuse of the objects.

Capturing Mobile: Nailing Jelly to a Tree

At the time of this writing, the number and type of mobile devices just keeps growing, and any code you write in PHP is bound to let some devices and/or browsers slip through the net. Even capturing the device may not be enough because some (like the iPad and the iPad Mini) have different screen resolutions in addition to different screen sizes. Suffice it to say that if you plan to create web pages for viewing on different devices, you will want a module in your system that can be updated without breaking your program. So, no matter what the latest technique is to detect and respond to multiple devices, be prepared for change. You can plan to start all over from scratch to incorporate new devices, such as Microsoft's Surface, or you can be prepared with a module that can be incorporated into an existing application where changes will not break the system.

At this point, you may be thinking, "I could write a better algorithm for sorting out devices and browsers." You probably could, and in fact, you'll probably have to because as new devices and browsers are introduced, they will have to be incorporated into a program that needs to use device/browser information. However, if you preserve the structure of the two methods, `findDevice()` and `findBrowser()`, you can make all the changes and improvements you want, and the larger program will not crash. You must imagine a much larger and more complex program and think about making changes. If you've ever had to revise a larger program, you know that a change can worm its way through the entire program and break it. Then your debugging becomes a nightmare. One of the main functions of OOP and design patterns is the capacity to change a module without breaking the entire program.

What About Speed?

Just about every programmer wants a program to run at optimum speed, and to do that, we look at the best algorithms. For now, though, we need to shift our attention to another kind of speed—the amount of time it takes to create and update a program. If a program cycles through an operation 100 million times, minor speed tweaks of that operation are important, but trying to squeeze a couple of microseconds from an operation that's used only once can be an expensive use of time. Likewise, having to revise an entire program because of a few lines of added code is an equally expensive use of time.

The Speed of Development and Change

Consider a contract you have to update and maintain a program for a customer. You have negotiated a set amount for ongoing updates, and you want both to satisfy your client and to spend a fair but limited amount of time on updates. For example, suppose your customer has weekly sales on different products requiring ongoing text and image updates. One solution may be to set up a weekly update using the `time()` function, and then all you have to do is add the most current image URL and text to a database. In fact, if you had the text and images ahead of time, you could go on vacation and let the PHP do the work while you're away. That would be a sweet maintenance deal, and you could keep several customers happy simultaneously.

Would you ever consider setting up a maintenance system where you had to rewrite the program every time you had to make a change? Probably not. That would be a very slow and expensive way of doing things. So where speed of revision is important, your program needs to consider the speed of both operation and development. Algorithms handle speed of operations, and design patterns handle speed of development.

The Speed of Teams

Another speed issue can be found in working with teams. When dealing with larger and more complex programs, teams need to agree on and understand a common plan and goal to effectively and efficiently create and maintain large programs. Among other things, OOP and design patterns provide a common language to speed along group work. References to "factories," "state machines," and "observers" all mean the same thing to those who understand OOP and design patterns.

Most importantly, design patterns provide a way of programming so that a team of programmers can work on separate parts that will go together. Think of an assembly line making automobiles—each team assembles a different part of the car. To do that, they need a pattern of development and an understanding of the relationship of one part to another. In this way, everyone can do their job knowing that someone else's job will fit with their work. They don't have to know the details of another worker's job. They just need to know that they're working from the same plan.

What's Wrong with Sequential and Procedural Programming?

"If it ain't broke, don't fix it" is a widely believed sentiment, and you may immediately agree with it if a solution works. However, such a mindset is the antithesis of progress and improvement. After all, for getting from one place to another, walking works just fine. However, for getting from one side of the country to the other, flying in a jet works much better. OOP and design patterns are improvements over sequential and procedural programming in the same way as flying is to walking.

Sequential Programming

Most programmers begin programming by writing one statement after another to create a series of lines that will execute a program. For example, the following is a perfectly good PHP sequential program that works:

```php
<?php

$firstNumber=20;
$secondNumber=40;
$total= $firstNumber + $secondNumber;
echo $total;

?>
```

The variables are abstract data types, and the arithmetic add operator (+) combines the values of two variables into a third variable. The echo statement prints out the total of the combined values to the screen.

Adding two numbers is a simple problem for PHP, and as long as you deal with simple problems, you can use simple solutions.

Procedural Programming

As programmers began to write longer and longer programs with more complex tasks, the sequences began to be entangled into what was called spaghetti code. A GOTO statement would allow sequential programmers to jump around in a program to complete a procedure, and so it was easy to become entangled.

With procedural programming came the function. A *function* is a little object where an operation can be called to perform a sequence with a single statement. For example, the following is a procedural version of the sequential program shown in the previous listing:

```php
<?php

function addEmUp($first,$second)
{
    $total=$first + $second;
    echo $total;
}
addEmUp(20,40);

?>
```

The functions (or *procedures*) allow programmers to group sequences into modules that can be reused in a program. Further, by having parameters, the programmer can enter different arguments into a function so that it can be used with different concrete values.

Like OOP, procedural programming uses modularity and reuse. However, procedural programming does not provide for classes where programming tasks can be bundled into objects. Class objects (instances of classes) can operate on their own data structures, and that cannot be done by functions alone. As a result, procedural programming requires long sequences to accomplish large tasks. Further, working in teams is more difficult with procedural programming because different team members cannot easily work on independent but interrelated classes, as can be done with OOP.

Pay Me Now or Pay Me Later

A while ago, I published a blog post titled "No Time for OOP and Design Patterns (*http://bit.ly/108IFSF*)." The post was in reaction to a number of developers who said reasonably that they did not have time to incorporate OOP or design patterns into their work even though they wanted to do so. They explained that a project would come along with a clear deadline, and in an effort to get it done on time, they'd cobble together a working program using sequential and procedural programming. Maybe they'd include a class or two if they had one that met a particular goal, but that was it.

In learning OOP and design patterns for PHP, you need to remember a couple of points, which were first made by Erich Gamma, Richard Helm, Ralph Johnson, and John Vlissides in *Design Patterns: Elements of Reusable Object-Oriented Software*:

- Designing object-oriented software is hard.
- Designing reusable object-oriented software is even harder.

Rather than looking at those statements as reasons *not* to learn OOP and design patterns, they stand as reasons why OOP and design patterns are so valuable. Knowledge adds value to any skillset. The more difficult the knowledge is to obtain, the more it is valued.

Don't expect to pick up OOP and design patterns easily and quickly. Rather, incorporate them a little at a time into your PHP programming. At some point you will see the value. Over time, you will develop more skills and understanding, and you will run into a project where you can reuse most of the program structures from a previous project. In a recent project, I decided to use a Strategy design pattern. It included a table with 105 fields, and the customer wanted a certain set of functionalities. By using a Strategy design, each of the strategies was a class with an algorithm to handle a fairly mundane PHP problem—filtering, updating, and deleting data in a MySQL database. It took a while to set it up, but once it was configured, it was easy to change (customers always want change!). Some time later, I was asked to do a similar kind of project using frontend and backend PHP with a MySQL database. Rather than starting over from scratch, I just pulled out the Strategy pattern, changed the algorithms, and had it up and running in no time. I got paid the same, but having worked smart, my customer got a much better piece of software than had I worked longer and dumber.

At some point, we have to stop our old habits and upgrade our skills. At this point in time, many programmers are updating their skills to accommodate mobile devices. If they do not, they'll lose out on many opportunities—eventually they may render their skills obsolete. Over time, we know that we'll have to update our skills to incorporate the benefits of the latest PHP release, new technology, or direction the industry takes.

OOP and design patterns contain concepts that transcend all of these changes, make us better programmers, and provide our customers with better software. It all starts with a first step. By taking the time now, you won't be scrambling for time to get a project done in the future. Besides, you will come out of the process as a better programmer, and that in and of itself is reason enough to learn OOP and design patterns.

Above all, learning OOP and design patterns is the pleasure of doing something well.

CHAPTER 2

Basic Concepts in OOP

*Two elements are needed to form a truth—a fact
and an abstraction.*

—Remy de Gourmont

*Beware how you trifle with your marvelous
inheritance, this great land of ordered liberty, for
if we stumble and fall, freedom and civilization
everywhere will go down in ruin.*

—Henry Cabot Lodge

*Everybody gets everything handed to them. The
rich inherit it. I don't mean just inheritance of
money. I mean what people take for granted
among the middle and upper classes, which is
nepotism, the old-boy network.*

—Toni Morrison

*Our normal waking consciousness, rational
consciousness as we call it, is but one special type
of consciousness, whilst all about it, parted from it
by the filmiest of screens, there lie potential forms
of consciousness entirely different.*

—William James

Abstraction

If you're new to OOP, don't expect everything to make sense right away. As you use OOP more and more, you'll experience little "aha!" moments when the pieces begin to come together. PHP does have important OOP features, and it has its own way of implementing these features in the language. If you are familiar with other OOP languages, you can be assured that PHP is different in places—like allowing constants to be a part of an interface. Understanding abstraction is a cornerstone in both OOP and design patterns, and the more you use it, the more sense it makes.

The notion of abstraction is so essential to both object-oriented programming and design patterns that it bears more than a fleeting consideration. The general idea of abstraction in computing is not unlike the abstractions we use every day in natural language. For example, the word *dog* denotes a phenomenon that has dog-like characteristics. If someone says, "look at the dog," they use the abstraction of dog (in other words, the word *dog*) to indicate a concrete instance of an animal with dog-like features. By using the words *dog* and *cat*, we can differentiate one from the other and point to lots of different dogs and cats. However, if we use the word "dog" to indicate a cat, we may be corrected. "That's not a dog. It's a cat." So while abstractions are general, they are specific enough so that we can differentiate specific instances.

In *Object-Oriented Design with Applications, 3rd Edition* (Addison-Wesley), Grady Booch, a pioneer in both OOP and design patterns, has a clear definition of *abstraction* that nicely sums it up:

> An abstraction denotes the essential characteristics of an object that distinguish it from all other kinds of objects and thus provide crisply defined conceptual boundaries relative to the perspective of the viewer.

Abstraction is important because it allows programmers to group and classify objects. To some extent, all classes are abstractions of a set of operations on data. Keep the following in mind about abstractions:

> Abstraction is the main tool used to deal with complexity. The more complex a problem, the more it requires abstractions to solve.

Think about this paradox: abstractions are concrete methods for handling complexity. We group similarities in reality (abstract concrete likeness) to make them more manageable to work with. So instead of, "my loyal, bold, furry-faced, tail-wagging, face-licking, wet-nosed friend whose name is SyntaxError," I can say, "my dog."

Abstract Classes

Besides regular classes, PHP also has what are called *abstract classes*. In OOP and design patterns, abstract classes provide an organizing mechanism for your project. An abstract class cannot be instantiated, but rather a concrete class (one you can instantiate) inherits its interface and any concrete properties from the abstract class.

Before continuing, the term *interface* needs to be examined. Familiar interfaces include user interfaces, hardware interfaces, and other kinds of linkages involving computer hardware and software. Another kind of interface is one that describes the outline of an object. To begin, consider a simple class with a single method:

```php
<?php
 class OneTrick
 {
     private $storeHere;
     public function trick($whatever)
     {
         $this->storeHere=$whatever;
         return $this->storeHere;
     }
 }

 $doIt=new OneTrick();
 $dataNow=$doIt->trick("This is perfect.");
 echo $dataNow;

 ?>
```

The central part of an interface is made up of all the signatures in the class defined by its operations (functions). A *signature* consists of an operation's name and parameters. Signatures also include the return data type, but because of the nature of data typing in PHP, we'll have to return to this third element of a signature further on in the section "Type Hinting: Almost Data Typing" (page 26). Figure 2-1 shows the trick() method's signature.

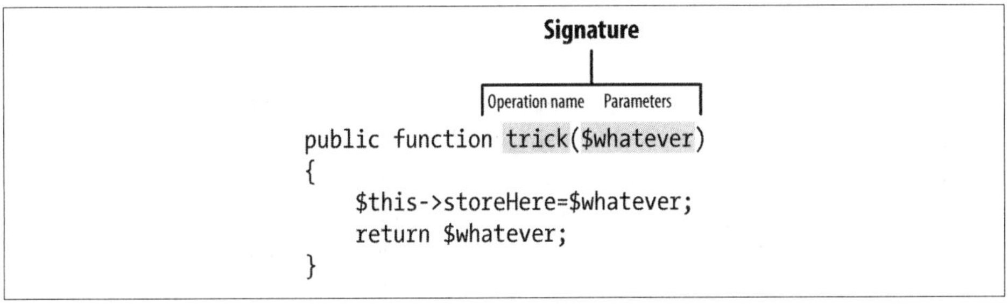

Figure 2-1. An operation's signature in PHP

When you take all of an object's signatures, it is the *interface*. For example, the One Trick class has one operation with one signature made up of the name trick() and a single parameter, $whatever.

Abstract Properties and Methods

To write the `trick()` function as an abstract one, include the interface but nothing else:

```
abstract public function trick($whatever);
```

If a class has at least one abstract method, it must be an abstract class. However, an abstract class can have concrete methods as well. For example, the following class is abstract and includes an abstract method:

```php
<?php
 abstract class OneTrickAbstract
 {
     public $storeHere;
     abstract public function trick($whatever);
 }
 ?>
```

In addition to the abstract method, you can see a single variable, `$storeHere`. A variable that is part of a class is a *property*. In some contexts, a reference to both properties and methods is simply *properties*, but for the most part *properties* refer to variables and constants (abstract data) and *methods* refer to functions (operations on the data).

PHP does not have *abstract properties* as such. You can declare a property with no assigned value and treat it as an abstract property, but unlike abstract methods, you are not forced to use them.

If you declare an abstract method in an abstract class, you must implement it in each child class that inherits the parent. It might help to think about methods in abstract classes as being like a contract that forces a set of hierarchies for all subclasses, so that they must all follow the same standards. For now, begin thinking of abstract classes as you would containers that can be filled with just about anything and placed on ships, trucks, and trains. The containers, like abstract classes, are part of a larger structure.

A class that inherits from a class is a *child class*, and the abstract class (or any other class from which another class has inheritance) is the *parent class*. The following shows how to implement the abstract class, `OneTrickAbstract`:

```php
<?php
include_once('OneTrickAbstract.php');

class OneTrickConcrete extends OneTrickAbstract
{
    public function trick($whatever)
    {
        $this->storeHere="An abstract property";
        return $whatever . $this->storeHere;
    }
}
```

```
$worker=new OneTrickConcrete();
echo $worker->trick("From an abstract origin...");
?>
```

Abstract methods can be implemented in any way you want as long as you include the method's signature and correct visibility. In this case, that signature includes the name "trick" and a single parameter, $whatever, and the visibility is public. The following are all legitimate implementations of the trick() method:

```
public function trick($whatever)
{
    $echo $whatever;
}
```

Or:

```
public function trick($whatever)
{
    $half=$whatever/2;
    return $half;
}
```

Or:

```
public function trick($whatever)
{
    $this->storehere=25;
    $quarter=$whatever * 100;
    return ($quarter / $this->storehere);
}
```

You may wonder what the point is in an abstract method if you can revise it as long as you maintain the signature and visibility. In the "Inheritance" (page 34) section of this chapter, you will be able to see more clearly why inheriting the interface is important.

While abstract classes generally have some abstract methods, you can add as many concrete methods and properties as you want in addition to any abstract methods that must be implemented. However, an abstract class can consist of nothing but concrete methods.

PHP 5.4 has a structure called *Traits* that are mechanisms for code reuse where multiple inheritance is not allowed. A class may inherit one class and then at the same time use a Trait that functions something like multiple inheritance. They will not be used in the examples in this book and are mentioned here in case there may be some pattern example in another language that uses multiple inheritance that you would like to implement in PHP.

Interfaces

Another OOP and design pattern building block is an *interface*. Like most abstract classes, interfaces have abstract methods. However, you cannot include concrete methods in an interface or variables as in an abstract class. (In an exception to abstractness, you can include concrete constants in an interface, but that is a unique feature of PHP interfaces.) The salient point about interfaces is that they are important structural elements in OOP and design patterns.

To create an interface, use the `interface` statement instead of `class`. As a general convention, interfaces begin with the letter *I* or *i*; in this book, we'll use a capital *I* followed by a capital letter describing the interface. This is followed by abstract methods, but the abstract statement is not used. The following is a simple interface with three methods:

```php
<?php
interface IMethodHolder
{
    public function getInfo($info);
    public function sendInfo($info);
    public function calculate($first,$second);
}
?>
```

To implement an interface, use the `implements` statement instead of `extend` as is done with abstract classes. Note that the listing uses the `include_once()` function to make the interface available to the class implementing it:

```php
<?php
include_once('IMethodHolder.php');

class ImplementAlpha implements IMethodHolder
{
    public function getInfo($info)
    {
        echo "This is NEWS! " . $info . "<br/>";
    }
    public function sendInfo($info)
    {
        return $info;
    }
    public function calculate($first,$second)
    {
     $calulated = $first * $second;
     return $calulated;
    }
    public function useMethods()
    {
        $this->getInfo("The sky is falling...");
        echo $this->sendInfo("Vote for Senator Snort!") . "<br/>";
        echo "You make $" . $this->calculate(20,15) . " in your part-time
         job<br/>";
    }
}

$worker=new ImplementAlpha();
```

```
$worker->useMethods();
?>
```

When you test the program, you should see the following output:

```
This is NEWS! The sky is falling...
Vote for Senator Snort!
You make $300 in your part-time job
```

Note that in addition to implementing the three methods in the interface, the Imple mentAlpha class includes a third method, useMethods(). As long as you implement the full number of methods in the interface, you can add as many other methods and properties as you need.

Interfaces and Constants

While you cannot include variables in interfaces, you can include constants. In order to use constants, you need the *scope resolution operator* (::). The double colon operator can be used to allow access to constants, both in classes and through an interface implementation. The general format can be seen in the following code samples:

```
$someVariable= InterfaceName::SOME_CONSTANT;
```

For example, the following interface has constants used in a MySQL connection:

```
<?php
interface IConnectInfo
{
    const HOST ="localhost";
    const UNAME ="phpWorker";
    const DBNAME = "dpPatt";
    const PW ="easyWay";
    function testConnection();
}
?>
```

Implement the interface just like any other PHP interface. The values of the constants can then be passed using the scope resolution operator in the implementation:

```
<?php
include_once('IConnectInfoMethod.php');

class ConSQL implements IConnectInfo
{
    //Passing values using scope resolution operator
    private $server=IConnectInfo::HOST;
    private $currentDB= IConnectInfo::DBNAME;
    private $user= IConnectInfo::UNAME;
    private $pass= IConnectInfo::PW;

    public function testConnection()
    {
```

```
        $hookup=new mysqli($this->server, $this->user, $this->pass,
          $this->currentDB);

        if (mysqli_connect_error())
        {
            die('bad mojo');
        }

        print "You're hooked up Ace! <br />" . $hookup->host_info;

        $hookup->close();
    }
}
$useConstant = new ConSQL();
$useConstant->testConnection();
?>
```

The only method is `testConnection()`, but your interface could be made up of nothing but constants if you wanted. The values are passed to the class properties (private variables in the example) using the name of the interface (`IConnectInfo`), the scope resolution operator, and the name of the constant.

Abstract Classes and Interfaces: Two Types of Interfaces

One of the more confusing concepts in OOP and design patterns is differentiating abstract classes and interfaces. Keep in mind that both have *interfaces*, general outlines of methods. The set of all signatures defined by the methods in a class is the interface of the class (or object). So, you may often find a reference to a pattern's interface referring to an abstract class as well as an interface. The reference is to the set of all signatures.

Gamma et al. note that, "An object's interface characterizes the complete set of requests that can be sent to the object." This means that if your `Client` class is aware of an object's interface, it knows what it can request and how to request it. So while both abstract classes and interfaces have interfaces of their own, abstract classes can have concrete methods (operations) and properties as well.

Much of understanding design patterns relies on understanding the general use of the term *interface* as it applies to the set of signatures in an object (a class).

Type Hinting: Almost Data Typing

One of the important structural elements in the abstraction in OOP and design patterns is *typing data* to an interface instead of an implementation. This means that the reference to the data is through the parent class, typically an interface or abstract class. (In this context, *interface* is used to refer to either an interface or abstract class.)

The basic format for type hinting is as follows:

```
function doWork(TypeHint $someVar)...
```

Type hints must be the name of a class or interface. In design pattern work, an abstract class or interface is preferred because it does not bind the type of an implementation, just the structure. The following example shows an interface with two implementations of the interface and a class that uses an interface in type hinting to establish a loose but clear bind.

Interface

```
//IProduct.php
<?php
interface IProduct
{
    function apples();
    function oranges();
}

?>
```

FruitStore Implementation

```
//FruitStore.php
<?php
include_once('IProduct.php');

class FruitStore implements IProduct
{
    public function apples()
    {
        return "FruitStore sez--We have apples. <br/>";
    }

    public function oranges()
    {
        return "FruitStore sez--We have no citrus fruit.<br/>";
    }
}
?>
```

CitrusStore Implementation

```
//CitrusStore.php
<?php
include_once('IProduct.php');

class CitrusStore implements IProduct
{
    public function apples()
    {
        return "CitrusStore sez--We do not sell apples. <br/>";
    }
```

```php
        public function oranges()
        {
            return "CitrusStore sez--We have citrus fruit.<br/>";
        }
    }

    ?>
```

Object with type hinting

```php
    //UseProducts.php
    <?php
    include_once('FruitStore.php');
    include_once('CitrusStore.php');

    class UseProducts
    {
        public function __construct()
        {
            $appleSauce=new FruitStore();
            $orangeJuice=new CitrusStore();
            $this->doInterface($appleSauce);
            $this->doInterface($orangeJuice);
        }

        //IProduct is type hint in doInterface()

        function doInterface(IProduct $product)
        {
            echo $product->apples();
            echo $product->oranges();
        }
    }

    $worker=new UseProducts();
    ?>
```

When you test the UseProducts class, the output displays the following:

```
    FruitStore sez--We have apples.
    FruitStore sez--We have no citrus fruit.
    CitrusStore sez--We do not sell apples.
    CitrusStore sez--We have citrus fruit.
```

What you see on the screen are different implementations of the IProduct interface. The crucial feature to note is that in the doInterface() method, the *type hint* of IProduct recognizes both of the classes that implemented the IProduct interface. In other words, instead of recognizing one as a FruitStore instance and the other as a CitrusStore instance, it recognizes their common interface IProduct.

In practical terms for development, enforcing data types ensures that any object (class) used in conjunction with a given method where code hinting is used will have a given interface. Further, if an interface (either an abstract class or interface) is used as the code hint, the binding is much looser; it is bound to the interface instead of a specific implementation. As your programs get bigger, you can make changes as long as you adhere to an interface. At the same time, you can do so without getting entangled in concrete implementations.

You cannot use scalar types like string or int for code hints, but you can use arrays, interfaces (as in the previous example), and classes. So while not as flexible as some other languages, the implementation of class typing in PHP through type hinting serves a crucial function in OOP and design pattern programming.

Encapsulation

Often when you read about *encapsulation* you will encounter the phrase *information hiding*. The phrase is not inaccurate, but it makes more sense once you understand encapsulation; it's not always helpful in explaining encapsulation to begin with the concept of information hiding. Instead, a better beginning is the image of *compartments*. Grady Booch provides the following description:

> Encapsulation is the process of *compartmentalizing the elements of an abstraction* that constitute its structure and behavior; encapsulation serves to separate the contractual interface of an abstraction and its implementation.

Once a big complex problem has been modularized into solvable subproblems, encapsulation is a way of taking the smaller abstractions and compartmentalizing them.

Everyday Encapsulation

You encounter encapsulation in everyday life. Take, for example, going for a drive in your car. The car is made up of many objects, and you have little idea of how most of them work. The ignition starts the engine, but you may not know much about the battery-powered starter motor, the details of the internal combustion engine, or the electrical system in your car. You just put the key in the ignition and rotate it to start the car. The complexities of the details are hidden from you, and you have access to them in only certain ways. You are working with an encapsulated system. You don't need to know how something works, you just need to know how to access control mechanisms—think of it as a user interface (UI) for your car.

As you are driving down the road with the window down, suppose that a car pulls up next to you, and a person sticks her arm out the window of the other car and tries to grab your steering wheel and steer your car. You can think of that as *breaking encapsulation*. You don't want that to happen, so you roll up your window so that no one outside the car has *access* to the encapsulated cocoon of you driving your car.

In programming, encapsulation is what makes an object *an object*. An object has certain features that surround it so that access to its functionality is controlled by the structure of the program—just like the structure of your car controls access to its many parts. A class is encapsulated through limited access to its methods and properties. You don't want outside influences to take control of the properties of the class and use them or change their state except through explicit routes—just like you don't want someone to grab the steering wheel away from you. So when you encounter *information hiding* in the context of encapsulation, what it means is that the details of a module may be hidden so that the module may be used through the appropriate access channels and not through the module's details.

Protecting Encapsulation through Visibility

In PHP, the term *visibility* refers to the access to the properties of a class. (The term *access* is used in other languages and *accessors* for the types of access.) Like other OOP languages, PHP uses three kinds of visibility: private, protected, and public. These visibilities are ways that programs can be encapsulated and accessed for use.

Private

The easiest way to encapsulate a program element is to make it *private*. That means the property can be accessed only from within the same class; it's visible only to elements in the same class. Consider the following class:

```php
<?php
class PrivateVis
{
    private $money;

    public function __construct()
    {
        $this->money=200;
        $this->secret();
    }

    private function secret()
    {
        echo $this->money;
    }
}
$worker=new PrivateVis();
?>
```

The constructor function automatically launches the class when the class is instantiated. Because the constructor function is part of the `PrivateVis` class, it can access all of the private properties and methods. In order to reference a property or method in the same class, PHP requires that the `$this` statement be used with the object. Further, the private method, `secret()`, can access the private property (variable), `$money`, because they are both part of the same class. Objects external to the class can see only the result of the secret( ) method's output. It cannot in any way alter the state of the method or property in the class.

By instantiating the class through the public __construct function (constructor function), another object has access to the private properties (variables or constants) and methods.

Protected

While private visibility of a property provides access only to elements within the same class, *protected* visibility allows access to both the same class and child classes. You can incorporate protected visibility with both abstract and concrete methods. The following example shows how using an abstract class and a concrete implementation use protected visibility:

```php
<?php
//ProtectVis.php
abstract class ProtectVis
{
    abstract protected function countMoney();
    protected $wage;

    protected function setHourly($hourly)
    {
        $money=$hourly;
        return $money;
    }
}
?>
```

When a child class extends an abstract class with protected methods, it must implement the abstract method before using it. The child class can use the protected concrete method without further implementation:

```php
<?php
//ConcreteProtect.php
include_once('ProtectVis.php');

class ConcreteProtect extends ProtectVis
{
    function __construct()
    {
        $this->countMoney();
    }
    protected function countMoney()
    {
        $this->wage="Your hourly wage is $";
        echo $this->wage . $this->setHourly(36);
    }
}
```

```
$worker=new ConcreteProtect();
?>
```

Note that the abstract method countMoney() incorporates the inherited setHourly() method. All inherited properties and methods require the $this statement. The initial access to the protected properties is through the public constructor function.

While not as encapsulating as private visibility, protected visibility has the capacity to encapsulate larger structures in a program. A parent class, whether abstract or concrete, and its child classes make up the larger structure.

Public

Access to an encapsulated object is through *public* visibility. To be useful, at least some of the methods in a class must be visible, even if it's only the constructor function. Of course, all constructor methods are *public*. So, if your program includes a constructor function, it has public access through the instantiation of the class by an object outside the class. For example, the following code shows how a single public access method can use private methods and properties in a class:

```
<?php
//PublicVis.php
class PublicVis
{
    private $password;
    private function openSesame($someData)
    {
        $this->password=$someData;
        if($this->password=="secret")
        {
            echo "You're in!<br/>";
        }
        else
        {
            echo "Release the hounds!<br/>";
        }
    }
    public function unlock($safe)
    {
        $this->openSesame($safe);
    }

}
$worker=new PublicVis();
$worker->unlock("secret");
$worker->unlock("duh");
?>
```

Often, public methods or properties are included to maintain a way to communicate with an object without the automatic launching of a constructor method. In PublicVis, both the $password property and openSesame() method are private. However, the unlock() method is public and because it is part of the PublicVis class, it can access the private properties and method of that class.

Getters and Setters

In order to maintain encapsulation while at the same time having accessibility, OOP design suggests using *getters* and *setters* (also called *accessors* and *mutators*, respectively). Instead of accessing a class directly and either obtaining or changing property values through direct assignment, the getter/setter function does this for you. In general, the use of getters and setters must be done judiciously; too many can break encapsulation. The following example shows one use of getters and setters in a PHP class:

```php
<?php
//GetSet.php
class GetSet
{
    private $dataWarehouse;

    function __construct()
    {
        $this->setter(200);
        $got= $this->getter();
        echo $got;
    }

    private function getter()
    {
        return $this->dataWarehouse;
    }

    private function setter($setValue)
    {
        $this->dataWarehouse=$setValue;
    }
}
$worker=new GetSet();

?>
```

The getter/setter functions are private, and so access is encapsulated. Further, in this implementation, the setter value is inside the class and so it functions as a rather large data holder.

In dealing with data in object-oriented systems, Allen Holub, in *Holub on Patterns* (Apress) suggests the following:

> Don't ask for the information you need to do the work; ask the object that has the information to do the work for you.

In the GetSet class example, instantiation of the class:

```php
$worker=new GetSet();
```

does that nicely. It does not expose the implementation details. However, in isolation, the GetSet class doesn't look too useful because the only way to assign a value is to hardcode it into the class.

In part, the purpose of design patterns is to set up the communication links between objects. Much of what passes as OOP misuses getters and setters, and making access public to them only breaks encapsulation. The following explanation, from "Single Responsibility Applied to Methods" (*http://tinyurl.com/9256gey*), of object-oriented programming compared to procedural programming by David Chelimsky helps clear up the role of communications in OOP:

> In procedural programming, a process is expressed in one place in which a series of instructions are coded in order. Whereas in OO, a process is expressed as a succession of messages across objects. One object sends a message to another, which does part of the process and then sends a new message off to another object, which handles part of the process, etc. You modify a process by reorganizing the succession of messages rather than changing a procedure.

The process of maintaining encapsulation while communicating between objects (classes) is part of a design pattern's job. Working out a way to establish communication without breaking encapsulation can be tricky, and so design patterns become a sort of "cheat sheet" on how to set up a program using communicating classes.

Inheritance

At its core, *inheritance* is a simple concept. A class that extends another class has all of the other class' properties and methods. This allows developers to create new classes that extend the functionality of other classes. For example, if you have a class, Furry Pets, you can extend it to Dogs and Cats with both classes inheriting the properties of FurryPets while extending it to differentiate Dogs and Cats. The following shows a simple PHP example:

FurryPets.php
```php
<?php
//FurryPets.php
class FurryPets
{
    protected $sound;
    protected function fourlegs()
    {
        return "walk on all fours";
    }
```

```php
    protected function makesSound($petNoise)
    {
        $this->sound=$petNoise;
        return $this->sound;
    }
}
?>
```

Dogs.php

```php
<?php
//Dogs.php
include_once('FurryPets.php');
class Dogs extends FurryPets
{
    function __construct()
    {
        echo "Dogs " . $this->fourlegs() . "<br/>";
        echo $this->makesSound("Woof, woof") . "<br/>";
        echo $this->guardsHouse() . "<br/>";
    }

    private function guardsHouse()
    {
        return "Grrrrr" . "<br/>";
    }
}
?>
```

Cats.php

```php
<?php
//Cats.php
include_once('FurryPets.php');
class Cats extends FurryPets
{
    function __construct()
    {
        echo "Cats " . $this->fourlegs() . "<br/>";
        echo $this->makesSound("Meow, purrr") . "<br/>";
        echo $this->ownsHouse() . "<br/>";
    }

    private function ownsHouse()
    {
        return "I'll just walk on this keyboard." . "<br/>";
    }
}

?>
```

Client.php

```php
<?php
//Client.php
include_once('Dogs.php');
```

```
include_once('Cats.php');
class Client
{
    function __construct()
    {
        $dogs=new Dogs();
        $cats=new Cats();
    }
}
$worker=new Client();
?>
```

The Client class makes the requests, and constructor functions in the dogs and cats objects generate the following output:

```
Dogs walk on all fours
Woof, woof
Grrrrr

Cats walk on all fours
Meow, purrr
I'll just walk on this keyboard.
```

The fourlegs() method generates identical output for both objects; the make sSound() output depends on the argument in the parameter; and finally, each class has its own unique method—guardsHouse() and ownsHouse().

Inheritance helps structure the different classes that may make up a program. However, in order to keep the binding between classes loose, inheritance typically comes from abstract classes, and it is shallow—a single level of child classes. If programs are bound to deep levels of inheritance of concrete classes, even simple changes in the parent classes can wreak havoc on the child classes.

Polymorphism

At its base, polymorphism refers to many forms, but that's not very helpful unless you understand it in the context of OOP. The real value of polymorphism is that objects with the same interface can be called to do different things. In a large complex structure (a great big program), additions and changes can blow the hinges off your program unless it has a common interface (from a parent class or interface). For example, the following program has two classes that share a common interface. The implementations of the interface are quite different:

```
<?php
//Poly.php
interface ISpeed
{
    function fast();
    function cruise();
    function slow();
```

```php
    }

class Jet implements ISpeed
{
    function slow()
    {
        return 120;
    }

    function cruise()
    {
        return 1200;
    }

    function fast()
    {
        return 1500;
    }
}

class Car implements ISpeed
{
    function slow()
    {
        $carSlow=15;
        return $carSlow;
    }

    function cruise()
    {
        $carCruise=65;
        return $carCruise;
    }

    function fast()
    {
        $carZoom=110;
        return $carZoom;
    }
}

$f22=new Jet();
$jetSlow=$f22->slow();
$jetCruise=$f22->cruise();
$jetFast=$f22->fast();
echo "<br/>My jet can take off at $jetSlow mph and cruises at $jetCruise mph.
However, I can crank it up to $jetFast mph if I'm in a hurry.<br/>";

$ford=new Car();
$fordSlow=$ford->slow();
$fordCruise=$ford->cruise();
$fordFast=$ford->fast();
```

```
echo "<br/>My car pokes along at $fordSlow mph in a school zone and cruises at
$fordCruise mph on the highway. However, I can crank it up to $fordFast mph
if I'm in a hurry.<br/>";
?>
```

The two implementations of the ISpeed interface by the Jet and Car classes are very different. However, when making changes or additions within a given structure of a program, I can request or use the interface methods without having to worry about whether my program will crash or not.

One Name with Many Implementations

The easiest way to see polymorphism is in the different implementations of an interface, as was done in the previous *Poly.php* example. The Jet class simply implements each method to return a primitive value, and the Car class first passes a primitive value to a variable and returns the variable's value. Both used the same interface.

One caution about using polymorphism with PHP classes and interfaces is that the return types are not included in a PHP function's signature. For example, a signature in C# would include both the type of return data and whether or not a return is expected. For example, consider the following C# snippet where an interface is declared:

```
//C# Interface
interface IFace
{
    string stringMethod();
    int numMethod(int intProp);
    void noReturnMethod();
}
```

The C# language does not require the keyword function to be included in any of its methods—just the signature, made up of the return data type, name, and parameters (if any). So the first method—stringMethod()—expects a string to be returned, and any implementation of the method must include the return keyword. Likewise, the second method—numMethod()—expects an integer to be returned, and the method must include an integer parameter. Again, any implementation requires a return statement. However, the third method—noReturnMethod()—has a return type of void. That means that no return statement is expected in the implementation of the method. In fact, if a return were included in the implementation of the method with a void data type, it would cause an error and failure.

In PHP, where no return information is included in the method's signature, you can run into possible trouble if you have mixed implementations with different data types and with and without return values. The value of polymorphism is that even though the forms may be different, you should be able to depend on the interface to guide your implementations. The more information in the interface—such as what type of behavior (returned data or not) and data type is expected—the easier it is to have different forms that still work together. In the *Poly.php* example, all of the methods included an integer and a return statement. So while PHP does not have a very strong signature, you can enforce it in your planning and implementation. You can do so using comment statements in your interface. For example:

```
//PHP Interface
interface IFace
{
//@return string
function stringMethod();

//@return integer and use integer property
    function numMethod($intProp);

    //do not use return
    function noReturnMethod();
}
```

If you have an *extended virtual signature* in your interfaces (including abstract classes) using comments, you can extend the advantages of a strongly typed language.

Built-In Polymorphism in Design Patterns

As you look at the different design patterns in this book and elsewhere, you should be aware that a good deal of the polymorphism is built right into the design pattern. For example, the Strategy design pattern includes a Strategy interface with different algorithms making up the implementations. The Strategy declares an interface that is common for the different algorithms that can be derived from Strategy. For example, a PHP Strategy design may include different implementations of the interface for different actions on a database, such as update, delete, or insert. By maintaining a common interface, new algorithms for specialized updates, selections, or searches can be added without fear of crashing the program that handles data manipulation with a MySQL table.

Easy Does It

This chapter has included the most key OOP concepts in one place you will find in this book. However, as you read each chapter and design pattern, you will find that these concepts will be reintroduced by pointing to some aspect of the design pattern or in a PHP implementation of a design pattern. So keep in mind that what may not make sense now should become clearer as you continue with the design patterns. Chapter 3 introduces some key design pattern concepts that are based on OOP concepts and ideas.

Use Page Stick-ems

On all of my OOP and design pattern books, I have different colored plastic stick-ems. They go by the names of "index tabs," "page markers," and any number of other labels, but whatever they're called in your local office supply store, get some to mark points that you will have to return to and reread. If you use a tablet, such as an iPad or Kindle to do your reading, use the electronic bookmarks. Depending on the reader (and software) you use, the page markers function differently.

Use highlighters judiciously. In some of my books I highlighted everything, which is the same as highlighting nothing. Some documents on my tablet, I can highlight using selection, but again, use highlighting with some caution.

CHAPTER 3

Basic Design Pattern Concepts

Large organization is loose organization. Nay, it
would be almost as true to say that organization is
always disorganization.

—Gilbert K. Chesterton

If you only have a hammer, you tend to see every
problem as a nail.

—Abraham Maslow

Because things are the way they are, things will not
stay the way they are.

—Bertolt Brecht

The MVC Loosens and Refocuses Programming

Way back in the 1970s when user interfaces (UIs) were fairly primitive, a programmer decided to separate key elements of what was required in a *graphical user interface* (GUI). Each of the parts was given a specific task, and each part communicated with the other parts. The parts were grouped into *domain objects* and *presentation objects*. The domain objects were for modeling what perception the user was given of the real world, and the presentation objects were what was viewed on the screen. The parts were divided into a *model*, a *view*, and a *controller*, and the Model-View-Control (MVC) design pattern came into being.

The domain element in the MVC is the model. The model is responsible for what is variously called the data, business, or application logic. For example, take a thermostat. Within the thermostat is a value that represents a temperature, either the actual ambient temperature or a value where a heater is turned *Off* or *On*. Somewhere in that thermostat you have a set of data that can be envisioned as set into variables:

```
$a = current temperature
$b = turn off heater
$c = turn on heater
```

At a given time, the actual values may be:

```
$a=65;
$b=67;
$c=64;
```

Those values are generated by the controller settings and a thermometer that reads the ambient temperature. It doesn't matter where or how the values are generated; that's the business of the model.

The presentation part of the MVC has two elements: the view and controller. The view, in the thermostat example, is a window that shows the temperature and settings to the viewer. The model provides the ambient temperature, and the controller provides the on/off temperature sent to the view for display. The controller is the device that adjusts the on/off values. (The view displays the controller, however.) Figure 3-1 illustrates the MVC in a thermostat.

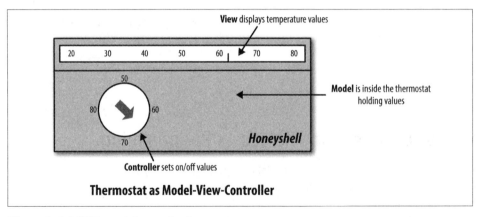

Figure 3-1. MVC participants in thermostat

A thermostat hanging on the wall and a virtual one represented in a computer program are different in that the view communicates to the controller how the user input is to be handled. Remember that in a computer display, the UI is actually part of the view in that the user can see it for making changes. The view then communicates changes by the user to the controller, which in turn sends the information to the model. Figure 3-2 shows the same object in a class diagram.

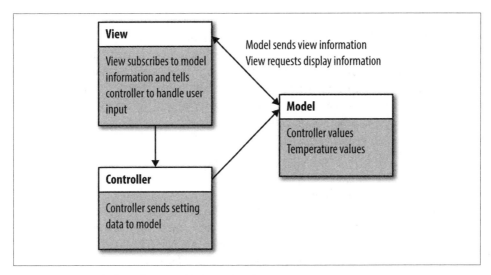

Figure 3-2. MVC class diagram

The MVC seems to have as many variations as there are implementations. Because of its simplicity and utility, it has been used and misused a good deal. However, the point remains that it stands as a structure that provides loose coupling between its parts. For example, suppose you want to change the view from an analog view to a digital view. That's easy to do because the model and controller are self-contained entities and really don't care what the view displays. Likewise, the controller can change from settings in Fahrenheit to Celsius, and as long as the model is sent the information, it doesn't care what temperature format is used.

The importance of the MVC lies more in the demonstration of loose coupling than in direct functionality. By separating out the different elements (or participants) in accomplishing a task, the MVC added a good deal of flexibility required in large programs. The larger the program, the more the program required the modular flexibility in the MVC.

Basic Principles of Design Patterns

While the MVC is an important point in the development of design patterns, it is only a starting point. The use, misuse, and overuse of the MVC in programming are well documented. When overemployed, it is not unlike building a house with a single tool—a hammer—to take care of all sawing, measurement, and drilling tasks.

In the landmark publication *Design Patterns: Elements of Reusable Object-Oriented Software* by Erich Gamma, Richard Helm, Ralph Johnson, and John Vlissides (best known as *The Gang of Four* or simply *GoF*), the MVC is used to begin a discussion of the many tools that make up design patterns. The MVC is credited with decoupling views and models by establishing a subscribe/notify protocol between them. However, GoF go on to show that many different and fundamental design patterns not only make up the MVC, but there is also a far greater range of common patterns for the kinds of work that computer programmers do, wholly apart from MVC. So, rather than looking at design patterns tied in some way to MVC, we need to examine design patterns apart from the MVC. We need instead to examine the principles of design patterns in general and each design pattern in its own right.

Why Gang of Four?

I am no lover of jargon or clubby idioms, and the reference to *Design Patterns: Elements of Reusable Object-Oriented Software* by Erich Gamma, Richard Helm, Ralph Johnson, and John Vlissides simply as *Gang of Four* or *GoF* may rankle some as sophomoric. The original name was tagged onto Jiang Qing, Zhang Chunqiao, Yao Wenyuan, and Wang Hongwen, leaders of the Chinese Communist Party who were kicked out after Mao Zedong's death. They were held responsible for the excesses in the Cultural Revolution that almost destroyed China. (There's also a rock band named Gang of Four based on the same discredited group of Chinese leaders.) However, with four authors with an aptly titled book that is too long with its full name or too short—*Design Patterns*—the GoF name stuck. It is unequivocal in its meaning, and there's no in-group nod because you happen to know the reference. It's a handy convenience universally understood by OOP and design pattern programmers and nothing more.

The First Design Pattern Principle

This first principle is a tricky one for PHP: *program to an interface, not an implementation*. In the simplest form, programming to an interface instead of an implementation means to set your variable as an instance of an abstract class or interface data type instead of a concrete implementation. By programming to an interface, you decouple the design from the implementation in such a way that you could (for example) easily replace a complex database implementation with a much simpler mock implementation for testing purposes. In languages that include data typing in variable declarations, you simply name the interface as the data type instead of the concrete class the variable instantiates. For example, in a strongly typed language, you may have the following:

*Interface **IAlpha***
> Name of interface

*Class **AlphaA***
> Implements **IAlpha**; AlphaA is data type **IAlpha**

*Variable **useAlpha***
> Declares type as **IAlpha** (for example, IAlpha useAlpha)

useAlpha
    Instantiates new **AlphaA**()

You cannot declare a variable to be of an abstract parent (abstract class or interface) data type in PHP because you cannot declare a data type without instantiating an instance of a class. Further, you cannot instantiate an object from an abstract class. A variable can "get" a data type by instantiating a concrete object using the following format:

```
$useAlpha = new AlphaA();
```

The variable named `$useAlpha` is an instance of the class `AlphaA` and is considered to be of that *data type*. So `$useAlpha` is of the data type `AlphaA`, a concrete implementation of a concrete class. At the same time, however, while an instance is the data type of a concrete class, it is also of the data type of the concrete class' parent. That bears repeating:

> An object instance is the data type of the object it instantiates and the data type of the object's parent.

How can that be done without strong typing? In PHP, you can program to an interface using code hinting.

Using Interface Data Types in Code Hinting

In Chapter 2, the section "Type Hinting: Almost Data Typing" (page 26) showed an example of using code hinting with the interface `IProduct`. Two different classes, `FruitStore` and `CitrusStore`, both implemented the same interface. Using code hinting, both were able to operate as arguments where a method with a code hinting parameter of `IProduct` was in force. That code hint specified the `IProduct` data type as a requirement for the argument. By closely examining a segment of that code, you can see how the operations were coding to an interface. Figure 3-3 shows the first step in a PHP operation programming to an interface: instantiating objects to be instances of interface implementations (see "Type Hinting: Almost Data Typing" (page 26) for the full program).

```
                    Instances of concrete implementations of IProduct
    public function __construct()
    {
        $appleSauce=new FruitStore();
        $orangeJuice=new CitrusStore();
        $this->doInterface($appleSauce);
        $this->doInterface($orangeJuice);
    }
```

Figure 3-3. Instantiating concrete implementations of IProduct

Figure 3-3 instantiations show *exactly the opposite* of what the principle of programming to an interface suggests: the variables are instantiated as instances of concrete implementations instead of the interface they share. What you cannot see in PHP because of weak data typing is that the concrete implementations are data types of the interface as well.

When type hinting is used, the programmer must include an object of the specified type hint. If that type hint is an interface, then the program will work exactly as though you are typing to an interface. Figure 3-4 shows the details of that process.

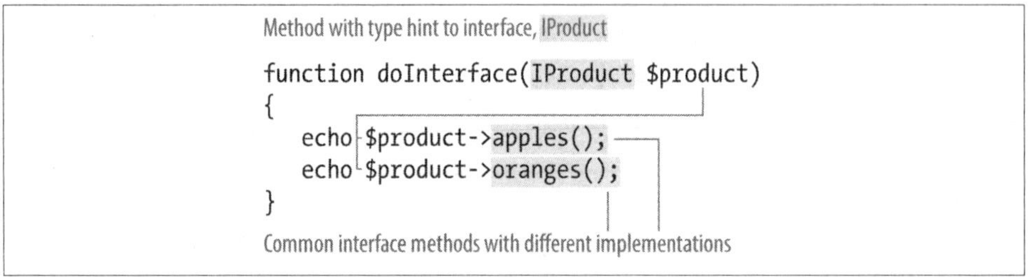

Method with type hint to interface, IProduct

```
function doInterface(IProduct $product)
{
    echo $product->apples();
    echo $product->oranges();
}
```
Common interface methods with different implementations

Figure 3-4. Method with type hinting to interface, IProduct

In looking at 3-3 and 3-4, you can see that the key method is doInterface(). It contains the type hint. When either the concrete instances of the two concrete implementations (FruitStore or CitrusStore) are used as arguments in the doInterface() method, the output is predictable. As long as any other implementation of the interface maintains the IProduct interface (including return data types), it won't matter how complex the program becomes. Your changes and additions will work the way you expect them to work, and they will not damage some other part of the program.

Abstract Classes and Their Interfaces

To help clarify the principle of programming to an interface instead of an implementation, the examples employ interfaces created using the keyword *interface*. Before continuing, though, understand that the concept of *interface* refers to the methods and their signatures, not necessarily the keyword, *interface*. Every class has an interface made up of its methods' signatures. Because most design patterns seldom include an extension from a concrete class, you need to understand that an extension from an abstract class is similar to the implementation of an interface.

In this next example, a simple abstract class is extended by two simple implementations. Then, a client class using type hinting shows how you can program to the interface using an abstract class. Comments in the code help to enforce the expected return values.

First, the abstract class `IAbstract` has a protected property (`$valueNow`), two protected abstract methods (`giveCost` and `giveCity`), and a public function that is not abstract, `displayShow`:

```php
<?php
abstract class IAbstract
{
    //Property available to all implementations
    protected $valueNow;

    /*All implementations must include the following 2 methods: */
    //Must return decimal value
    abstract protected function giveCost();
    //Must return string value
    abstract protected function giveCity();

    //This concrete function is available to all
    //class implementations without overriding
    //the contents

    public function displayShow()
    {
        $stringCost =$this->giveCost();
        $stringCost = (string)$stringCost;
        $allTogether=("Cost: $" . $stringCost . " for " . $this->giveCity());
        return $allTogether;
    }
}
?>
```

Next, two different extensions of the abstract class have different implementations of the abstract methods:

```php
//NorthRegion.php
<?php
include_once('IAbstract.php');

class NorthRegion extends IAbstract
{
    //Must return decimal value
    protected function giveCost()
    {
        return 210.54;
    }
    //Must return string value
    protected function giveCity()
    {
        return "Moose Breath";
    }
}
?>
```

```
//WestRegion.php
<?php
include_once('IAbstract.php');

class WestRegion extends IAbstract
{
    //Must return decimal value
    protected function giveCost()
    {
        $solarSavings=2;
        $this->valueNow=210.54/$solarSavings;
        return $this->valueNow;
    }
    //Must return string value
    protected function giveCity()
    {
        return "Rattlesnake Gulch";
    }
}
?>
```

With two different implementations of an abstract class, you can see that programming to an interface in this context really means the interface of the class and not an interface structure as used with the keyword *interface*. Finally, the Client class sets up a method that includes code hinting that specifies the abstract class as the interface:

```
<?php
include_once('NorthRegion.php');
include_once('WestRegion.php');

class Client
{
    public function __construct()
    {
        $north=new NorthRegion();
        $west= new WestRegion();
        $this->showInterface($north);
        $this->showInterface($west);
    }

    private function showInterface(IAbstract $region)
    {
        echo $region->displayShow() . "<br/>";
    }
}
$worker=new Client();
?>
```

The output shows the following:

```
Cost: $210.54 for Moose Breath
Cost: $105.27 for Rattlesnake Gulch
```

The amounts are different for the different regions because the abstract methods are implemented differently by the two concrete classes NorthRegion and WestRegion. If an incorrect data type is used (a string, for example), you will see the following kind of error message:

```
Catchable fatal error: Argument 1 passed to Client::showInterface()
must be an instance of IAbstract, string given, called in /Library/
```

So, in its own way, type hinting can help your programs move toward programming to an interface instead of an implementation.

To see how useful this style of programming is, add SouthRegion and EastRegion implementations of the IAbstract abstract class. Remember to use a decimal value for the giveCost() method and a string value for the giveCity(). Likewise, maintain the rest of the interface for both, and add them to the Client class. You should see how easy it is to make additions and changes as long as you maintain the interface.

The Second Design Pattern Principle

Some OOP programmers equate object reuse with inheritance. A class may be a rich collection of properties and methods, and by extending it you get to reuse all of those object elements without having to recode. Extend the class, add the required new properties and methods, and you're ready to go. Eventually, extension can create problems in the form of tightly bound objects. It is within the context of overinheritance that the second principle is grounded: *favor object composition over class inheritance.*

So what's the difference between object composition and class inheritance? This proposition does not imply getting rid of inheritance. Instead, it means that in developing programs where there's an opportunity to use composition, use it instead of inheritance. In doing so, the child classes do not become bloated with unused properties and methods.

Basic Composition Using a Client

To see the difference between using inheritance and composition, a simple example illustrates using a parent and child class (inheritance) and two separate classes (composition). Before looking at the code, Figure 3-5 shows a general idea of the difference between using inheritance and composition.

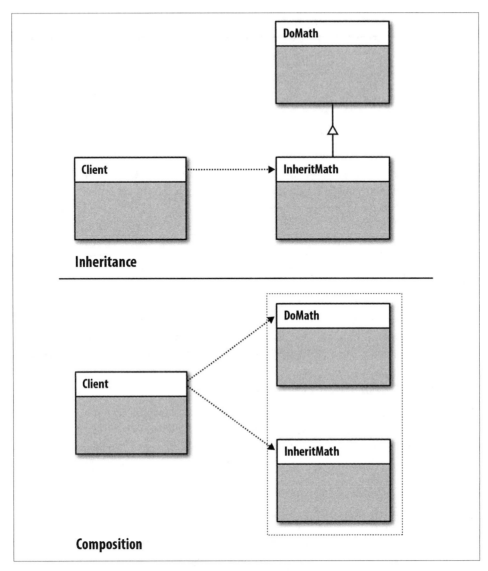

Figure 3-5. Inheritance and composition

Using inheritance, the client can make a single instantiation for the math and text functionality. With composition, the client uses two different instances to gain access to the functionality of both classes. Composition within a design pattern typically refers to composition within a participant in the pattern.

First, look at the code using inheritance. The first class (parent class) is a simple one that has methods for addition and division:

```php
<?php
//DoMath.php
class DoMath
{
    private $sum;
    private $quotient;

    public function simpleAdd($first,$second)
    {
        $this->sum=($first + $second);
        return $this->sum;
    }

    public function simpleDivide($dividend, $divisor)
    {
        $this->quotient=($dividend/$divisor);
        return $this->quotient;
    }
}
?>
```

The second class is for adding text functionality. One method converts numbers to strings and the other sets up a formatted output. It inherits all of the DoMath functionality through extension:

```php
<?php
//InheritMath.php
include_once('DoMath.php');
class InheritMath extends DoMath
{
    private $textOut;
    private $fullFace;

    public function numToText($num)
    {
        $this->textOut=(string)$num;
        return $this->textOut;
    }

    public function addFace($face, $msg)
    {
        $this->fullFace= "<strong>" . $face . "</strong>: " . $msg;
        return $this->fullFace;
    }
}
?>
```

The Client class instantiates the InheritMath class and is able to use all of the functionality inherited from the DoMath class as well as the included classes for text work:

```php
<?php
//ClientInherit
include_once('InheritMath.php');
```

```php
class ClientInherit
{
    private $added;
    private $divided;
    private $textNum;
    private $output;

    public function __construct()
    {
        $family=new InheritMath();
        $this->added=$family->simpleAdd(40,60);
        $this->divided=$family->simpleDivide($this->added,25);
        $this->textNum=$family->numToText($this->divided);
        $this->output=$family->addFace("Your results",$this->textNum);
        echo $this->output;
    }
}
$worker=new ClientInherit();
?>
```

The output is a formatted calculated value:

```
Your results: 4
```

That output used four different methods, two of which were inherited from a parent class.

Turning to composition, the Client class uses two separate classes, each containing two methods. The DoMath class is identical to the parent class in the inheritance example, so begin by examining the DoText class:

```php
<?php
//DoText.php
class DoText
{
    private $textOut;
    private $fullFace;

    public function numToText($num)
    {
        $this->textOut=(string)$num;
        return $this->textOut;
    }

    public function addFace($face, $msg)
    {
        $this->fullFace= "<strong>" . $face . "</strong>: " . $msg;
        return $this->fullFace;
    }
}
?>
```

The DoText class looks a lot like the InheritMath class, and it is. However, it does not inherit the DoMath class.

In using composition in this example, the client uses both of the separate classes, and the results are identical. However, the client must instantiate two objects instead of one. Otherwise, the client used in composition is very similar to the one used with inheritance:

```php
<?php
//ClientCompose.php
include_once('DoMath.php');
include_once('DoText.php');

class ClientCompose
{
    private $added;
    private $divided;
    private $textNum;
    private $output;

    public function __construct()
    {
        $useMath=new DoMath();
        $useText=new DoText();
        $this->added=$useMath->simpleAdd(40,60);
        $this->divided=$useMath->simpleDivide($this->added,25);
        $this->textNum=$useText->numToText($this->divided);
        $this->output=$useText->addFace("Your results",$this->textNum);
        echo $this->output;
    }
}
$worker=new ClientCompose();
?>
```

The results are the same, but the Client class has to include multiple classes. That may seem like an argument to favor inheritance, but composition in larger programs avoids the problem of maintaining each child class with multiple levels of inheritance and the possible errors that can occur. For instance, a change in the parent class can ripple down to the child implementation that interferes with an algorithm used by the child class.

Delegation: The IS-A and HAS-A Difference

In the context of design patterns, you will see classes that use other classes in their construction. When one class passes off a task to another class, that is *delegation*. It's what makes composition so powerful.

With inheritance, each child *IS-A* part of another class or classes. With composition, objects may *USE-A* different class or group of classes for a series of tasks. This does not mean that inheritance should not be used. In fact, most design patterns include inheritance and composition used together. Instead of using inheritance in a long series of child, grandchild, great-grandchild, *ad infinitum*, a design pattern approach encourages using shallow inheritance and using the functionality of more than a single class. This approach helps to avoid tight binding and crashes occurring when changes are made to designs where concrete classes have child classes.

Design Patterns as a Big Cheat Sheet

When working out when and how to use delegation, how much inheritance should be included, and how to ensure reuse in OOP programming, design patterns can be seen as a big cheat sheet. You can quickly look up the general designs that use class diagrams to display where inheritance and composition are employed. Using a Unified Modeling Language (UML), you can learn to look at a class diagram and quickly see the different parts (called *participants*). (Chapter 4 covers the details of using UMLs to work with design patterns with PHP.)

Organization of Design Patterns

This book follows the organization of design patterns laid out by the Gang of Four. In the most general sense, design patterns are organized by purpose and scope. Design pattern purpose has been organized into three classifications:

- Creational
- Structural
- Behavioral

This classification is a general view of patterns in terms of what goal they are designed to accomplish. Scope has two categories:

- Class
- Object

This section looks at these ordering categories and explains how they can be handy in selecting and understanding design patterns.

Creational patterns

As the name implies, creational patterns are ones used to create objects. More specifically, they abstract the instantiation process. As a program comes to depend more on composition, it depends less on hardcoded instantiations and more on a flexible set of behaviors that can be arranged into a more complex set. Creational patterns provide ways to encapsulate knowledge about which concrete classes a system uses and hide information about instance creation and composition.

Structural patterns

The patterns concerned with the structure of compositions are structural. The *structural class patterns* employ inheritance to compose interfaces or implementations. The *structural object patterns* describe ways to compose objects to establish new functionality. Understanding structural patterns contributes to understanding and using interrelated classes as participants in a design pattern.

Behavioral patterns

By far, the largest number of patterns is behavioral object ones. The focal point of these patterns is algorithms and the assignment of responsibilities between objects. Gamma et al. note that these design patterns describe more than the patterns of objects or classes. They describe the patterns of communication between classes and object.

Class category

The first of the two scope categories is *class*. The focus in these patterns is on the relationships between classes and their subclasses. Of the 24 design patterns in their book, GoF include only four in the class scope. The relationships are established through inheritance, and because GoF emphasize composition over inheritance, it is no surprise. Patterns in class scope are static and thereby fixed at compile time.

Object category

While most design patterns are in the *object scope*, several use inheritance as well as those in *class scope*. What differentiates design patterns in object scope is that the focus is on objects that can be changed at runtime, making these patterns more dynamic.

Choosing a Design Pattern

Part of learning design patterns is learning to select the most appropriate one. Keep in mind that design patterns are not templates. They are general strategies that deal with general problems that crop up in object-oriented programming. This book includes one design pattern from each of the three *purpose* categories and the two *scope* categories. In addition, it includes three chapters (Chapter 12 through Chapter 14) that tackle common uses of PHP with MySQL where design patterns will come in handy. The three patterns discussed in these final chapters are all of the object scope and behavioral purpose type, the largest category in the GoF catalog.

What Causes Redesign?

One of the first considerations in selecting a design pattern is to ask, "What causes redesign?" For example, suppose you have set up an online help desk. Users make requests and a database stores responses. However, you can plan on both the types of help request and the help responses changing. If your program depends on specific operations, making changes can cause problems. So instead of having hardcoded operations to satisfy a request, a *Chain of Responsibility* design pattern provides a way to allow the request to be passed along a chain to give more than one object a chance to handle it.

This book provides guidance on what kinds of problems different design patterns can solve. The chapters and patterns provide the context for understanding not only the general principles of design patterns but also specific cases of problems handled by particular patterns.

What Varies?

One thing to consider in choosing a design pattern is what will vary in a design. Instead of looking at the cause of redesign, this approach looks at what you want to be able to change without redesign. As you will see, the focus switches to encapsulating the concept that varies. Table 3-1 shows the nine design patterns this book explains divided into purpose, scope, and aspects of the pattern that can vary.

Table 3-1. Design pattern purpose, scope, and variation

Purpose	Scope	Name	What Can Vary
Creative	Class	Factory Method	Subclass of object instantiated
	Object	Prototype	Class of object instantiated
Structural	Class	Adapter*	Interface of object
	Object	Adapter* Decorator	Object responsibility without subclassing
Behavioral	Class	Template Method	Steps in algorithm
	Object	State	States of objects
	Object	Strategy	An algorithm
	Object	Chain of Responsibility	Object that can fulfill request
	Object	Observer	Number of objects that depend on other objects; how many dependent objects can stay up to date

 *The Adapter pattern has two configurations: one class and one object. Chapter 7 examines both.

Each of the patterns has a *general* use. The variation must be understood in context, and as we look at each pattern, the variation becomes clearer.

Unique Problem Solving: Are Design Patterns Canned Answers?

Because design patterns are solutions to recurring and common problems in programming, some misconstrue them as "canned answers" and programming "straitjackets." That's like saying that the loop structure in PHP is a programming constraint. Loops, like design patterns, were introduced to deal with recurring programming problems; in the case of the loop, dealing with repetitions. Having a single loop take care of 100 iterations sure beats writing 100 sequential lines. Likewise, using design patterns with loose coupling beats having to rewrite an entire program every time you make a change. So, just like you'll find many different uses and implementations of loop structures, you'll find a lot of different design pattern implementations.

What Is the Difference Between Design Patterns and Frameworks?

Design patterns are smaller architectural elements and more abstract than frameworks. Further, design patterns are less specialized than frameworks. As a result, design patterns are more reusable and flexible than frameworks.

The advantage of a framework, somewhat like the advantage of a template, is that they are more instructive. They are clearer guides to the structures of problem solving. What they make up for in ease of use they give up in architectural flexibility. Using a framework, building applications goes much faster, but what you can build is constrained by the framework itself. A framework can contain object-oriented structures, and often frameworks will be stacked, each layer handling one aspect of a larger design. Some features of frameworks are shared in design patterns, but design patterns are not as specialized, large, or concrete as frameworks.

CHAPTER 4

Using UMLs with Design Patterns

*Reality seems valueless by comparison with the
dreams of fevered imaginations; reality is therefore
abandoned.*

—Emile Durkheim

*The earliest phase of social formations found in
historical as well as in contemporary social
structures is this: a relatively small circle firmly
closed against neighboring, strange,
or in some way antagonistic circles.*

—Georg Simmel

*Neither the life of an individual nor the history of
a society can be understood without
understanding both.*

—C. Wright Mills

Why Unified Modeling Language (UML)?

In their book, *Design Patterns: Elements of Reusable Object-Oriented Software*, Gamma, Helm, Johnson, and Vlissides (Addison-Wesley) employ a UML that may have slight variations from 1990s era UML standards, as well as contemporary UML 2.0 standards. However, those variations are slight, and by employing the GoF version of a UML, the reader will be able to compare the design patterns using PHP in this book with the Gang of Four's original work. So whatever arguments may exist about the best UML for programming, you will find strict consistency between the UML in this book and the original work by Gamma and his associates.

If you are not familiar with UMLs, you will need patience. As you work with design patterns, they will become clearer in the context of the design and specific usage with PHP. Because of the minimum data typing used in PHP, implementing a design directly from a UML is very difficult until you are able to make the adjustments for data type and understanding the pattern itself.

Class Diagrams

Previous chapters displayed some simple class diagrams, and this section shows more details of class diagrams and how to use them with design patterns. In general, design pattern class diagrams display relations and communication between participants (classes and interfaces). For example, Figure 4-1 shows a typical class diagram of a design pattern. In this particular diagram, you will find five participants:

- **Client (implied)**
- *Creator*
- **ConcreteCreator**
- *Product*
- **ConcreteProduct**

Each of the participants is a class or interface (abstract class or interface). The names of interfaces are in italics whereas concrete classes are in bold roman text. Note that the Client is shown in a light gray box. That means that it is implied in the pattern, and in the case of the Factory Method pattern, the Client class is not part of the pattern.

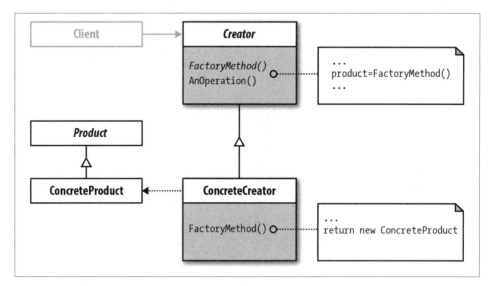

Figure 4-1. Class diagram (Factory Method)

The Client class is often an integral part of design patterns; sometimes it is implied, and sometimes it is absent from the diagram altogether. Clients make requests from the main program, and the arrows help to show the different relations between the Client and the main part of the program. Often, programmers use the name "main" to indicate the client, but with design patterns, the "main" terminology is misleading. The main part of the program is in the interrelated participants and not the client.

Figure 4-2 is the same pattern minus the pseudocode annotations to provide a clearer focus on the fundamental elements in the pattern.

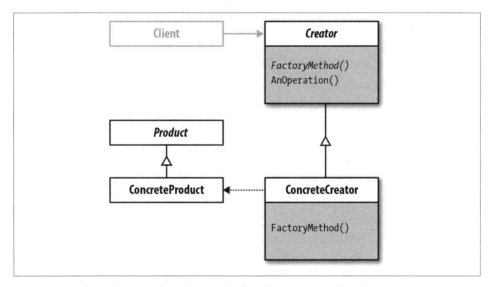

Figure 4-2. Class diagram (Factory Method without annotations)

The Factory Method pattern instantiates objects through a *factory* (Creator) to separate the instantiation process from the requestor. The client wants (requests) a product of some sort, but instead of instantiating it directly from the ConcreteProduct, it is directed (as seen in the class diagram) to make the request through the Creator. Without class diagrams, knowing where to direct the client to make a request would be ambiguous, as would all participant relations. Class diagrams provide a view of the design pattern so that you can quickly see the relationships illustrated in the UML. The exact nature of relationships is specific, and the following sections help break down the symbols used for the pattern participants and the connections.

Participant Symbols

The Gang of Four refer to the classes and interfaces that make up a design pattern as *participants*. The name of the participant is in boldface. Interfaces (interfaces and abstract classes) are italicized. Some participants are shown with a line beneath the name with a list of key methods. Abstract methods are italicized, and concrete methods are in normal type face. Figure 4-3 shows a close look at the Creator interface.

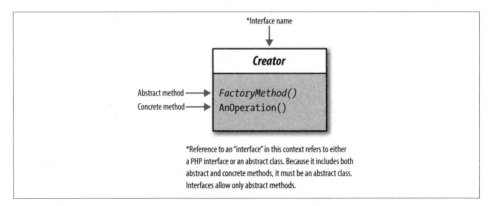

Figure 4-3. Elements in an interface participant

In concrete implementations of interfaces, the abstract methods are concrete as well. Figure 4-4 shows the implementation of the Creator interface.

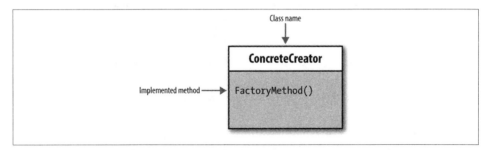

Figure 4-4. Concrete class and method from abstract class or interface

Note that the method, called AnOperation() in the interface, is not included in the concrete class. That's because it has been implemented already and inherited by the ConcreteCreator. However, the FactoryMethod() must be implemented because it was an abstract method in the parent class.

A final notation associated with participants is the *pseudocode annotations*. Figure 4-5 shows a clearer view of the annotations removed from the Factory Method pattern.

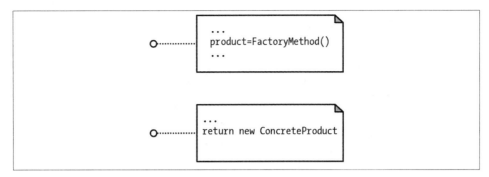

Figure 4-5. Pseudocode annotations

Pseudocode annotations provide further information about the structure of the design pattern. They are designed to give the developer a better sense of different code expectations with participants.

What's the Best UML?

Like most things in OOP and design patterns, the best resource is the original source. As noted, the UML in this book is that used by the Gang of Four, but the root of UMLs can be found in works by Booch, Jacobson, and Rumbaugh. They were the original developers of UML in the mid-1990s and proposed their Unified Modeling Language to the Object Management Group (OMG), a standards group for the computer industry. It was adopted as the industry standard in 1997 and has been revised as models have changed and refined. A great resource for UMLs can be found in Chapter 5 of *Object-Oriented Analysis and Design with Applications, 3rd Edition* (Addison-Wesley). This 100-page chapter provides good details on one of the most up-to-date versions of the OMG UML. The 2005 edition of *Unified Modeling Language User Guide, 2nd Edition*, by Booch, Jacobson, and Rumbaugh provides almost 500 pages of UML detail. So, if you want to delve into UMLs, you can find what you want in these resources.

Relationship Notations

Pseudocode annotations provide further information about the structure of the design pattern. They are designed to give the developer a better sense of different code expectations with participants (see Figure 4-6).

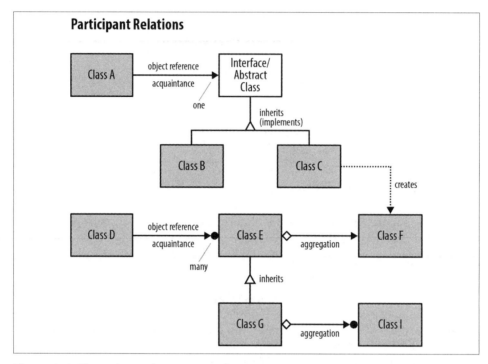

Figure 4-6. Class relationships

The associations and their meanings may vary in different renditions of the UML and this collage is a somewhat simplified UML of the relations that can be found in Chapter 1 of *Design Patterns: Elements of Reusable Object-Oriented Software*, where you can find more details if desired. In case you wish to use additional design patterns with PHP not covered in this book, you will be familiar with the UML used by GoF.

Acquaintance Relations

The basic and possibly the most common relationship between participants in a design pattern is the *acquaintance*. An acquaintance relationship is where one participant holds a reference to another participant. It is represented by a simple arrow between the Client and ISubject and the Proxy and RealSubject, as shown in a Proxy design pattern in Figure 4-7.

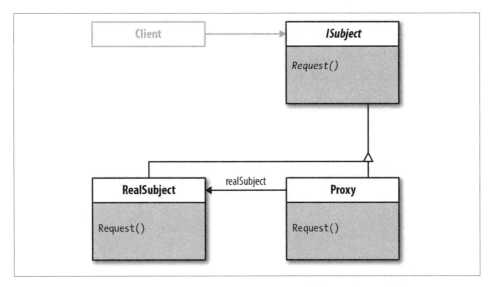

Figure 4-7. Association relations between Client *and* ISubject *and between* Proxy *and* RealSubject

In order to see a concrete example of such an association, the following listing of the Proxy class shows what an association would look like in PHP:

```php
<?php
class Proxy extends ISubject
{
    private $realSubject;

    protected function request()
    {
        $this->realSubject=new RealSubject();
        $this->realSubject->request();
    }

    public function login($un,$pw)
    {
        //Evaluates password etc.
        if($un==="Professional" && $pw==="acp")
        {
            $this->request();
        }
        else
        {
            print "Cry 'Havoc,' and let slip the dogs of war!";
        }
    }
}
?>
```

Generally, when one class holds a reference to another class, it would merely need to have a declaration. In a strongly typed language like C# where declarations include the data type, the "association" reference would look like the following:

```
private RealSubject realSubject;
```

As you can see in the Proxy listing, there's also a declaration for a private variable with the same name:

```
private $realSubject;
```

The problem is that the variable can be instantiated as any data type. So, in order to hold a reference, the variable either has to be extended from a concrete instantiation of the variable, or it must be instantiated in the class where it is declared. In this case, it is instantiated:

```
$this->realSubject=new RealSubject();
```

So now, the Proxy class holds a reference to the RealSubject class and has an acquaintance relation with it.

Aggregation Relationship

The Gang of Four point out that no single code set can demonstrate what an aggregate relationship looks like, so keep in mind that the example used here simply shows what an implemented design pattern (Strategy) using aggregation looks like. In some respects, an aggregate relation is like an acquaintance relation but stronger. As Gamma et al. note, aggregation implies that an aggregate object and its owner have identical lifetimes. That is something like heart and lungs. As long as the heart keeps pumping blood, the lungs can move oxygenated blood throughout the system. Each is independent as an operating organ, but if one stops, so will the other.

The Strategy design pattern includes an aggregate relationship between the Context class and the Strategy interface, as shown in Figure 4-8.

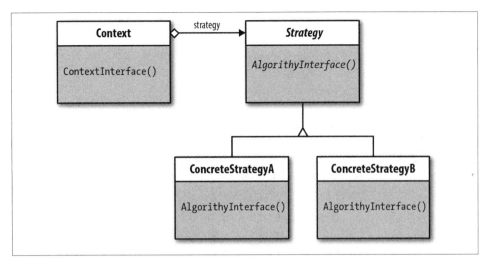

Figure 4-8. Strategy class diagram with aggregate relationship between `Context` class and `Strategy` interface

Now, look at a PHP listing of a `Context` class:

```php
<?php

class Context
{
    private $strategy;

    public function __construct(IStrategy $strategy)
    {
        $this->strategy = $strategy;
    }

    public function algorithm($elements)
    {
        $this->strategy->algorithm($elements);
    }
}

?>
```

The code hint reference is to the `IStrategy` interface. (The interface name is `IStrat egy` of the Strategy participant in the design pattern.) In this way, you can see that the `Context` class holds a reference to the Strategy interface through code hinting and without having to instantiate an implementation of `IStrategy` in the `Context` participant (class). The `Client` class will have to provide a concrete strategy implementation when instantiating an instance of the `Context` class. For example, a client making a request would include a `ConcreteStrategyA`:

```php
<?php
interface IStrategy
{
    public function algorithm($elements);
}

?>
```

As can be seen in the simple IStrategy interface, it has a single method, algo
rithm(). However, the Context class appears to have implemented the algorithm()
method. Actually, the Context class is configured with a concrete implementation of
IStrategy through the constructor function. The important feature of the relationship
is to note how the two objects form an *aggregation* and how they have identical lifetimes.

Of all the relations, the aggregate relation is the most difficult to explain and understand
because of its many variations. Rather than attempt further explanation at this time and
risk oversimplifying and misrepresenting it, as you go through the design patterns in
the book that use this aggregation, its specific use will be explained.

Inheritance and Implementation Relations

The Gang of Four uses the same notation for inheritance and implementation: a triangle.
Figure 4-9 shows an abstract class and interface with child classes.

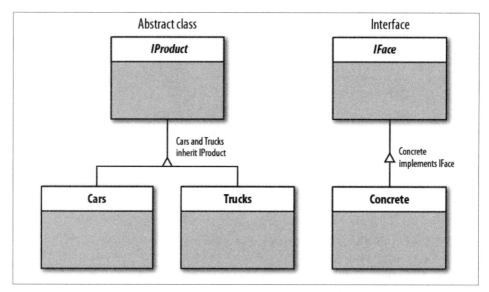

Figure 4-9. Inheritance and implementation use the same triangle notation

Single inheritance or implementation uses a single triangle (triangle-on-a-stick), whereas indications of multiple inheritance or implementation display the triangle lying flat on the common connecting lines to the concrete classes.

You may wonder why GoF chose to use the same triangle symbol for both inheritance and implementation. In part, it is because virtually all design patterns that use inheritance from a class do so from an abstract class. Abstract classes imply implementation of the abstract methods, so whether interfaces or abstract classes are employed, implementation is part of the relationship. In many places in their book, GoF use abstract classes and interfaces interchangeably (referring to them simply as *interfaces*) because both include interfaces used by the child classes. Likewise, in many design patterns, it does not matter whether abstract classes or interfaces are used in the pattern. In one implementation of the design pattern, the programmer will use an abstract class, and in another implementation of the same design pattern, interfaces are used.

Polymorphism in the Use of Terms

One of the difficulties some encounter in reading the Gang of Four's book is that they use certain terms interchangeably. After initial struggles, you may be ready to write the authors and tell them to get their terms straight, but it turns out that just like polymorphism in programming, there's polymorphism in writing. The following are some examples and how to handle them:

Interfaces
> GoF refers to both abstract classes and interfaces as *interfaces*. What they're referring to (as am I) is the collection of unimplemented methods and properties that make up the abstract class or interface. The important feature is the capacity of either to have loose binding in a pattern.

Implementation
> Just like the use of the term *interface*, you will find the term *implements* used in different contexts. Both abstract classes and interfaces must be implemented to some extent. Any abstract method in an abstract class needs to be implemented by a child class, and so even though a child class inherits the interface of an abstract class, it also must implement at least some of the abstract methods in the abstract class. So, a general reference to a concrete class implementing an abstract class or an interface points to both the inheritance and the implementation when abstract classes are involved. It's just easier to say "implemented" rather than "inherited and implemented." Besides, it points to the wiggle room that the child class has to nail down a concrete implementation.

Operation

Throughout the book, including in class diagrams, you'll run into the term *operation*. In general, it refers to a piece of the program that *does something*. The operation might be synonymous with *function* or *method*, or it might refer to several different things that occur between classes. For example, the reference might be to code that instantiates an instance from a concrete class in a design pattern. You might run across a reference to the operation that wraps ClassB to instantiate an instance of ClassC. The *operation* in that case may be only part of a function or simply a statement in a constructor.

Flexible thinking

Throughout this book and the Gang of Four's, you will need to think about programming in a different way. Think in terms larger than working out an algorithm, and especially think about *relationships* between objects. This may involve some algorithmic thinking, but for the most part, by placing things in the context of their relationship to one another and a larger context, everything will make more sense. Good algorithms will always be important, but they live in methods or objects. What's important is the interplay between objects and how to use and reuse them. If used correctly, object-oriented components can always handle a new algorithm. As long as the objects have good relations with other objects, algorithm changes should not interfere with the overall program. That's why you need to think *relations* and not a sequence of coding that will handle an immediate problem.

Creates Relations

When one object creates an instance of another in a design pattern, the notation is a dashed line with an arrow pointing to the object that has been instantiated. You will see this kind of relationship in patterns that use factories such as the Factory Method (see Chapter 5) or Abstract Factory design patterns, but you will encounter it in some other patterns as well. Figure 4-10 shows a class diagram of the Factory Method with the `ConcreteCreator` using a `factoryMethod()` to create instances of `ConProductA` and `ConProductB`. The `Client` holds references to both the `Creator` and `Product` interfaces so that it can specify the exact product request.

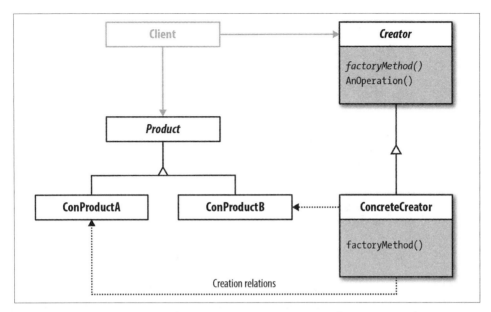

Figure 4-10. Creates relations between a concrete creator and concrete products

In the discussion of acquaintance relationships between classes using PHP, in some cases it may be necessary to instantiate a class to hold reference to another class or interface. Such instantiation is due to creating a data type to hold the reference and not for using the instantiated object. Where this is necessary in PHP, do not use the dashed line. The relation is acquaintance, and even though an instance is created, it is only for establishing the acquaintance.

Multiple Relations

Sometimes you will see a class diagram where the arrows in acquaintance or aggregation relations have a ball at the end of the arrows, as in Figure 4-11.

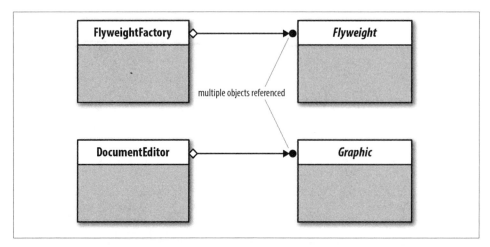

Figure 4-11. Black ball indicates multiple objects referenced

The black ball means that multiple objects are being referenced or aggregated. The Flyweight pattern is used to reference multiple instances of shared objects or different objects.

Object Diagrams

Unlike a class diagram that shows the classes, object diagrams show only the instances and arrows indicating the object referenced. The naming convention employed is a class instance name headed by the lowercase letter *a*. So, an instance of a class named Cli ent would be aClient. The text in the lower half of the object diagram modules is the name of the target object or a method.

A good example of using an object diagram can be found in the Chain of Responsibility design pattern. The pattern is used where more than a single object may handle a request, such as a help desk application. The client issues a request and then a handler interface passes on the request until a concrete handler is found to deal with the request. Figure 4-12 illustrates the chain.

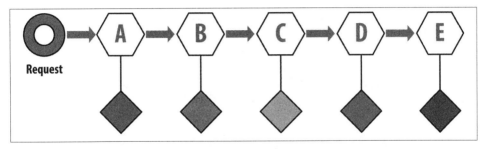

Figure 4-12. A Chain of Responsibility pattern passes a request along a chain of handlers

In Figure 4-12, the request is passed from A to B to C and so on until the request can be handled and terminates to search for a handler. Figure 4-13 shows the same process in an object diagram.

Figure 4-13. Object diagram of Chain of Responsibility pattern

Object diagrams provide another way of viewing a specific implementation of a design pattern and the relations between the objects generated through the pattern. They can help clarify object relations.

Interaction Diagrams

The final diagram GoF uses is one to trace the order in which requests are executed. These interaction diagrams are like object diagrams in the naming of objects, but their timeline is vertical—from top to bottom. Solid lines with arrowheads point to the direction of the request, and dashed lines with arrowheads indicate instantiation. Figure 4-14 shows the same Chain of Responsibility sequence as Figure 4-13, but in an interaction diagram. (The gray time direction arrow and time labels have been added but do not appear in the actual diagrams.)

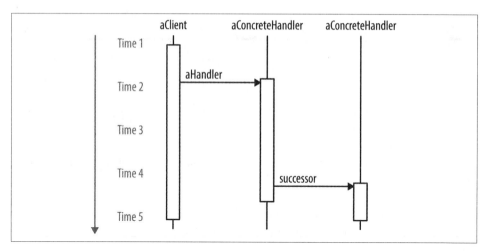

Figure 4-14. Interaction diagram of Chain of Responsibility pattern

The vertical rectangles indicate the time at which the object is active. As can be seen in Figure 4-14, the client object is active the entire time, the first concrete handler becomes active with the request from the client, and the second concrete handler does not become active until the request is passed from the first concrete handler.

The Role of Diagrams and Notations in Object-Oriented Programming

Before going on to examine the first design pattern and implementing it in PHP, I want to pause a moment and look at what we're trying to do with diagrams and notations. Just in case we forget, diagrams and the notations associated with them are explaining, examining, and building design patterns. The extent to which they are useful in assisting us, we can employ them. However, the second they are not useful, they should be abandoned and new ones created.

For years, the only programming diagram I knew was the old flowchart. It looks fine, and while I rarely used them for program planning or as guides for writing a program, I understood their use. However, in looking at them now, I realize they might be very bad tools for object-oriented programming. Flowcharts are guides to sequential programming. In contrast, the UMLs developed for OOP look and feel different. They break up a program into modules called classes, and notations show relations and interactions.

Tools for UMLs

If you look, you can probably find tools that will help draw UMLs, but I'd recommend against it. In *Unified Modeling Language User Guide, 2nd Edition*, when discussing automated UML tools, Grady Booch points out the following:

> Given automated support for any notation, one of the things that tools can do is help bad designers create ghastly designs much more quickly than they ever could without them.

If you treat the UMLs as aids for thinking, you'll probably be better off as far as your code designs are concerned and understand design patterns a lot better. For example, Figure 4-15 shows the kind of diagram (Strategy design pattern) I've used with PHP projects to good effect.

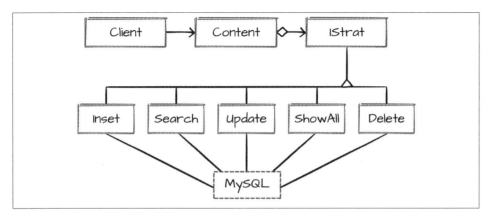

Figure 4-15. Sketching out design on paper

As I start working on the project, I'll make more sketches with more details, annotations, comments, and bits of code. I am forced to think while I sketch out the pattern and its details. With larger projects and groups of programmers, some kind of UML drawing tools may be handy for communication between programmers for the sake of clarity. At this time, though, pencil and paper stand as my main UML tools (I like to use the discarded pages from my cartoon-a-day calendar).

Other UMLs

As far as UMLs go, rather than thinking of "standards," think of how they can be usefully employed. Booch suggests a *diagram taxonomy* divided into Structure and Behavior Diagrams, with Interaction Diagrams being a major subtype of the behavior category. Of these, I have found *statecharts* to be especially useful for thinking about designs using state machines—the State design pattern in particular. The statecharts help the developer focus on states, change of states, triggers, and transitions. So while statecharts are not part of the UML set GoF uses, they can be handy for thinking through problems that involve state machines like those in State design patterns. (See Chapter 10, *The State Design Pattern*, for examples of statecharts.)

For getting started with design patterns, besides becoming familiar with the notations, learn about what the notations mean. For example, knowing the meaning of aggregation is more important than knowing it is represented by a line with a diamond on its tail and an arrowhead on its head. Further, if you start using the design pattern UML, you can better frame programming problems as having design pattern solutions. By using a pencil and a piece of paper, your thought process will be better connected than if you use automated tools, and you'll have a better chance of understanding design patterns.

PART II

Creational Design Patterns

Imagination is the beginning of creation. You imagine what you desire, you will what you imagine and at last you create what you will.

—George Bernard Shaw

Without culture, and the relative freedom it implies, society, even when perfect, is but a jungle. This is why any authentic creation is a gift to the future.

—Albert Camus

If the Lord Almighty had consulted me before embarking on creation thus, I should have recommended something simpler.

—Alfonso the Wise

Creational design patterns are those that focus on the instantiation process. These patterns are designed to conceal the creation process from the instances created and encapsulate knowledge used by the objects. The five creational design patterns listed by Gamma, Helm, Johnson, and Vlissides include:

- Abstract Factory
- Builder
- Factory Method
- Prototype
- Singleton

Of these five, the Factory Method and Prototype have been selected as examples of creational designs implemented in PHP. The Factory Method is the only one of the five that is included in the class scope category of design patterns, and it is a relatively simple yet informative pattern. The Prototype pattern is in the object category, and it can be implemented using the PHP __clone() method. Objects are instantiated (created) on the basis of prototype, and then further objects are cloned from the instantiated object. I think you will find this pattern easy to use and quite handy.

Of the uses of creational patterns, the most interesting is that they are important—indeed critical—as programs and systems evolve to depend more on object composition than on class inheritance. As programs become systems made up of objects composed of other objects, the creation of any single object should not depend on the creator. In other words, objects should not be tightly bound to the processes that create the objects. In this way, object composition is not hindered by any specific feature of the requesting object. The design patterns in Part II illustrate how the creational process is optimally achieved. Figure II.1 provides an overview of how creational patterns work.

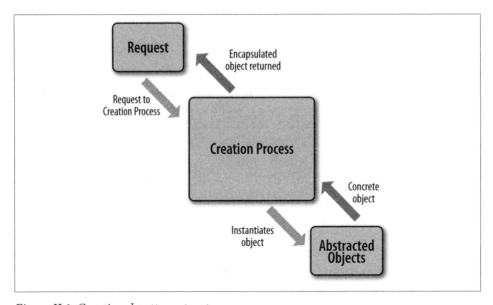

Figure II.1. Creational pattern structure

CHAPTER 5

Factory Method Design Pattern

Women's movements would form among the
factory workers, a great mobilisation that
destroyed the old models.

—Emma Bonino

Design is the method of putting form and content
together. Design, just as art, has multiple
definitions; there is no single definition. Design can
be art. Design can be aesthetics. Design is so simple,
that's why it is so complicated.

—Paul Rand

Create your own method. Don't depend slavishly
on mine. Make up something that will work for
you! But keep breaking traditions, I beg you.

—Constantin Stanislavski

What Is the Factory Method Pattern?

As part of the creational category of design patterns, the Factory Method pattern is involved with creating *something*. In the case of the Factory Method, the *something* created is a product that is not tied to the class that creates it. Instead, in order to maintain loose coupling, the client makes the request through a factory. The factory then makes the requested product. Another way of thinking about it is that the Factory Method frees the product from the requestor. Figure 5-1 shows a class diagram of the Factory Method.

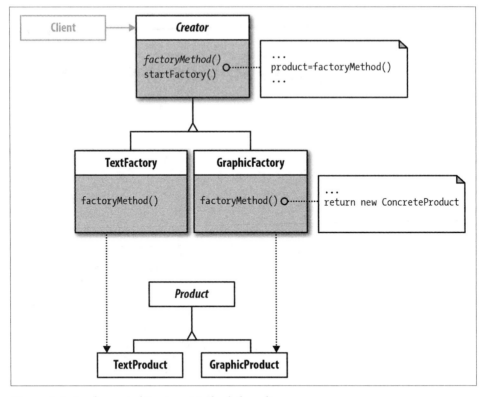

Figure 5-1. Implemented Factory Method class diagram

The Client class is implied. As you can see in Figure 5-1, the Client holds a reference to the Creator (factory interface) for requesting a graphic or text product. However, it does not instantiate the product it requests. The concrete factories instantiate the requested product. Imagine that you want to order chocolate cupcakes with black and orange frosting for a Halloween party. You call the baker (creator) who then makes the cupcakes (product) for you. You are not involved with the creation of the object that you requested but you still get the cupcakes requested.

When to Use the Factory Method

In part, design patterns are selected based on what you want to be able to change. In Chapter 3, Table 3-1 shows that the Factory Method should be used when the subclass of an object instantiated can vary. In the examples in this chapter, all of the subclasses of the Project interface vary; they are different countries. As you will see, the projects developed are objects made up of text (write-ups) and graphics (maps). At the outset, we assume that the developer does not know how many countries there will be. In other words, the number and types of objects are unknown. A class cannot anticipate the number of objects it must create, and so you do not want the class tightly bound to the classes it may have to create.

If a class has a finite and known number of objects it must create, the class can be built so that the finite number of objects can be created in a predictable manner. For example, if you are making a world map application with separate objects for the seven continents, you can be fairly certain that they are not going to vary. On the other hand, if you are creating a site for different species of insects, you can be fairly certain that new ones will be discovered, change, and become extinct over a relatively short period of time. A programming product to deal with that kind of variation needs to have a good deal of flexibility built into it. This is the kind of project where you would want to consider using a Factory Method design.

A Minimalist Example

To get started with the Factory Method design pattern, this first example returns only text. It is for a project where the developer knows that he will have to create different text and graphic items for a project that involves maps and text write-ups. He has no idea of exactly how many graphic-text pairs he has to create, and he's not even sure what the client wants to add. He's been told that a map graphic is required and that descriptive text needs to be added as well. So, to get started, he creates a small Factory Method design to output text information to the screen, one displaying "graphic" information and the other "text" information. If done correctly, it should not be difficult to make changes to accommodate any number of text and graphics.

Factory Work

The first step is to set up the factory: a Creator interface. For the interface, this implementation uses an abstract class. In looking carefully at the class diagram, one of the code annotations indicates a concrete method, startFactory(). From the fact that a concrete method is used in the interface, we know that the interface must be an abstract class instead of an interface. Interfaces can have only abstract methods, so it must be an abstract class. In addition, the design requires an abstract method, factoryMethod(). In an abstract class, all such methods need to be designated as abstract; otherwise, they are treated as concrete methods. *Creator.php* shows the code for this first pattern participant:

```php
<?php
//Creator.php
abstract class Creator
{
    protected abstract function factoryMethod();

    public function startFactory()
    {
```

```
        $mfg= $this->factoryMethod();
        return $mfg;
    }
}
?>
```

Note that the pseudocode annotation indicates that the startFactory() method needs to return a *product*. In the implementation, startFactory() expects that the factory Method() will return a product object. So, the concrete implementation of the factor yMethod() needs to build and return a product object implemented from a Product interface.

The two concrete factory classes extend Creator and implement the factoryMethod. The factoryMethod() implementation returns a text or graphic product through a Product method, getProperties(). The TextFactory and GraphicFactory implementations incorporate these elements:

```php
<?php
//TextFactory.php
include_once('Creator.php');
include_once('TextProduct.php');
class TextFactory extends Creator
{
    protected function factoryMethod()
    {
        $product=new TextProduct();
        return($product->getProperties());
    }
}
?>
```

```php
<?php
//GraphicFactory.php
include_once('Creator.php');
include_once('GraphicProduct.php');
class GraphicFactory extends Creator
{
    protected function factoryMethod()
    {
        $product=new GraphicProduct();
        return($product->getProperties());
    }
}
?>
```

Both factory implementations are similar other than the fact that one creates a Text Product and the other a GraphicProduct instance.

The Product

The second interface in the Factory Method design pattern is the `Product`. In this first minimalist implementation, a single method, `getProperties()`, is to be implemented by all text and graphics properties:

```php
<?php
//Product.php
interface Product
{
    public function getProperties();
}
?>
```

Set up as a method with no properties, we can decide with the implementation exactly what we want to do with the `getProperties()` method. In PHP, given the signature of a name and visibility, we can do anything we want with this abstract method, including having a return value, and as long as the name and visibility conform to the signature, we're good to go.

You can see where *polymorphism* comes in with this implementation of the Factory Method in the `getProperties()` method. It is going to be used to return either "text" or "graphics," but we know that as long as it has the correct signature, it's going to deliver what we want. The exact same method, `getProperties()`, has many (poly) different forms (morphs). In this case, one of the forms returns text and the other graphics:

```php
<?php
//TextProduct.php
include_once('Product.php');
class TextProduct implements Product
{
    private $mfgProduct;

    public function getProperties()
    {
        $this->mfgProduct="This is text.";
        return $this->mfgProduct;
    }
}
?>
```

You may be thinking, "Big deal, all this does is return a string variable." At this point, that is true. However, you can put anything you want in the implementation, and the Factory Method design will create and return it to the `Client` for use. So, where you see the output "This is text," or "This is a graphic," imagine any object you may possibly want to create and use. This next implementation returns an abstract graphic in a message with a "text graphic":

```php
<?php
//GraphicProduct.php
include_once('Product.php');
```

```
class GraphicProduct implements Product
{
    private $mfgProduct;

    public function getProperties()
    {
        $this->mfgProduct="This is a graphic.<3";
        return $this->mfgProduct;
    }
}
?>
```

Each of the two factory and product implementations override the abstract methods to create two different factories and products while conforming to the interfaces implemented.

The Client

The final participant in this pattern is implied: the client. We do not want the Client class to make a request directly to the product. Instead, we want the request to go through the Creator interface. Later, if we add products or factories, the client can make the same request to a much richer variety of products without breaking the application:

```
<?php
//Client.php
include_once('GraphicFactory.php');
include_once('TextFactory.php');
class Client
{
    private $someGraphicObject;
    private $someTextObject;

    public function __construct()
    {
        $this->someGraphicObject=new GraphicFactory();
        echo $this->someGraphicObject->startFactory() . "<br />";
        $this->someTextObject=new TextFactory();
        echo $this->someTextObject->startFactory() . "<br />";
    }
}

$worker=new Client();
?>
```

If everything works as expected, the output is:

```
This is a graphic.<3
This is text.
```

Note that the `Client` object made no direct request to the product but instead made it through the factory. Importantly, the client leaves the characteristics of the product up to the product implementations.

Accommodating Class Changes

The real value of a design pattern is not the speed of the operations but in the speed of development. In simple applications, like this current example of a Factory Method, it can be difficult to see. However, as we begin making changes, the value becomes more apparent.

Adding Graphic Elements

The first step will be to change a product to include loading a graphic image into an HTML document. In and of itself, adding graphics to a web page is quite simple, but as your PHP program becomes more complex, it can become trickier. The following shows the changed `GraphicProduct` class:

```php
<?php
//GraphicProduct.php
include_once('Product.php');
class GraphicProduct implements Product
{
    private $mfgProduct;

    public function getProperties()
    {
        $this->mfgProduct="<!doctype html><html><head><meta charset='UTF-8' />";
        $this->mfgProduct.="<title>Map Factory</title>";
        $this->mfgProduct.="</head><body>";
        $this->mfgProduct.="<img src='Mali.png' width='500' height='500' />";
        $this->mfgProduct.="</body></html>";
        return $this->mfgProduct;
    }
}
?>
```

Again you can see polymorphism at work. The same `getProperties()` method now has an entirely different implementation. Does this mean that the client will have to change its request? No. In requesting a graphic, the `Client` class just drops the text request as the following shows:

```php
<?php
//Client.php
include_once('GraphicFactory.php');
class Client
{
    private $someGraphicObject;
    private $someTextObject;
```

```php
    public function __construct()
    {
        $this->someGraphicObject=new GraphicFactory();
        echo $this->someGraphicObject->startFactory() . "<br />";
    }
}

$worker=new Client();
?>
```

That simple request is the same as was made in the initial client. However, because the GraphicProduct object changed, so does the output, as shown in Figure 5-2.

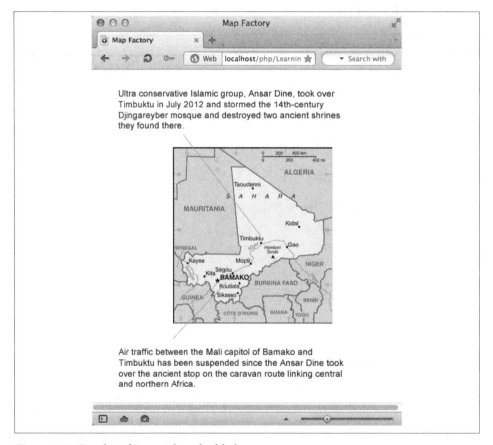

Figure 5-2. Graphic object with embedded text

In looking at Figure 5-2, you can see that the graphic includes text, but that text is part of the graphic image and not HTML text placed in the document.

Coordinating Products

Getting products in PHP is not that difficult, but as a site grows and becomes more complex, keeping the changes simple increases in importance. The next step is to work with the text and graphics so that they can be placed together in a document.

As you can see in Figure 5-2, the text has been integrated into the image, so all that the change has accomplished is to demonstrate that graphics can be loaded into a page without having to change the client's request from the GraphicFactory class. Can the same be done when more than two products have to be coordinated?

Taking materials from the CIA's *World Factbook*, a map and write-up have been stitched together, as shown in Figure 5-3.

Figure 5-3. Coordinated text and graphic objects

The Factory Method helps to simplify demands made by growing and increasingly complex sites where new products are introduced. To create the site shown in Figure 5-3 requires changes only in the text and graphic products. All of the other participants in the application stay the same, as requests depend on the interfaces and not the concrete products.

Changing the Text Product

The changes to the text product are relatively simple. The returned product will include some formatting and a header, but the same variable is returned to the requesting client and displayed on the screen. The following listing shows the changes in the TextProduct class:

```php
<?php
//TextProduct.php
include_once('Product.php');
class TextProduct implements Product
{
    private $mfgProduct;

    public function getProperties()
    {
        //Begin heredoc formating
        $this->mfgProduct =<<<MALI
<!doctype html>
<html><head>
<style type="text/css">
header {
    color: #900;
    font-weight: bold;
    font-size: 24px;
    font-family: Verdana, Geneva, sans-serif;
}
p {
    font-family: Verdana, Geneva, sans-serif;
    font-size: 12px;
}
</style>
<meta charset="UTF-8"><title>Mali</title></head>
<body>
<header>Mali</header>
<p>The Sudanese Republic and Senegal became independent of France in
1960 as the Mali Federation. When Senegal withdrew after only a
few months, what formerly made up the Sudanese Republic was
renamed Mali. Rule by dictatorship was brought to a close in 1991
by a military coup that ushered in a period of democratic rule.
President Alpha KONARE won Mali's first two democratic presidential
elections in 1992 and 1997. In keeping with Mali's two-term
constitutional limit, he stepped down in 2002 and was succeeded by
Amadou TOURE, who was elected to a second term in 2007 elections
that were widely judged to be free and fair.
 A military coup overthrew the government in March 2012, claiming
that the government had not adequately supported the Malian army's
fight against an advancing Tuareg-led rebellion in the north.
Heavy international pressure forced coup leaders to accelerate
the transition back to democratic rule and, to that end,
Dioncounda TRAORE was installed as interim president on 12 April 2012
    </p>
```

```
        </body></html>
MALI;
            return $this->mfgProduct;
        }
    }
    ?>
```

The changes in the text object appear to be substantial, but the single Product method, getProperties(), still maintains the same interface, returning a property object to a factory request. The heredoc format allows developers to write HTML code without having to put every line in quotes, and within the heredoc variable PHP variables and constants are accepted. (In the *Helper Classes* section further on in this chapter, you will see how a "Helper" class takes care of formatting.)

Changing the Graphic Product

In looking at the graphic object class, we see the same method and interface as when it merely returned text with no HTML formatting:

```
<?php
//GraphicProduct.php
include_once('Product.php');
class GraphicProduct implements Product
{
    private $mfgProduct;

    public function getProperties()
    {
        $this->mfgProduct="<img style='padding: 10px 10px 10px 0px';
        src='Mali.png' align='left' width='256' height='274'>";
        return $this->mfgProduct;
    }
}
?>
```

Just like the text product and the magic of polymorphism, the getProperties() method is proving to be as resilient as a cockroach. Nothing has been changed in the factory objects, and the same request from the Client has been issued, changing the request from "text" to a "graphic" product.

Adding New Products and Parameterized Requests

Thus far you've seen that changing the graphic and text will not tangle up a Factory Method design, but what happens when you start adding more maps and text write-ups? Will it be necessary to add a new concrete factory class every time a new country is added? That would mean a new factory and product would need to be added for each new country; it's time to look at a parameterized Factory Method design. Figure 5-4 shows one such Factory Method implementation.

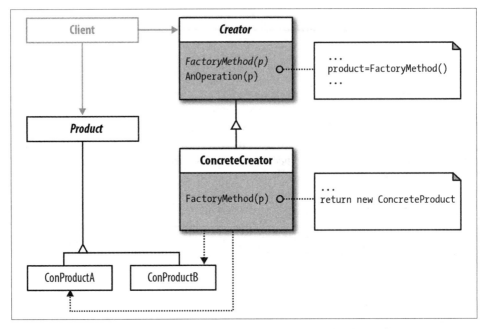

Figure 5-4. Single concrete creator with responsibility for multiple products

The class diagram in Figure 5-4 shows a number of differences from the initial class diagram. Both are accurate depictions of the Factory Method design pattern—they accomplish the same goals—but they are different in their implementation.

One of the key differences between the parameterized Factory Method and the initial design shown in Figure 5-1 is that the client holds references to the factory and the product. In the parameterized request, the Client class must name the product, not just the product factory. The parameter in the factoryMethod() operation is a product passed by the client; so the client must reference the concrete product it wants. However, that request is still through the Creator interface. So, even though the client has a reference to a product, it is still separated from the product through the Creator.

One Factory and Multiple Products

In most respects, the parameterized Factory Method is simpler because the client has to deal only with a single concrete factory. The factory method operation has a single parameter that directs the creation to the desired product. In the initial design, each product had its own factory and no parameter to pass; it relied on unique factories for each product.

As far as implementing more products from the parameterized Factory Method, all that needs to be done is to implement more concrete ones with the Product interface.

Further, since the product should contain both text and graphics, instead of having separate products for the two, in this example, a single class can handle them both as a unified entity without breaking the principle that each class should have only a single responsibility. The single responsibility is to display text and graphics depicting a country. Since the application is a simple one, the responsibility of each Product class is fairly simple as well.

The New Factories

The new factories—Creator and CountryCreator—are similar to the old, but they include both a parameter and code hinting. The code hinting allows development to proceed by programming to the interface (Product) and not the concrete implementation of the Product interface:

```php
<?php
//Creator.php
abstract class Creator
{
    protected abstract function factoryMethod(Product $product);

    public function doFactory($productNow)
    {
        $countryProduct=$productNow;
        $mfg= $this->factoryMethod($countryProduct);
        return $mfg;
    }
}
?>
```

As can be seen in the new Creator abstract class, both the factoryMethod() and the startFactory() operations expect a parameter. Further, because the code hinting requires a Product object and not a specific implementation of the Product, it can be used with any concrete instance of the Product.

The concrete creator class, CountryCreator, implements the factoryMethod() with the necessary parameter *with code hinting*. Of course, the class inherits the startFactory() method that will be used by the Client:

```php
<?php
//CountryFactory.php
include_once('Creator.php');
include_once('Product.php');
class CountryFactory extends Creator
{
    private $country;

    protected function factoryMethod(Product $product)
    {
        $this->country=$product;
        return($this->country->getProperties());
```

```
        }
    }
    ?>
```

The concrete creator class includes a private variable, $country, that holds the specific product requested by the client. It then uses the Product method, getProperties(), to return to the client.

The New Products

The changes in the concrete products do not change the original Product interface. It is exactly like it was originally:

```php
<?php
//Product.php
interface Product
{
    public function getProperties();
}
?>
```

That means the concrete products must also have the same interface, and as you will see, they do. However, the new implementations contain both graphics and text. The text is embedded in the class itself (something you would probably get from a text file or a database) and a graphic that is called up with a simple <img src...> tag. The following class represents an example with text and a graphic map culled from the CIA's *World Factbook* (*http://1.usa.gov/akOFIK*):

```php
<?php
//TextProduct.php
include_once('FormatHelper.php');
include_once('Product.php');

class KyrgyzstanProduct implements Product
{
    private $mfgProduct;
    private $formatHelper;

    public function getProperties()
    {
        $this->formatHelper=new FormatHelper();
        $this->mfgProduct=$this->formatHelper->addTop();
        $this->mfgProduct.=<<<KYRGYZSTAN
        <img src='Countries/Kyrgyzstan.png' class='pixRight' width='600'
            height='304'>
        <header>Kyrgyzstan</header>
        <p>A Central Asian country of incredible natural beauty and proud
            nomadic traditions, most of Kyrgyzstan was formally annexed to
            Russia in 1876. The Kyrgyz staged a major revolt against the
            Tsarist Empire in 1916 in which almost one-sixth of the Kyrgyz
            population was killed. Kyrgyzstan became a Soviet republic in 1936
```

and achieved independence in 1991 when the USSR dissolved. Nationwide
demonstrations in the spring of 2005 resulted in the ouster of
President Askar AKAEV, who had run the country since 1990.
Subsequent presidential elections in July 2005 were won overwhelmingly
by former prime minister Kurmanbek BAKIEV. Over the next few years,
the new president manipulated the parliament to accrue new powers
for himself. In July 2009, after months of harassment against
his opponents and media critics, BAKIEV won re-election in a
presidential campaign that the international community deemed
flawed. In April 2010, nationwide protests led to the resignation
and expulsion of BAKIEV. His successor, Roza OTUNBAEVA, served as
transitional president until Almazbek ATAMBAEV was inaugurated in
December 2011. Continuing concerns include: the trajectory of
democratization, endemic corruption, poor interethnic relations,
and terrorism.

```
        </p>
KYRGYZSTAN;
        $this->mfgProduct .=$this->formatHelper->closeUp();
        return $this->mfgProduct;
    }
}
?>
```

The output has not changed from the original Factory Method that had separate factories for graphics and text. Figure 5-5 shows what you can expect to see.

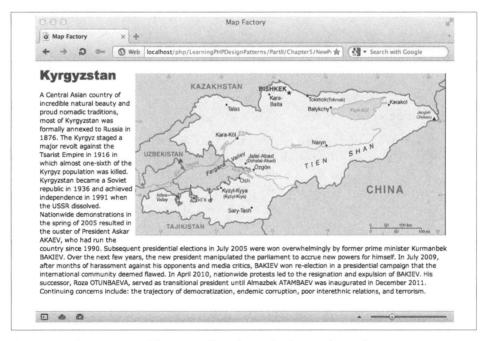

Figure 5-5. Parameterized factories allow for multiple specific products

You may have noticed that the image is on the right instead of the left, and it is larger compared to the map of Mali, but otherwise, it's almost the same. Something new is the addition of an instance of a class named `FormatHelper`. It is a "helper" class that needs to be explained in the context of design patterns and this particular implementation, but first, the `Client` class needs to be re-examined because it too has changed—it requires a parameter.

The Client with Parameters

Initial examples in this chapter show how the client simply made a request through the factory interface for the specific product factory. With the changes made, the `Client` class now has to include a parameter:

```php
<?php
//Client.php
include_once('CountryFactory.php');
include_once('KyrgyzstanProduct.php');
class Client
{
    private $countryFactory;

    public function __construct()
    {
        $this->countryFactory=new CountryFactory();
        echo $this->countryFactory->doFactory(new KyrgyzstanProduct());
    }
}

$worker=new Client();
?>
```

Helper Classes

A helper class in a design pattern is a class that has some task that is better handled by a separate object instead of incorporated into one of the participants. You might think of a helper class in the same way you would an external CSS file. You could add the same CSS to each and every class, but it is far more efficient to pack it into a single file and reuse it by incorporating a `<link>` tag that calls a stylesheet. Likewise, if you have a certain set of HTML formatting tags that are reused, they can be packaged into another object for reuse. The following shows the helper class used with this application:

```php
<?php
class FormatHelper
{
    private $topper;
    private $bottom;

    public function addTop()
    {
```

```
        $this->topper="<!doctype html><html><head>
        <link rel='stylesheet' type='text/css' href='products.css'/>
        <meta charset='UTF-8'>
        <title>Map Factory</title>
        </head>
        <body>";
        return $this->topper;
    }

    public function closeUp()
    {
        $this->bottom="</body></html>";
        return $this->bottom;
    }
}
?>
```

Not only does it provide an HTML wrapper, it also calls the CSS file, *products.css*. For convenience, the helper class has HTML code that is added to the top and bottom of a typical HTML page placed into two different public methods, addTop() and close Up(). In this way, the instantiated concrete product can be placed between the correct HTML formatting tags.

The CSS stylesheet also provides options for the developer and designer. Two CSS classes allow for left and right image alignment choices:

```
@charset "UTF-8";
/* CSS Document */
img
{
    padding: 10px 10px 10px 0px;
}

.pixRight
{
    float:right; margin: 0px 0px 5px 5px;
}

.pixLeft
{
    float:left; margin: 0px 5px 5px 0px;
}

header
{
    color:#900;
    font-size:24px;
    font-family:"Arial Black", Gadget, sans-serif;
}

body
{
```

```
        font-family:Verdana, Geneva, sans-serif;
        font-size:12px;
}
```

You can even think of a CSS file as a "helper" class. Likewise, you may wish to add some JavaScript or jQuery scripts as external helpers to the larger design.

File Diagram

An unofficial diagram that I've found helpful is a *file diagram*. Basically, it consists of a picture of the files and folders used in a design pattern with the relationship notations indicating links. It's a lot like a Class diagram but provides a picture of the actual files in use. Figure 5-6 shows a file diagram of the final Factory Method used in this chapter.

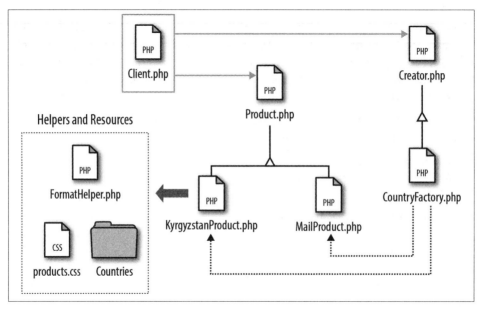

Figure 5-6. Added helpers and resources

As you can see in the diagram, the helpers and resources, while not part of the design pattern, are used by the products. A dashed box indicates they are separate from the pattern itself, and the large arrow indicates that they are used by the concrete products.

Product Changes: Leave the Interface Alone!

One of the big advantages of using a design pattern is the ease with which you can make changes in a class and not disrupt a much larger program. The secret to making it easy is to keep the same interface but change the contents.

One change that would simplify matters is taking the text out of the concrete products. By placing the write-ups into text files and then loading them into variables, not only would it be easier to change the text contents, but the concrete classes would be a lot cleaner as well.

In the new concrete product, a little routine adds the text to a private variable, $coun tryNow. So, instead of having a big messy jumble of text, the concrete product has five lines of code to place the write-up into a variable. The following shows a new product (Moldova) with a new way of handling the text:

```php
<?php
//MoldovaProduct.php
include_once('FormatHelper.php');
include_once('Product.php');

class MoldovaProduct implements Product
{
    private $mfgProduct;
    private $formatHelper;
    private $countryNow;

    public function getProperties()
    {
        //Loads text writeup from external text file
        $this->countryNow = file_get_contents("CountryWriteups/Moldova.txt");

        $this->formatHelper=new FormatHelper();
        $this->mfgProduct=$this->formatHelper->addTop();
        $this->mfgProduct.="<img src='Countries/Moldova.png' class='pixRight'
            width='208' height='450'>";
        $this->mfgProduct .="<header>Moldova</header>";
        $this->mfgProduct .="<p>$this->countryNow</p>";
        $this->mfgProduct .=$this->formatHelper->closeUp();
        return $this->mfgProduct;
    }
}
?>
```

As you can see, all of the messy text is gone. However, what remains the same—and is crucial to remain unchanged—is the getProperties() interface. As long as you keep an eye on the interface, making changes or additions in a Factory Method design pattern will not result in a crash. This is true even though an additional external resource has been added. Figure 5-7 shows that the new results are like the old results but with a different country.

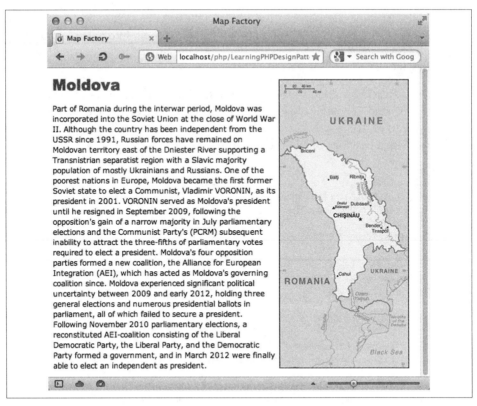

Figure 5-7. Created with external resources

As your products become more complex—something beyond simple placement of text and graphics in an HTML document—the more important the interface becomes. Fortunately, maintaining a single interface is much easier than attempting to maintain any number of classes and objects. That is why using the Factory Method simplifies the complex creation process: it maintains a common interface.

CHAPTER 6

Prototype Design Pattern

Originality is nothing but judicious imitation. The most original writers borrowed one from another.

—Voltaire

We forfeit three-quarters of ourselves in order to be like other people.

—Arthur Schopenhauer

Act that your principle of action might safely be made a law for the whole world.

—Immanuel Kant

What Is the Prototype Design Pattern?

The Prototype design pattern is interesting in its use of a *cloning* technique to replicate instantiated objects. New objects are created by copying prototypical instances. In this context, *instances* refer to instantiated concrete classes. The purpose is to reduce the cost of instantiating objects by using cloning. Rather than instantiating new objects from a class, a clone of an existing instance can be used instead. Figure 6-1 shows the Prototype class diagram.

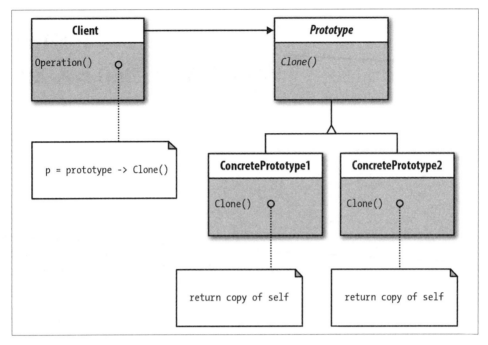

Figure 6-1. Prototype class diagram

Note that the Client class is an integral part of the Prototype design pattern. The client creates an instance of a concrete prototype through the Prototype interface that includes a clone method of some sort. Fortunately, PHP has a built-in clone() method that can be used within the design pattern. As you will see, the basics of the design are quite simple.

When to Use the Prototype Pattern

The Prototype pattern should be used in any application where your project requires that you create several instances of a prototypical object. For example, in research on evolutionary development, scientists often use fruit flies. They reproduce quickly and have a greater probability of generating a mutation, the fundamental evolutionary change event. For example, a typical study may use 15 million fruit flies, and because females may be laying eggs almost as soon as they emerge (within hours), the chance of finding and recording mutations is much greater than with other creatures, such as elephants, which have a 22-month gestation period. In recording mutations, the male and female prototypes serve as a base, and mutations are a clone of any male or female instance. Thus, from two instantiations (one male and one female), you can clone as many mutations as required with no further need to create another instance from the concrete classes.

The Prototype pattern has also been used to create an organizational structure where a finite number of positions can be created and filled based on the actual organization. Prototypes have been used where a drawing object has been created using composition and then cloned for different versions. A final example could be in game development where a prototype warrior could be cloned to add numbers and types to an army.

The Clone Function

The key to working with the Prototype design pattern in PHP is understanding how to use the built-in function, __clone(). While somewhat odd in relation to what you've probably done in PHP programming, it's very easy. In order to see how to use the method, look at the following little program. (You really don't need to extend an abstract class that contains an abstract __clone() method, but the examples all show an abstract class including a __clone() method, and so this might prove useful in the further Prototype examples in this book.)

```php
<?php
//CloneMe.php
abstract class CloneMe
{
    public $name;
    public $picture;
    abstract function __clone();
}

class Person extends CloneMe
{
    public function __construct()
    {
        $this->picture="cloneMan.png";
        $this->name ="Original";
    }

    public function display()
    {
        echo "<img src='$this->picture'>";
        echo "<br />$this->name <p />";
    }

    function __clone() {}
}
$worker=new Person();
$worker->display();

$slacker = clone $worker;
$slacker->name="Cloned";
$slacker->display();
?>
```

The concrete class Person is an extension of the CloneMe abstract class. In the example, an instance of Person is instantiated by $worker. So now, $worker is a Person object. Next, a second instance variable, $slacker, clones the $worker instance of Person. It has access to the same properties as $worker and can change them just as a direct instance of the Person class would be able to do. Figure 6-2 shows the results.

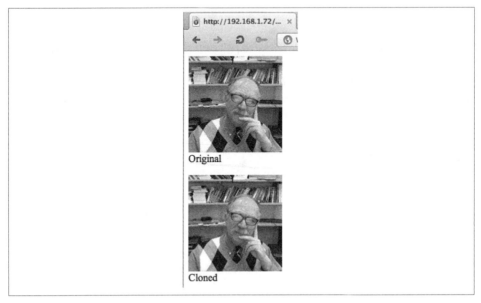

Figure 6-2. The original object and a clone in browser

The __clone() method cannot be accessed directly. Rather, if a __clone() method has been included in a class definition, using the following format:

```
$anotherInstance = clone $someInstance;
```

the clone keyword instantiates another instance of the same class as that of the cloned instance. The PHP documentation notes:

> An object copy is created by using the clone keyword (which calls the object's __clone() method (*http://bit.ly/122mJtB*) if possible). An object's __clone() method (*http://bit.ly/122mJtB*) cannot be called directly.

Constructor Does Not Relaunch with Clone

There's one catch to the cloning process: the clone does not launch the action in the constructor function. Clones can use default assigned values generated by the constructor, but if a constructor generates an action such as printing a message as soon as it is instantiated, the clone will not display that message ("Hello, clone!"). The following example shows how a constructor sends out a message upon instantiation but not on a clone operation:

```php
<?php
class HelloClone
{
    private $builtInConstructor;
    public function __construct()
    {
        echo "Hello, clone!<br />";
        $this->builtInConstructor="Constructor creation<br />";
    }

    public function doWork()
    {
        echo $this->builtInConstructor;
        echo "I'm doing the work!<p />";

    }
}
//Launch constructor
$original=new HelloClone();
$original->doWork();

//Clone does not launch constructor
$cloneIt = clone $original;
$cloneIt->doWork();

?>
```

The original instantiation displayed the message "Hello, clone!" but the clone operation did not. The following output shows the results:

```
Hello, clone!
Constructor creation
I'm doing the work!

Constructor creation
I'm doing the work!
```

What this means for the Prototype design pattern (and any other use of cloning) is that you should not depend on your constructor function for any significant output or return. However, that may not be a bad thing. In fact, it may be a good programming practice.

The Constructor Function Should Do No Real Work

In discussing unit testing, Miško Hevery, who develops coding guidelines for Google, points out that a constructor should do no real work (*http://bit.ly/1a9MWr*). The comment was made in the context of unit testing (testing parts of a program), but it certainly may apply to design patterns. Hevery's main point is that when a class instantiates and initializes its collaborators, the result tends to be an inflexible and prematurely coupled design. In the same vein, when a constructor function outputs anything, it provides no options for the client other than to shoot out what the constructor sends, even if it does not want it—or at least does not want it at a given time.

Hevery's point does not mean that a constructor function cannot assign values to properties when needed. Likewise, the client's constructor can be a good deal different from the other participants of a pattern because it is making requests of the participants.

One way to deal with the concept that constructors should do no real work is to omit constructor functions in pattern classes unless you have a good reason to include them. Otherwise, allow operations to be called when needed and let the client take care of instantiation and cloning chores. So, while we can find limitations in using the __clone() function, those limitations may aid in better OOP programs.

A Minimalist Prototype Example

In this first example, consider an experiment using fruit flies. The goal of the research is to set up a prototype fruit fly and then, whenever a mutation occurs, build the mutation. With 50 million flies, you'll get a lot of mutations, but you're interested only in the fly's eye color, the number of wing beats per second, and the number of unit eyes since the fruit fly eye contains hundreds of light-sensing units, each with its own lens and set of light receptor cells, and they may vary based on gender and reproduction. Other mutations are possible, but this study examines only those three variables.

Studying Fruit Flies

The reason for selecting the Prototype for a fruit fly study is that it provides a starting point from which to measure mutation. The concrete classes set up a baseline for standard values for fruit flies, and mutations can be measured as deviations from the baseline. An abstract class provides the baseline variables (all of them are public for ease of the example use).

The abstract class interface and concrete implementation

The two concrete class implementations of the prototype (IPrototype) represent the fly genders, the variable (gender), and gender behaviors (mating and producing eggs). The abstract class also includes an abstract method based on the __clone() method.

```php
<?php
//IPrototype.php
abstract class IPrototype
{
    public $eyeColor;
    public $wingBeat;
    public $unitEyes;
```

```php
    abstract function __clone();
}
?>
```

The two implementations of IPrototype differentiate between gender using constants labeling one MALE and the other FEMALE. The male has a $mated Boolean variable set to true after the male has mated and the female has a $fecundity variable containing a numeric value representing how capable the fly is at reproducing (its number of remaining eggs):

```php
<?php
//MaleProto.php
include_once('IPrototype.php');
class MaleProto extends IPrototype
{
    const gender="MALE";
    public $mated;

    public function __construct()
    {
        $this->eyeColor="red";
        $this->wingBeat="220";
        $this->unitEyes="760 ";
    }
    function __clone(){}
}
?>
```

Importantly, both concrete implementations of IPrototype have an implemented __clone() method even though the implementation is nothing more than adding two curly braces to the statement. The __clone() method is built into PHP with encapsulated code that will do the required work for this particular design pattern; so an "implementation" can be nothing more than adding the signature of a function:

```php
<?php
//FemaleProto.php
include_once('IPrototype.php');
class FemaleProto extends IPrototype
{
    const gender="FEMALE";
    public $fecundity;

    public function __construct()
    {
        $this->eyeColor="red";
        $this->wingBeat="220";
        $this->unitEyes="760 ";
    }
    function __clone(){}
}
?>
```

Both implementations include literals (actual numbers, strings, or Booleans) for the assigned values. In this way, the mutations can be measured as a deviation from these values.

The Client

While not rare in design patterns, the Client class is included as an *integral participant* in the Prototype design pattern. The reason for this is that while the concrete implementations of the child classes serve as templates for the instances, the work of actually cloning the instances using the same template is carried out by the Client class.

The two concrete implementations of the prototype are very simple and use direct value assignments to the shared variables of eyeColor, wingBeat, and unitEyes; they don't even have getter/setter methods. For now, that's fine because the focus is on seeing how those properties are used by the cloned implementations of the classes' instances; $fly1 and $fly2 are instantiated from the concrete classes and $c1Fly, $c2Fly, and $updatedCloneFly are all clones of one or the other of the two class instances.

```php
<?php
//Client.php
function __autoload($class_name)
{
    include $class_name . '.php';
}
class Client
{
    //For direct instantiation
    private $fly1;
    private $fly2;

    //For cloning
    private $c1Fly;
    private $c2Fly;
    private $updatedCloneFly;

    public function __construct()
    {
        //Instantiate
        $this->fly1=new MaleProto();
        $this->fly2=new FemaleProto();

        //Clone
        $this->c1Fly = clone $this->fly1;

        $this->c2Fly = clone $this->fly2;
        $this->updatedCloneFly = clone $this->fly2;

        //update clones
        $this->c1Fly->mated="true";
        $this->c2Fly->fecundity="186";
```

```php
        $this->updatedCloneFly->eyeColor="purple";
        $this->updatedCloneFly->wingBeat="220";
        $this->updatedCloneFly->unitEyes="750";
        $this->updatedCloneFly->fecundity="92";

        //Send through type hinting method
        $this->showFly($this->c1Fly);
        $this->showFly($this->c2Fly);
        $this->showFly($this->updatedCloneFly);
    }

    private function showFly(IPrototype $fly)
    {
        echo "Eye color: " . $fly->eyeColor . "<br/>";
        echo "Wing Beats/second: " . $fly->wingBeat . "<br/>";
        echo "Eye units: " . $fly->unitEyes . "<br/>";
        $genderNow=$fly::gender;
        echo "Gender: " . $genderNow . "<br/>";
        if($genderNow=="FEMALE")
        {
            echo "Number of eggs: " . $fly->fecundity . "<p/>";
        }
        else
        {
            echo "Mated: " . $fly->mated . "<p/>";
        }
    }
}
$worker=new Client();
?>
```

With multiple class references, it's easier to use the PHP __autoload() method than
the include_once method. In this way, no matter how many participants or helper
classes the Client class references, all classes are automatically included. The downside
of using __autoload() while learning design patterns is that the include_once method
shows all of the classes in use. Throughout the rest of the book, one or the other of the
techniques for including classes in external files is employed depending on how useful
a specific class referenced class name is to understanding the program. (Filenames are
based on class names.)

The following output shows two unchanged clones of the male and female concrete
classes (the "template" classes) and the third is the output of a "mutated" clone indicated
by purple eyes and a different number of eye units. The number of eggs is within a
standard deviation and is not considered a mutation.

```
Eye color: red
Wing Beats/second: 220
Eye units: 760
Gender: MALE
Mated: true
```

```
Eye color: red
Wing Beats/second: 220
Eye units: 760
Gender: FEMALE
Number of eggs: 186

Eye color: purple
Wing Beats/second: 220
Eye units: 750
Gender: FEMALE
Number of eggs: 92
```

The Prototype depends on the Client to use the concrete prototypes through a cloning process. The Client is the participant in the design that performs the cloning, and because cloning is the key element in the Prototype design, that makes the Client a fundamental participant and not simply a requesting class.

Adding OOP to the Prototype

The minimalist example focuses on the relationships between the participants and the outcome. To keep the amount of code to the minimum to "see" the structure, the classes were not built with the kind of encapsulation we expect from an OOP application. In other words, the participants in the pattern implementation are fairly skeletal so that the relationship between the classes is easier to see. For instance, in the minimal implementation of the Prototype, the Client is able to change prototype property values directly—that is, by simple assignment. For example, the client changed the mutant eye color using the following code:

```
$this->updatedCloneFly->eyeColor="purple";
```

No method in the abstract or concrete prototype classes included getter/setter methods or some other structure to better encapsulate the properties.

The Modern Business Organization

On the creational side of design patterns, modern business organizations may be good candidates for the Prototype implementation. As bureaucratic hierarchies, they model many of the same characteristics that object-oriented programming does. This next Prototype example is still relatively simple, with the focus on understanding class relationships, but it is better encapsulated along the lines expected by OOP. The class diagram in Figure 6-3 shows its participants and general structure.

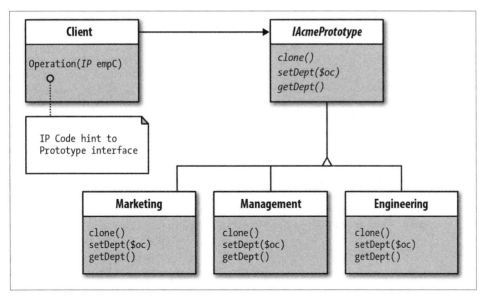

Figure 6-3. Organizational Prototype class diagram

The software engineering corporation depicted is typical of modern organizations. The Engineering Department is responsible for creating the product, Management handles coordinating and organizing resources, and Marketing is in charge of sales, promotion, and overall marketing of the product.

Encapsulation in the Interface

The first thing that this Prototype implementation does is add OOP to the program's interface—an abstract class. Like all Prototype interfaces, this one includes an abstract cloning operation. However, it also includes both abstract and concrete getters and setters. The abstract getter/setter pair leaves the specific implementation up to the three concrete prototype implementations. The other getter/setter methods are more generally applicable to such things as employee names, ID codes, and photos. Not that all of the properties are protected, so even though the concrete getters and setters have public visibility, the protected visibility of the properties used in the operations affords a degree of encapsulation:

```php
<?php
//IAcmePrototype.php
abstract class IAcmePrototype
{
    protected $name;
    protected $id;
    protected $employeePic;
    protected $dept;
```

```php
//Dept
abstract function setDept($orgCode);
abstract function getDept();

//Name
public function setName($emName)
{
    $this->name=$emName;
}

public function getName()
{
    return $this->name;
}
//ID
public function setId($emId)
{
    $this->id=$emId;
}

public function getId()
{
    return $this->id;
}

//Employee Picture

public function setPic($ePic)
{
    $this->employeePic=$ePic;
}

public function getPic()
{
    return $this->employeePic;
}

    abstract function __clone();
    }

    ?>
```

With the getter/setter methods set, the values for any of the properties are through inherited protected variables. With this arrangement, the extended classes and their instances are better encapsulated.

The Interface Implementations

Each of the three IAcmePrototype child classes must implement the "dept" (department) abstract methods along with the __clone() method. Likewise, each concrete prototype class includes a constant, UNIT, with an assigned value that can be used by instances, whether implemented directly or a clone, for identification. Begin by looking at how the Marketing class has been structured:

```php
<?php
//Marketing.php
include_once('IAcmePrototype.php');
class Marketing extends IAcmePrototype
{
    const UNIT="Marketing";
    private $sales="sales";
    private $promotion="promotion";
    private $strategic="strategic planning";

    public function setDept($orgCode)
    {
        switch($orgCode)
        {
            case 101:
            $this->dept=$this->sales;
            break;

            case 102:
            $this->dept=$this->promotion;
            break;

            case 103:
            $this->dept=$this->strategic;
            break;

            default:
            $this->dept="Unrecognized Marketing ";
        }
    }

    public function getDept()
    {
        return $this->dept;
    }

    function __clone(){}
}
?>
```

The setDept() method is implemented using a single parameter. Instead of directly entering the name of the department within the marketing unit, the method expects a numeric code. If it were expecting an object derived from a class, the method could be built using a type hint for an object/interface type, but type hinting does not allow scalar types such as int. Using a switch/case statement with the argument as a comparative variable, the class enforces one of three acceptable cases or defaults to "Unrecognized Marketing." Once a match is made, the operation uses a private variable that has an assigned value. Again, this helps to encapsulate both the class and setter method. The getter method (getDept()) uses the same private variables.

The other two prototype implementations are similar, but note that each has different departments stored in private variables. Likewise, each has a different value for the constant, UNIT:

```php
<?php
//Management.php
include_once('IAcmePrototype.php');
class Management extends IAcmePrototype
{
    const UNIT="Management";
    private $research="research";
    private $plan="planning";
    private $operations="operations";

    public function setDept($orgCode)
    {
        switch($orgCode)
        {
            case 201:
            $this->dept=$this->research;
            break;

            case 202:
            $this->dept=$this->plan;
            break;

            case 203:
            $this->dept=$this->operations;
            break;

            default:
            $this->dept="Unrecognized Management";
        }
    }

    public function getDept()
    {
        return $this->dept;
    }
    function __clone(){}
}
?>
```

The values expected in the switch/case statement are different in all three concrete prototype implementations. Likewise, the name and values of the private properties are different as well:

```php
<?php
//Engineering.php
```

```php
include_once('IAcmePrototype.php');
class Engineering extends IAcmePrototype
{
    const UNIT="Engineering";
    private $development="programming";
    private $design="digital artwork";
    private $sysAd="system administration";

    public function setDept($orgCode)
    {
        switch($orgCode)
        {
            case 301:
            $this->dept=$this->development;
            break;

            case 302:
            $this->dept=$this->design;
            break;

            case 303:
            $this->dept=$this->sysAd;
            break;

            default:
            $this->dept="Unrecognized Engineering";
        }
    }

    public function getDept()
    {
        return $this->dept;
    }
    function __clone(){}

}
?>
```

With all three concrete prototype implementations, each unique for its use but respecting the interface, a single instance of each can be created and then cloned by as many instances as needed. The Client class will fill this last role.

The Organizational Client

The basic setup for the Client is very simple. The plan is to create a single instance of each concrete prototype and then clone each one as the following outline shows:

- Marketing Instance
  — Marketing clone
  — Marketing clone

- Management Instance
  — Management clone
- Engineering Instance
  — Engineering clone
  — Engineering clone

Only the clones will be used. The information for each unique case is to be assigned to the clones using the getter/setter methods. The following code for the client shows this implementation:

```php
<?php
//Client.php
function __autoload($class_name)
{
    include $class_name . '.php';
}

class Client
{
    private $market;
    private $manage;
    private $engineer;

    public function __construct()
    {
        $this->makeConProto();

        $Tess=clone $this->market;
        $this->setEmployee($Tess,"Tess Smith",101,"ts101-1234","tess.png");
        $this->showEmployee($Tess);

        $Jacob=clone $this->market;
        $this->setEmployee($Jacob,"Jacob Jones",102,"jj101-2234","jacob.png");
        $this->showEmployee($Jacob);

        $Ricky=clone $this->manage;
        $this->setEmployee($Ricky,"Ricky Rodriguez",203,"rr203-5634","ricky.png");
        $this->showEmployee($Ricky);

        $Olivia=clone $this->engineer;
        $this->setEmployee($Olivia,"Olivia Perez",302,"op301-1278","olivia.png");
        $this->showEmployee($Olivia);

        $John=clone $this->engineer;
        $this->setEmployee($John,"John Jackson",301,"jj302-1454","john.png");
        $this->showEmployee($John);
    }

    private function makeConProto()
```

```
    {
        $this->market=new Marketing();
        $this->manage=new Management();
        $this->engineer=new Engineering();
    }

    private function showEmployee(IAcmePrototype $employeeNow)
    {
        $px=$employeeNow->getPic();
        echo "<img src=$px width='150' height='150'><br/>";
        echo $employeeNow->getName() . "<br/>";
        echo $employeeNow->getDept() . ": " . $employeeNow::UNIT . "<br/>";
        echo $employeeNow->getID() . "<p/>";
    }

    private function setEmployee(IAcmePrototype $employeeNow,$nm,$dp,$id,$px)
    {
        $employeeNow->setName($nm);
        $employeeNow->setDept($dp);
        $employeeNow->setID($id);
        $employeeNow->setPic("pix/$px");
    }
}
$worker = new Client();
?>
```

The client's constructor class holds three private properties to be used to instantiate one each of the three concrete prototype classes. The makeConProto() method generates the necessary instances.

Next, an "employee" instance is created using the clone technique. The cloned instance then sends unique instance information to a setter method (setEmployee()) that uses type hinting for the IAcmePrototype interface. However, note that it employs type hinting only for the first parameter. None of the other parameters have type hinting, and they do not have to be derived from the IAcmePrototype interface. All of the setter methods from the IAcmePrototype abstract class as well as the implemented set Dept() methods from the concrete prototype classes are used by the cloned "employee."

In order to use the data for each employee, the Client class uses the inherited getter methods. Figure 6-4 shows a simple output for each of the five employee clones.

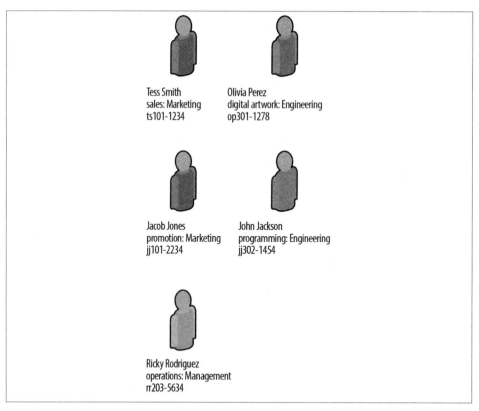

Tess Smith
sales: Marketing
ts101-1234

Olivia Perez
digital artwork: Engineering
op301-1278

Jacob Jones
promotion: Marketing
jj101-2234

John Jackson
programming: Engineering
jj302-1454

Ricky Rodriguez
operations: Management
rr203-5634

Figure 6-4. Clones from the organization

You can add as many clones as required, and all you will ever need is a single instantiation of one of the concrete prototype classes. Instead of having several instances of the concrete classes, you have a single class instantiation and several clones.

Making Changes, Adding Features

The important point, perhaps the fundamental point, to keep in mind is that design patterns allow the developer to add and change a program without having to start all over. For example, suppose that the president of the company decides that a new division should be added to the company—Research, for instance. Would that be difficult to do? Not at all. A Research class could extend the IAcmePrototype abstract class and implement the abstract getter/setter methods to reflect the division's organization. Note that the getter/setter methods in the Client class use code hinting to the interface and not a concrete implementation of the abstract class. So, as long as the added unit implements the interface correctly, it will slip into the application without making a wave or requiring refactoring of the other participants in the program.

In addition to adding more concrete classes, making changes within each class is just as easy and undisruptive. For example, suppose the marketing division of the organization decides that they need a special online marketing division apart from the current departments they have. The switch/case operation would need a single new case and a new private property (variable) to describe the added department. This change would not affect the other participants, encapsulated in their classes. The bigger the application, the more important it is that the change does not cause disruption, and as you can see, the Prototype design pattern allows for both consistency and change.

Dynamic Object Instantiation

In looking at the Client class, you may be thinking that with a real organization, you'd have a lot more employees, and hardcoding them in a client doesn't seem to be a very smart way of dealing with the problem. That's absolutely true, and so we need to consider how to dynamically create clones from data stored in a database, an XML file, or somewhere other than a line of code in a client.

When you use a record from a database, you can pass that data to a PHP program to handle it. However, the data are not stored as instances of a concrete class but instead as numeric or string data of some kind. Take, for example, the following bit of data from the Client class:

```
$Tess=clone $this->mar;
$this->setEmployee($Tess,"Tess Smith",101,"ts101-1234","tess.png");
$this->showEmployee($Tess);
```

The data in the setEmployee() method arguments would normally come from a database and feed into the Client. The first parameter expects an object with the IAcmePrototype interface. So, the question is, how do you dynamically create (clone) an object based on data coming from a database?

Variables to objects

PHP seems to be one of the most considerate languages around when it comes to dynamic creation. The process to take a variable and instantiate a class in PHP is quite simple. The following code creates an instance of a class from a value in a variable:

```
//Class name = MyClass
$myVar = "MyClass";
$myObj =new $myVar;
```

That's it. The variable $myObj has just instantiated an instance of MyClass.

The code is equivalent to the following:

```
$myObj = new MyClass();
```

Using these techniques, you can dynamically create and clone objects from data coming from a database, array, or anywhere else you program gets it data.

In the following example, imagine that instead of an array, the data are coming from a database. The same principles apply. Note also that it employs an interface instead of an abstract class:

```php
<?php
interface IPrototype
{
    const PROTO="IPrototype";
    function __clone();
}
class DynamicObjectNaming implements IPrototype
{
    const CONCRETE=" [Concrete] DynamicObjectNaming";

    public function __construct()
    {
        echo "This was dynamically created.<br/>";
    }

    public function doWork()
    {
        echo "<br/>This is the assigned task.<br/>";
    }

    function __clone() {}
}

$employeeData = array('DynamicObjectNaming','Tess','mar', 'John',
    'eng', 'Olivia','man' );
$don=$employeeData[0];
$employeeData[6]=new $don;
echo $employeeData[6]::CONCRETE;
$employeeData[6]->doWork();

$employeeName=$employeeData[5];
$employeeName = clone $employeeData[6];
echo $employeeName->doWork();
echo "This is a clone of " . $employeeName::CONCRETE . "<br/>";
echo "Child of: " . $employeeName::PROTO;
?>
```

When you run the program, you will see the following output:

```
This was dynamically created.
[Concrete] DynamicObjectNaming
This is the assigned task.

This is the assigned task.
This is a clone of [Concrete]
DynamicObjectNaming
Child of: IPrototype
```

Notice that in the initial instantiation, the constructor printed, "This was dynamically created." That's because the instantiation launched the operations in the constructor. However, in the cloning process, the cloned object did not launch the constructor. Nevertheless, the clone could use any assigned values generated from the initial instantiation of the class that was passed to the cloned object.

The Prototype in PHP Land

Because PHP is a server-side language and is a key tool for interacting with a MySQL database, the Prototype design pattern is an especially good option. Instead of having to create new objects for every element in a database, PHP can use the Prototype to create single instances of a concrete class and then clone the rest of the cases (records) from the database.

After looking at the cloning process compared with direct instantiation of an object from a class, you may well ask yourself, "What's the difference?" In other words: Why do clones use fewer resources than objects instantiated directly from a class? The big difference is in what you do not see. When an object creates an instance through cloning, it does not fire the constructor. In the DynamicObjectNaming class application, you saw an example of where the direct instantiation fired off the constructor and the clone did not. The clone had all of the properties of the original class and even parent interface, but it also inherited any values that had been passed to the instantiated object. Any values generated by the constructor function and stored in the object properties become a part of the object. So there is no need to rerun the constructor. If you find that your clones do need access to values generated by the constructor function but cannot access them, it's time to refactor your class so that instantiated instances have everything they need and can pass that on to the clone.

Overall, the Prototype can be applied in several different kinds of PHP projects where a problem solution calls for a creational pattern. This chapter has provided a couple of different examples, but now that you have a better idea of what the Prototype pattern does and how to use it, keep an eye open for opportunities to employ it. If you do, you can expect to save development time and improve your design for changes that may occur.

PART III

Structural Design Patterns

What we observe as material bodies and forces are nothing but shapes and variations in the structure of space.

—Erwin Schrodinger

A living cell requires energy not only for all its functions, but also for the maintenance of its structure.

—Albert Szent-Gyorgyi

Most of the dogmatic religions have exhibited a perverse talent for taking the wrong side on the most important concepts in the material universe, from the structure of the solar system to the origin of man.

—George G. Simpson

Structural design patterns examine how objects and classes are composed to form larger structures. In class structural design, new structures are created through multiple inheritance. One class inherits from more than a single parent class to create a new structure. More commonly, object structures combine different objects to form new structures. The following seven patterns have been designated as structural by Gamma, Helm, Johnson, and Vlissides:

- Adapter (class and object)
- Bridge
- Composite

- Decorator
- Façade
- Flyweight
- Proxy

Of these seven, two versions of the Adapter pattern—class and object—and the Decorator pattern are closely examined in Part III. The Adapter is important for bringing together two incompatible systems through an adaptation using either multiple inheritance or through composition. One of the thorny problems to deal with is that PHP does not have multiple inheritance, but as you will see, PHP has a workaround available for doing class category Adapters. Composition, on the other hand, is available for both object category Adapters and for the Decorator pattern. Figure III.1 provides a visualization of the Structural design patterns.

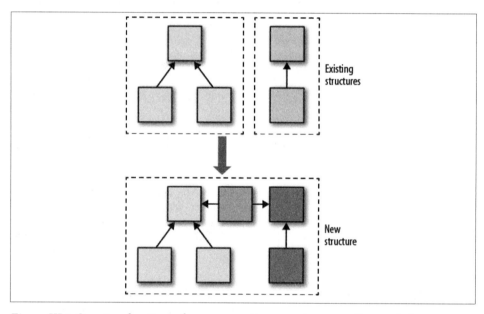

Figure III.1. Structural patterns focus on creating new structures from existing ones

The focal points for Structural design patterns lie in creating new structures without destroying the old ones. On top of that, the standard of loose coupling for reuse and change are both maintained and enhanced in the Structural patterns.

CHAPTER 7

The Adapter Pattern

It is not the strongest of the species that survives,
nor the most intelligent that survives. It is the one
that is the most adaptable to change.

—Charles Darwin

The measure of intelligence is the ability to change.

—Albert Einstein

Science always has its origin in the adaptation of
thought to some definite field of experience.

—Ernst Mach

What Is the Adapter Pattern?

This chapter is a two-for-one package: object and class Adapters. This chapter has many lessons, but one of the most interesting is seeing the difference between using inheritance and using composition. The class scope version of the Adapter design pattern uses inheritance, as can be seen in the class diagram in Figure 7-1.

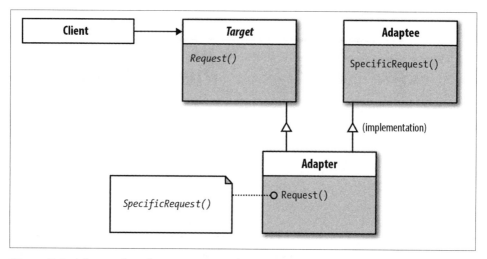

Figure 7-1. Adapter class diagram using inheritance

In the class diagram, one implementation of the pattern is to have one class with dual inheritance. As you will see, dual inheritance is not allowed in PHP 5, but there are alternatives to dual inheritance where the pattern can be correctly implemented with a combination of inheritance and implementation.

As you know, an important dictum of design patterns is to favor composition over inheritance. In looking at the second Adapter pattern, the Adapter participant uses composition to hold a reference to the Adaptee instead of inheritance.

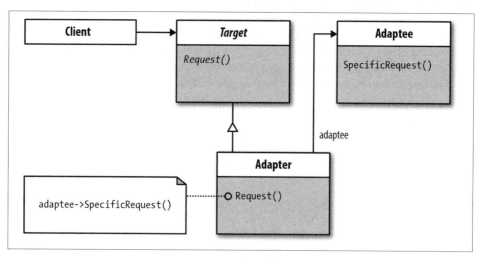

Figure 7-2. Adapter class diagram using composition

Generally, composition is favored over inheritance because the binding between participants is looser and allows for the advantages of reuse, structure, and revision without the disadvantages that tight binding brings with inheriting from concrete classes or classes containing implemented methods.

When to Use the Adapter Pattern

Adapters are easy to understand; we use them all the time. Most familiar are electrical adapters that you use to charge your mobile phone. You can't just plug your mobile phone into a standard outlet with your USB connector. Instead, you have to use an adapter that accepts the USB plug on one end and the electrical outlet on the other. Figure 7-3 shows a typical adapter arrangement used to recharge a mobile phone or computer.

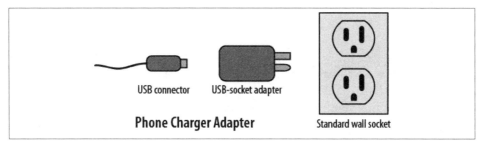

Figure 7-3. Adapters are common in electronics

In part, the answer to the question "When should I use an Adapter pattern?" is similar to the answer you would get when any adapter use comes into question. For example, if someone asked you how to recharge your mobile phone, you'd simply tell them to use an adapter so that the USB connecter and wall socket were compatible.

Breaking the problem down into its simplest parts, you have the following:

- USB connector—unchanged
- Standard wall socket—unchanged

You could get out your electrical tools and either change the USB connector or rewire the wall socket, but that would be a lot of extra work and you could possibly break the connector or socket (or both!). Or, you could get an adapter. Most likely you'll get an adapter. The same is true with software development.

Suppose you and your fellow developers have worked out a PHP program that allows you to easily create custom desktop web designs for your clients. Your system handles everything from the look and feel of the site to a MySQL database. Everything works smoothly for a multicolumn design and UX for laptop and desktop size screens. In fact, you have what looks a lot like a desktop CMS created with PHP.

One day some clients ask you to add a mobile version of their website. Your designers tell you that a horizontal design is out for mobile, and you'll have to redesign the look and feel. Likewise, your whole UX will have to be changed as well. After they whip up a mobile module, you find that it is incompatible with your desktop module. Figure 7-4 illustrates this problem.

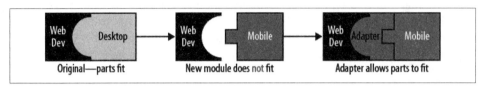

Figure 7-4. Adapter designs work on the same principle as an adapter for your mobile phone

Rather than changing the web development module that contains all of your classes and operations to link a web page with a database or change the new mobile module that has been painstakingly created for a mobile site, what would you do? The answer, just like when recharging your phone, is to use an adapter. In "The Adapter Pattern Using Composition" (page 131), you will find an example that reflects updating a system to include a module using the Adapter design pattern.

You will find a lot of uses for the Adapter pattern. Many web development professionals who use special vendor-supplied accelerators, UIs, or other enhancement modules often need an adapter of some sort to use with existing software. Likewise, if two different groups have developed incompatible modules, often it's less time-consuming to use an adapter than to have one or the other group redevelop its modules. (You also might want to encourage your development groups to communicate a little better in the future!)

The Adapter Pattern Using Inheritance

The class Adapter design pattern is relatively easy but less flexible than the object version of the Adapter. It is easier because it inherits its functionality from the Adaptee participant, and so there's less to recode in the Adapter. Of course, given a concrete Adaptee from which the Adapter inherits, the binding is relatively tight, and so in creating an application using a class Adapter pattern, one needs to be especially cognizant of where the adaptation is going to be.

Because the class adapter has dual inheritance, as suggested in Figure 7-1, the PHP example is doing some fancy footwork. Natively, PHP does not support dual inheritance.

(Don't feel bad, neither does Java.) You can find elaborate examples of where PHP fakes or simulates dual inheritance, but a better lesson is that PHP natively handles a combination of interface implementation and class inheritance. The following statement illustrates the correct structure of a statement that inherits a class while simultaneously implementing an interface:

```
class ChildClass extends ParentClass implements ISomeInterface
```

So, when implementing the class Adapter pattern, one of the participants needs to be a PHP interface participant.

A Minimal Example of a Class Adapter: The Currency Exchange

In looking for something both useful and minimal, a currency exchange/converter came to mind. Imagine a business website where the developer is selling both software services and products. Up to this point, all of the business was in the United States, where he could do all calculations in U.S. dollars. Without having to change a class that calculates how many dollars are involved in a transaction, the developer wants something that will handle exchanges in euros. By adding an Adapter, the program can calculate either dollars or euros.

To begin, suppose you have a perfectly good class, DollarCalc, that adds the values of purchased services and products and returns the total:

```php
<?php
//DollarCalc.php
class DollarCalc
{
    private $dollar;
    private $product;
    private $service;
    public $rate=1;

    public function requestCalc($productNow,$serviceNow)
    {
        $this->product=$productNow;
        $this->service=$serviceNow;
        $this->dollar=$this->product + $this->service;
        return $this->requestTotal();
    }

    public function requestTotal()
    {
        $this->dollar*=$this->rate;
        return $this->dollar;
    }
}
?>
```

In looking at the class, one of the properties is $rate, and the requestTotal() method calculates the value of a transaction using $rate. In this original form, the value is set at 1, and multiplies the value of the two parameters variable by 1, which has the effect of not multiplying the total value at all. However, the $rate variable is handy for providing customers with discounts or adding surcharges for enhanced service or products. This class is not part of the class Adapter pattern, but it is a starting point.

Enter the euro

The developer's client announces that her company has decided to expand to Europe and is going to kick things off small with entry into the Luxembourg market. You quickly learn that Luxembourg is part of the eurozone, and so you need to develop an application that does the same calculations in euros. You decide that you can make it just like DollarCalc, and all you do is change the names of the variables.

```php
<?php
//EuroCalc.php
class EuroCalc
{
    private $euro;
    private $product;
    private $service;
    public $rate=1;

    public function requestCalc($productNow,$serviceNow)
    {
        $this->product=$productNow;
        $this->service=$serviceNow;
        $this->euro=$this->product + $this->service;
        return $this->requestTotal();
    }

    public function requestTotal()
    {
        $this->euro*=$this->rate;
        return $this->euro;
    }
}
?>
```

Next, plug in the rest of your application to the EuroCalc class and you'll be good to go. However, you realize that all of the data for your customer is in dollars. In other words, you cannot "plug" in your system for the euro without redoing your entire program. You don't want to do that. You need an adapter for your EuroCalc.

Creating a euro adapter

At this point, we need to pause to get our bearings. Figure 7-5 shows the class diagram using the names of the classes in this implementation of the class Adapter pattern.

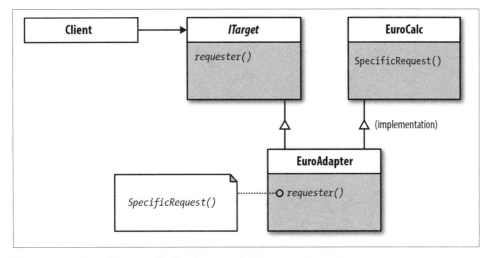

Figure 7-5. Class diagram for implemented Adapter using inheritance

Just as you can get an adapter to fit into European sockets, you can create an adapter for making your system work with euros. Fortunately, the class Adapter pattern is designed for such a situation. The first thing you need to do is to create an interface. In the class diagram the interface is named ITarget. It has a single method, reques ter(). The requester() is an abstract method that leaves up to the implementation exactly what will be done with it:

```php
<?php
//ITarget.php
//Target
interface ITarget
{
    function requester();
}
?>
```

The developer can now implement the requester() method to request euros instead of dollars.

In the inheritance version of the Adapter design pattern, the Adapter participant implements both the ITarget interface and the concrete class EuroCalc. Not much is required to create the EuroAdapter. Most of the work has been done in the EuroCalc class, a concrete class whose interface it inherits. All that's really necessary is to implement the requester() method so that it can translate dollar values into euro values:

```php
<?php
//EuroAdapter.php
//Adapter
include_once('EuroCalc.php');
```

```php
include_once('ITarget.php');
class EuroAdapter extends EuroCalc implements ITarget
{
    public function __construct()
    {
        $this->requester();
    }

    function requester()
    {
        $this->rate=.8111;
        return $this->rate;
    }
}
?>
```

The class version of the Adapter pattern is one of the few design patterns where you will see one concrete class inherit from another concrete class. Almost all inheritance in design patterns is from an abstract class that allows the concrete classes to implement the abstract methods and properties as needed. In other words, when thinking about class inheritance, think concrete classes inherit from abstract classes.

By both implementation and extension, the EuroAdapter class has the interfaces of both the interface and concrete class. Using the requester() method, it sets the rate value (exchange rate) so that the adaptee's functionality can be used without having to change it.

To see how it works, the Client class makes requests from both the EuroAdapter and the DollarCalc classes. As you can see, the original DollarCalc works fine, but it does not have the ITarget interface. The EuroAdapter class has both, and in using type hinting, either would comply with its own interface:

```php
<?php
//Client.php
//Client
include_once('EuroAdapter.php');
include_once('DollarCalc.php');

class Client
{
    private $requestNow;
    private $dollarRequest;

    public function __construct()
    {
        $this->requestNow=new EuroAdapter();
        $this->dollarRequest=new DollarCalc();
        $euro="&#8364;";
        echo "Euros: $euro" . $this->makeAdapterRequest($this->requestNow)  .
          "<br/>";
```

```
        echo "Dollars: $" . $this->makeDollarRequest($this->dollarRequest);

    }

    private function makeAdapterRequest(ITarget $req)
    {
        return $req->requestCalc(40,50);
    }

    private function makeDollarRequest(DollarCalc $req)
    {
        return $req->requestCalc(40,50);
    }
}

$worker=new Client();
?>
```

The output shows that the pattern can handle either dollars or euros now, thanks to the Adapter pattern:

```
Euros: €72.999
Dollars: $90
```

The calculation is a simple one, but with more complex calculations, the inheritance should provide the necessary interface and the implementation of the Target interface that sets up a class Adapter.

The Adapter Pattern Using Composition

The object version of the Adapter pattern uses composition instead of inheritance, but it accomplishes the same goal. By comparing the two versions of the Adapter pattern, you can see the advantages and disadvantages of using one type or the other. The class version allows the Adapter to inherit most of the functionality it needs with only a slight tweaking by the interface. With the object version, the Adapter participant *uses* the Adaptee and implements the Target interface. In the class version, the Adapter *is* an Adaptee and implements the Target interface.

From Desktop to Mobile

A common problem for PHP programmers is adapting to the mobile environment. Not too long ago, all you had to worry about was providing a site that would fit a range of desktop environments. A single layout worked for most desktops, and the designers made it look good. With mobile devices, designers and developers had to rethink not only the design elements of what a page shows in desktop and mobile environments, but also a way to switch from one to the other.

Using an object Adapter pattern, this example begins with a simple PHP class that brings up a simple page with text and graphics. For text, the example uses the placeholder text ("lorem ipsum") as filler stored in a text file. The CSS is simple as well, setting up a text-graphic relationship of text-left and graphic-right in an elementary two-column design. The CSS is stored as a separate CSS file.

Just the desktop

In order to understand the composition Adapter, you need to first look at the original class that later requires an adapter. It uses a straightforward but very loose interface:

```php
<?php
interface IFormat
{
    public function formatCSS();
    public function formatGraphics();
    public function horizontalLayout();
}
?>
```

It allows for many CSS and graphics choices, but one method implies a horizontal layout—something we know we don't want for a small mobile device. The implementation of the interface is quite simple, as you can see in the following class, Desktop:

```php
<?php
include_once("IFormat.php");
class Desktop implements IFormat
{
    private $head="<!doctype html><html><head>";
    private $headClose="<meta charset='UTF-8'>
<title>Desktop</title></head><body>";

    private $cap="</body></html>";
    private $sampleText;
    public function formatCSS()
    {
        echo $this->head;
        echo "<link rel='stylesheet' href='desktop.css'>";
        echo $this->headClose;
        echo "<h1>Hello, Everyone!</h1>";
    }
    public function formatGraphics()
    {
        echo "<img class='pixRight' src='pix/fallRiver720.png' width='720'
            height='480' alt='river'>";
    }

    public function horizontalLayout()
    {
        $textFile = "text/lorem.txt";
        $openText = fopen($textFile, 'r');
```

```
            $textInfo = fread($openText, filesize($textFile));
            fclose($openText);
            $this->sampleText=$textInfo;
            echo "<div>" . $this->sampleText . "</div>";
            echo "<p/><div>" . $this->sampleText . "</div>";
        }

        public function closeHTML()
        {
            echo $this->cap;
        }
    }
?>
```

Most of the code is formatting an HTML page for viewing. The text and image, along
with the header, represent minimum examples. The CSS has a stylesheet for color pa-
lette, the body text, a header, a "second column" in placing the image to the right of the
text, and padding around the image (any CSS with a far more elaborate design for
desktop works just as well, and you may want to substitute your own for this one):

```
@charset "UTF-8";
//desktop.css
/* CSS Document */
/*DDDCC5,958976,611427,1D2326,6A6A61*/
@media only screen and (min-device-width : 800px) {
}
body
{
    font-family:Verdana, Geneva, sans-serif;
    color:#1D2326;
    font-size:12px;
    background-color:#DDDCC5;
}

h1
{
    font-family:"Arial Black", Gadget, sans-serif;
    font-size:24px;
    color:#611427;
}

.pixRight
{
    float:right; margin: 0px 0px 5px 5px;
}

image
{
    padding: 10px 10px 10px 0px;
}
```

The CSS is saved in a file named *desktop.css* and is called through a PHP-generated HTML `<link>` tag.

Figure 7-6 shows the output of the PHP.

Figure 7-6. Simple desktop design with two columns

As you can see in Figure 7-6, the whole thing is way too wide for a small mobile device. So the goal will be to take the same content and adapt it for a mobile design.

Adapting to mobile. To get started, take a look at Figure 7-7, which shows the actual class names and operations that will be used in creating a mobile version of the website. I added the original interface for the `Mobile` class (`IMobileFormat`), but given the way in which the `MobileAdapter` is used, it implements the `IFormat` interface.

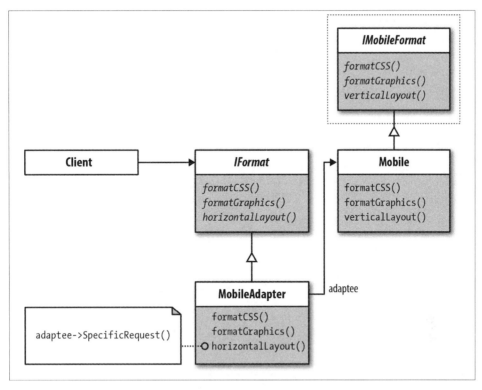

Figure 7-7. MobileAdapter in object Adapter class diagram

In looking at the IMobileFormat and the IFormat interfaces, you can see that they are incompatible: one has a method horizontalLayout() and the other a verticalLay out() interface. However, using the MobileAdapter (Adapter), which inherits IFor mat (Target) originally used by the Desktop class, the Mobile (Adaptee) class can now interact compatibly with other implementations of the IFormat interface.

Not surprisingly, the Adapter pattern is also known as the *wrapper* pattern. The Adapter (MobileAdapter) participant "wraps" the Adaptee (Mobile) participant so that the Adaptee can use the same interface as itself. To see how the wrapping process works, start with the IMobileFormat interface and the Mobile class, which is almost identical to the Desktop class except for the fact that it has a different interface:

```php
<?php
interface IMobileFormat
{
    public function formatCSS();
    public function formatGraphics();
    public function verticalLayout();
}
?>
```

Keep in mind that this process is designed to let two incompatible interfaces work together. The differences are small, but as you know, when converting from a desktop to a mobile design the key difference is that one can be organized horizontally into columns and the other uses vertical organization. The IMobileFormat is implemented by the following Mobile class (it looks almost identical to the Desktop class):

```php
<?php
include_once('IMobileFormat.php');
class Mobile implements IMobileFormat
{
    private $head="<!doctype html><html><head>";
    private $headClose="<meta charset='UTF-8'>
<title>Mobile</title></head><body>";

    private $cap="</body></html>";
    private $sampleText;
    public function formatCSS()
    {
        echo $this->head;
        echo "<link rel='stylesheet' href='mobile.css'>";
        echo $this->headClose;
        echo "<h1>Hello, Everyone!</h1>";
    }
    public function formatGraphics()
    {
        echo "<img src='pix/fallRiver960.png' width=device-width
            height=device-height alt='river'>";
    }

    public function verticalLayout()
    {
        $textFile = "text/lorem.txt";
        $openText = fopen($textFile, 'r');
        $textInfo = fread($openText, filesize($textFile));
        fclose($openText);
        $this->sampleText=$textInfo;
        echo "<p/><div>" . $this->sampleText . "</div>";
        echo "<p/><div>" . $this->sampleText . "</div>";
    }

    public function closeHTML()
    {
        echo $this->cap;
    }
}
?>
```

As noted, it looks a lot like the Desktop class, but the graphics are set up differently, with a different graphic. It also calls a different CSS file. The CSS file includes an @media statement to provide different resolutions flexibility:

```
@charset "UTF-8";
/* CSS Document */
/*DDDCC5,958976,611427,1D2326,6A6A61*/

@media only screen and (min-device-width : 640px) and (max-device-width : 960px)
{
    img { max-width: 100%; }
}

body
{
    font-family:Verdana, Geneva, sans-serif;
    color:#1D2326;
    font-size:24px;
    background-color:#DDDCC5;
}

h1
{
    font-family:"Arial Black", Gadget, sans-serif;
    font-size:48px;
    color:#611427;
}

image
{
    padding: 5px 5px 5px 0px;

}
```

The CSS, while important as far as the looks go, is used here only for formatting the appearance of the page on mobile devices. A designer could do a lot more. What's important is that different classes for desktop and mobile appearance need to work together. So now you can see the key Adapter participant that brings them all together:

```
<?php
include_once("IFormat.php");
include_once("Mobile.php");

class MobileAdapter implements IFormat
{
    private $mobile;

    public function __construct(IMobileFormat $mobileNow)
    {
        $this->mobile = $mobileNow;
    }
```

```php
    public function formatCSS()
    {
        $this->mobile->formatCSS();
    }

    public function formatGraphics()
    {
        $this->mobile->formatGraphics();
    }

    public function horizontalLayout()
    {
        $this->mobile->verticalLayout();
    }

}
?>
```

As you can see, the `MobileAdapter` is instantiated with a Mobile object instance. Note also that the `IMobileFormat` is used in type hinting to ensure that the argument is a Mobile object. What makes the Adapter participant interesting is how it implements the `horizontalLayout()` method to include the `Mobile` object `verticalLayout()` method. In fact, all of the `MobileAdapter` methods wrap a `Mobile` method. It just so happens that one of the methods in the adapter participant is not in the interface of the adapter (`verticalLayout()`). They could all be different, and the adapter would just wrap them in one of the methods in its own interface (`IFormat`).

The Client class as participant

The final step is to launch the application using the `MobileAdapter` class. Keep in mind that the `Client` class is an integral part of the design pattern, and even though it is just making requests, it must do so in a way that is consistent with the intent and design of the Adapter pattern:

```php
<?php
include_once('Mobile.php');
include_once('MobileAdapter.php');
class Client
{
    private $mobile;
    private $mobileAdapter;

    public function __construct()
    {
        $this->mobile = new Mobile();
        $this->mobileAdapter = new MobileAdapter($this->mobile);
        $this->mobileAdapter->formatCSS();
        $this->mobileAdapter->formatGraphics();
        $this->mobileAdapter->horizontalLayout();
        $this->mobile->closeHTML();
```

```
    }
}

$worker=new Client();

?>
```

The Client class in the Adapter design must wrap an instance of the Adaptee (Mobile) to help integrate it into the Adapter itself. The Client instantiates the Adapter using the Adaptee as a parameter in the Adapter instantiation. So the client must create an Adaptee object first (new Mobile()) and then an instance of the Adapter (new MobileAdapter($this->mobile).

The Client class makes most of the requests through the MobileAdapter instance. However, to close up the code, it uses the instance of the Mobile class. Because the application requires no special implementation of the closeHTML() method, the Cli ent launches the method directly from the Mobile instance.

Figure 7-8 shows the same content configured for a mobile device. In this example the device is an iPhone.

Figure 7-8. The mobile adaptation with single column

A lot has been written about how to design and configure mobile web applications, and any design can be used with the Adapter pattern. The point is that starting with a Desktop design (of clearly humble origins), the Adapter was able to pick up and use a different design appropriate for mobile devices without disrupting any implementation of the original desktop design.

Desktop and Mobile Design: Mobile First

While this example began with desktop design and used an Adapter pattern to create a mobile design, mobile developers and designers suggest that a better plan is to begin with a mobile design and create an adapter to create a desktop design. The reason is that with mobile, you need to start with the bare essentials of content and then add any whistles and bells as you develop/design for a larger viewing environment. (See *Head First Mobile Web* by Lyza Danger Gardner and Jason Grigsby [O'Reilly]). Further on in this book, Chapter 14 examines using PHP design patterns to build a content management system (CMS) that delivers the same information to various mobile and desktop environments. One of the strong features of PHP is its ability to distinguish between devices and dynamically supply the right kind of information.

Adapters and Change

PHP programmers live with change. Different versions of PHP change, new functionalities are added and others taken away. Likewise, big and small changes in PHP sometimes accompany MySQL changes. For example, the `mysql` extension was upgraded to `mysqli`, and PHP developers needed to adapt to the new API in `mysqli`. Would an Adapter design be appropriate here? Probably not. Depending on how your program is configured, an Adapter would or would not work. All of the connecting and interaction code could be rewritten, but that's not exactly what the Adapter pattern is supposed to do. That's like rewiring your USB connector to plug into a standard wall socket. However, if all of your old `mysql` code existed in modules, you could change the module (class) and swap in a new module with the same interface but using `mysqli` instead of `mysql`. I don't think a swap is the same as an adapter, but it's in the same spirit. In an Adapter, nothing in the original code changes. All code changes are in the Adapter.

Where the Adapter is most useful is where two incompatible interfaces need to be used together. The Adapter "marries" the interfaces. You can think of the Adapter as a marriage counselor; it resolves the differences by creating a common interface. It saves the separate parts from wholly rewriting themselves so that they can function together.

CHAPTER 8

Decorator Design Pattern

*Charm, in most men and nearly all women,
is a decoration.*

—E. M. Forster

*This wasn't just plain terrible, this was fancy
terrible. This was terrible with raisins in it.*

—Dorothy Parker

*The ornament of a house is the friends who
frequent it.*

—Ralph Waldo Emerson

*She well knew the great architectural secret of
decorating her constructions, and never
condescended to construct a decoration.*

—Anthony Trollope

What Is the Decorator Pattern?

As a structural pattern, the Decorator adds to an existing structure. With the Adapter pattern, the addition to an existing structure is by adding an adapter class that resolves incompatible interfaces. The Decorator adds objects to existing objects. Also called wrapper (as was also the Adapter), the Decorator participant wraps the Component participant with concrete components. Figure 8-1 shows the class diagram, but before going over it, several details need to be considered.

First of all, the Decorator is one of the few design patterns that includes one abstract class inheriting another abstract class. As you can see in Figure 8-1, a looping aggregation connects the Decorator to the Component participant. (The looping line looks more like "wrapping" than the straight line used in the original Gang of Four's class diagram—see also the Freemans' *Head First Design Patterns*, page 91.) The Decorator can be said to "wrap" the Component.

The design creates both the component to be decorated and the decorators. Think of the Component participant as an empty room to be decorated with furniture and rugs—the furniture and rugs being concrete decorators. Note also that all of the participants share a common interface through the Component.

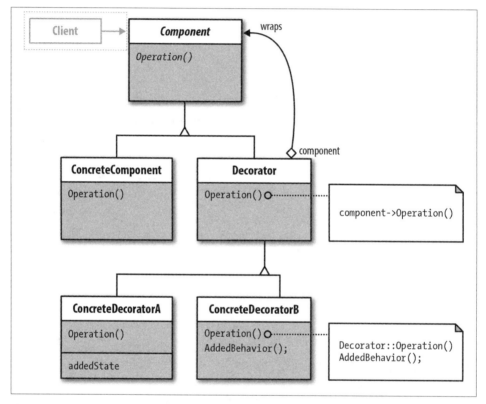

Figure 8-1. Decorator class diagram [Client implied]

The Client is included in the diagram but is really is not a part of the pattern—not even implied. Given the loose coupling, it could make a direct request to any of the concrete components or decorators. However, when using the Decorator pattern, the Client holds a reference to the Component interface.

When to Use the Decorator Pattern

The Gang of Four point out some very general guidelines for using the Decorator. Primarily, the Decorator is used when you want to add functionality to existing objects without affecting the other objects. If you have painstakingly created a website format for a customer with key components that work flawlessly, you don't want to have to upset the applecart when new functionalities are requested. For example, suppose your customers want to include video functionality in their websites after you have built all of the components originally requested. Instead of reworking your original components, you could "decorate" existing components with video functionality. In this way, you can maintain the original functionality while adding new functionality.

Another important feature of the Decorator design pattern can be found in projects where sometimes you need decoration and other times you don't. Suppose your fundamental site development model works just dandy with the majority of your customers. However, some want certain functionality that will help their particular needs. Not everyone wants or needs these additional functionalities. As a developer, you want to create sites that will meet their business goals, and so you need what the business schools call *customerization*—features unique to a specific business. With the Decorator pattern, you can include both the core functionality and then "decorate" those cores with functionality unique to the customer.

With the change that constantly occurs on the Web and Internet—not to mention the scope—the Decorator can be a huge asset in your kit of developer tools. It is a case where you can have your cake and eat it, too—or at least decorate it with sprinkles.

Minimalist Decorator

This first example whittles the Decorator down to the most basic participants, but it clearly illustrates a PHP application. The example depicts a web development business where the business plan has a basic website it markets with added enhancements available. However, the web developer is aware that while the basic plan may work for most customers, along the way they may want certain enhancements.

Another point this minimalist Decorator example makes is the ease with which a number of concrete decorators can be added. In addition to the three decorators provided in this example, see if you can add more. It's easy.

Further, because you can pick and choose which decorators to add, the business can control both the functionality and cost of a project. The ease of the Decorator includes both what can be used in a decoration and what does not have to be added.

The Component Interface

The Component participant is an interface, and in this case it will be an abstract class, IComponent. It has a single property, $site, and two abstract methods, getSite() and getPrice. It sets up the interface for both the concrete components and the abstract class for the Decorator participant:

```php
<?php
//IComponent.php
//Component interface
abstract class IComponent
{
    protected $site;
    abstract public function getSite();
    abstract public function getPrice();
}
?>
```

In PHP, abstract methods have a very small signature, and so while getSite() and getPrice() have an expected return, nothing can be provided further in the abstract method declaration to suggest the kind of return they should generate.

The Decorator Interface

The decorator interface in this example may surprise you. It is an abstract class that extends another abstract class! The purpose of the class is to maintain a reference to the component interface (IComponent) and by extending IComponent, its job is done:

```php
<?php
//Decorator.php
//Decorator participant
abstract class Decorator extends IComponent
{
    //Inherits both getSite() and getPrice()
    //This is still an abstract class and there's
    //no need to implement either abstract method here
    //Job is to maintain reference to Component
    //public function getSite() { }
    //public function getPrice() { }
}
?>
```

Like any other abstract class, you have the option of implementing methods and adding properties. However, the fundamental the role of the Decorator class is in this minimalist example is to keep a link to the component interface.

Before going on to the concrete component participant, take a look at the class diagram for this Decorator implementation in Figure 8-2.

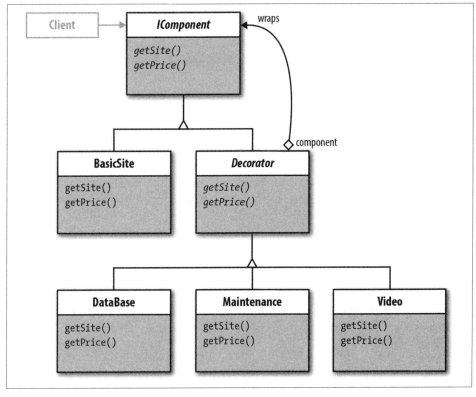

Figure 8-2. Class diagram for minimalist Decorator implementation

All of the participants have identical interfaces. In all implementations of the Decorator, you will find that both the concrete components and decorators have the same interfaces. Their implementations will be different, and both components and decorators can have added properties and methods beyond the basic interfaces. However, the lesson in this first example is that all concrete components and decorators share common interfaces.

Concrete Component

The single concrete component in this example generates a name for the site and a price ($1,200) for a basic site:

```php
<?php
//BasicSite.php
//Concrete Component
class BasicSite extends IComponent
{
    public function __construct()
    {
        $this->site="Basic Site";
```

```
        }
        public function getSite()
        {
            return $this->site;
        }
        public function getPrice()
        {
            return 1200;
        }
    }
    ?>
```

Both of the abstract methods are implemented using literal assignments ("Basic Site" and 1200), but the flexibility is not in changing the set values. Rather, the value of the "Basic Site" is changed by adding the values of the decorators. The following section shows how this is done.

Concrete Decorators

The concrete decorators in this example have the same interface as the concrete component. However, they inherit the interface from the `Decorator` abstract class and not the `IComponent` class. Remember, though, that all the `Decorator` does is to inherit the `IComponent` interface.

Maintenance

```php
<?php
//Maintenance.php
//Concrete decorator
class Maintenance extends Decorator
{
    public function __construct(IComponent $siteNow)
    {
        $this->site = $siteNow;
    }
    public function getSite()
    {
        $fmat="<br/>   Maintenance ";
        return $this->site->getSite() . $fmat;
    }
    public function getPrice()
    {
        return 950 + $this->site->getPrice();
    }
}
?>
```

If you look at the concrete constructor, you will see that it looks almost identical to the decorators. However, each of the concrete decorators adds its own value to the value of the concrete component it wraps. The remaining two concrete decorators are similar to the Maintenance decorator.

Video

```php
<?php
//Video.php
//Concrete decorator
class Video extends IComponent
{
    public function __construct(IComponent $siteNow)
    {
        $this->site = $siteNow;
    }
    public function getSite()
    {
        $fmat="<br/>   Video ";
        return $this->site->getSite() . $fmat;
    }
    public function getPrice()
    {
        return 350 + $this->site->getPrice();
    }
}
?>
```

Database

```php
<?php
//DataBase.php
//Concrete decorator
class DataBase extends Decorator
{
    public function __construct(IComponent $siteNow)
    {
        $this->site = $siteNow;
    }
    public function getSite()
    {
        $fmat="<br/>   MySQL Database ";
        return $this->site->getSite() . $fmat;
    }
    public function getPrice()
    {
        return 800 + $this->site->getPrice();
    }
}
?>
```

When you test the application, you can see that each individual price is added to the base cost. The names are formatted to add a couple of spaces to indent each decorator name.

One of the most important elements of the decorator implementations is in the constructor where a component type is expected. With only a single concrete component, it will be used in all of the instantiations of the decorator. When multiple components are used, the decorators can wrap some, all, or none of the components in the application.

The Client

While the Client class is not a part of the design pattern or even implied, using it correctly is crucial. Each decorator must "wrap" the component in its instantiation, as you saw in the previous section. First, though, it must create an instance of the Basic Site class to wrap:

```php
<?php
//Client.php
function __autoload($class_name)
{
    include $class_name . '.php';
}
class Client
{
    private $basicSite;

    public function __construct()
    {
        $this->basicSite=new BasicSite();
        $this->basicSite=$this->wrapComponent($this->basicSite);

        $siteShow=$this->basicSite->getSite();
        $format="<br/>  <strong>Total= $";
        $price=$this->basicSite->getPrice();

        echo  $siteShow . $format . $price . "</strong><p/>";
    }

    private function wrapComponent(IComponent $component)
    {
        $component=new Maintenance($component);
        $component=new Video($component);
        $component=new DataBase($component);
        return $component;
    }
}
$worker=new Client()
?>
```

Once the Client instantiates the BasicSite, a wrapComponent() method checks to make sure that the correct data type is in the argument (IComponent), and then instantiates each of the three decorators. (In a typical use of the Decorator pattern, only those selected would be included; comment out a couple to see how different combinations affect the total cost.)

When the `wrapComponent()` method returns the component (`$this->basicSite`), it has been changed and now contains the added decorations. The output shows that the concrete component instance is now wrapped with the three decorators, but keep in mind that the output is minimal:

```
Basic Site
   Maintenance
   Video
   MySQL Database
  Total= $3300
```

The `Client` could just as well have wrapped the decorators without the `wrapCompo nent()` method by the simple expedient of having the same sequence of statements in the constructor function. However, it was added to bring attention to the wrapping process in this pattern.

What About Wrappers?

Both the Adapter and Decorator patterns have the alternative name *wrapper*. In fact, some definitions describe a *wrapper* as an adapter. In case you're not certain about the definition of a wrapper, this is a good point to stop and take a look at wrappers in coding in general and PHP specifically.

Primitives in Wrappers

Perhaps the best way to start with wrappers is looking at wrapping a primitive. The following shows how an integer is wrapped in an object and retrieved:

```php
<?php
class PrimitiveWrap
{
    private $wrapeMe;
    public function __construct($prim)
    {
        $this->wrapeMe=$prim;
    }

    public function showWrap()
    {
        return $this->wrapeMe;
    }
}
$myPrim=521;
$wrappedUp=new PrimitiveWrap($myPrim);
echo $wrappedUp->showWrap();
?>
```

If you need a primitive in an object, such as the `PrimitiveWrap` one, it's a little more difficult than in some languages, where you can wrap it with a built-in wrapper. Some languages, like Java, have built-in wrapper classes for every primitive type, and so you don't have to build a class for a wrapper.

Built-in Wrappers in PHP

While not having wrappers for all primitives, PHP does have wrappers of its own. For instance, in Chapter 5, one example of a wrapper at work is the `file_get_con tents()` wrapper. It binds a named resource, such as a filename (or URL to a filename), to a stream. The following example uses a little poem by Ogden Nash to illustrate. First, the poem is saved as a text file (*celery.txt*):

```
<strong>Celery</strong><p/>
Celery, raw<br/>
Develops the jaw,<br/>
But celery, stewed,<br/>
Is more quietly chewed. <p/>
--Ogden Nash<br/>
```

The `file_get_contents()` wrapper opens *celery.txt*, and makes it available to the PHP program for output. The following shows this wrapper at work:

```php
<?php
class TextFileLoader
{
    private $textNow;
    public function __construct()
    {
        $this->textNow = file_get_contents ("celery.txt");
        echo $this->textNow;
    }
}
$worker=new TextFileLoader();
?>
```

The code generates the following output:

```
Celery

Celery, raw
Develops the jaw,
But celery, stewed,
Is more quietly chewed.

--Ogden Nash
```

The filename (*celery.txt*) is "wrapped" in the built-in `file_get_contents()` wrapper.

Design Pattern Wrappers

In Chapter 7, you saw how the Adapter participant in the object Adapter pattern "wrapped" the Adaptee. By doing so, it is able to create a compatible interface with the Adaptee. Likewise, in the minimal example of the Decorator pattern, you saw how the Decorator participants "wrapped" a component object to add responsibilities to an existing component without having to change it. The following code illustrates how the code in the Client wraps a component object ($component) in a decorator (Maintenance):

```
$component=new Maintenance($component);
```

Like the term *interface*, the word *wrapper* applied to computer programming has different uses in different contexts. In general, the term used in the context of design patterns refers to working with incompatible or added on interfaces, and wrappers represent the strategy used to reduce incompatibility.

Decorators with Multiple Components

While only a single concrete component is used in the minimalist example of the Decorator pattern, the use of more than a single component is common. For example, Figure 8-3 shows a class diagram with multiple concrete components.

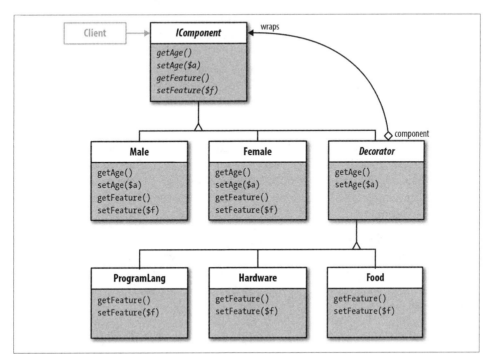

Figure 8-3. Multiple concrete components in Decorator pattern

The Male and Female classes represent concrete implementations of the IComponent abstract class. The Decorator adds properties in the form of arrays. Further on in this section, each of these will be examined closely.

Multiple Concrete Components

Including multiple concrete components is not a problem as far as implementation or decoration. As long as they have the same interface as the component that is passed to the decorators, either one (or one of several) can be wrapped in a concrete decorator, just like a program or system with a single component.

Concrete Decorators with Multiple States and Values

In Figure 8-3, the Decorator, which has inherited the IComponent abstract class interface implements some methods. A couple of things are going on here. First of all, the Decorator implements all of the methods that will not be used in setting the states of the decorations. Basically, the Decorator recognizes certain elements will not be changed in Components through decoration such as age and the name of the component. If the methods responsible for the components are implemented only in the Decorator, they don't have to be reimplemented in the concrete decorators. Secondly, as you can see in Figure 8-1, the Decorator class diagram indicates that it does implement at least some of the Component's interface. The method (Operation()) is not in italics, indicating that the method has been instantiated. The getAge() and setAge($a) methods are implemented but not used. If they were not implemented in the Decorator, they would have to be in each of the concrete decorators because all inherited abstract methods must be implemented in the child class.

The Developer Dating Service

To illustrate how to implement a Decorator with more than a single component, this next example sets up a dating service for software developers. The two components are Male and Female, and each can be decorated with different interests of those seeking dates. The components can be decorated with the same or different concrete decorations in any combination.

At the base, each should have a name and assigned age. We'll assume that age is not a decoration whereas in "real life" it often is. As for the concrete decorations, they will have different states. Not only will each decoration be something that can be added to the concrete components, as was done in the initial example, each concrete decoration can have different states.

Component interface

The component interface includes three properties and five methods. The $date property is used to identify the date as in "a date to go out on" and not a day/month/year kind of date object. The $ageGroup is set in a component and the $feature is a characteristic supplied by one of the concrete decorations:

```php
<?php
//IComponent.php
//Component interface
abstract class IComponent
{
    protected $date;
    protected $ageGroup;
    protected $feature;

    abstract public function setAge($ageNow);
    abstract public function getAge();
    abstract public function getFeature();
    abstract public function setFeature($fea);
}
?>
```

All methods are abstract and all properties are protected.

Concrete components

The two concrete methods are implemented as Male and Female. Each has a constructor that sets the $date value—an ID as "Male" or "Female." Getter/setter methods establish an age and any of the decorations that might be added:

```php
<?php
//Male.php
//Male Concrete Component
class Male extends IComponent
{
    public function __construct()
    {
        $this->date="Male";
        $this->setFeature("<br/>Dude programmer features: ");
    }
    public function getAge()
    {
        return $this->ageGroup;
    }
    public function setAge($ageNow)
    {
        $this->ageGroup=$ageNow;
    }
    public function getFeature()
    {
        return $this->feature;
```

```php
    }
    public function setFeature($fea)
    {
        $this->feature=$fea;
    }
}
?>
```

The initial feature set by both concrete components establishes them as male or female:

```php
<?php
//Female.php
//Female Concrete Component
class Female extends IComponent
{
    public function __construct()
    {
        $this->date="Female";
        $this->setFeature("<br />Grrrl programmer features: ");
    }
    public function getAge()
    {
        return $this->ageGroup;
    }
    public function setAge($ageNow)
    {
        $this->ageGroup=$ageNow;
    }
    public function getFeature()
    {
        return $this->feature;
    }
    public function setFeature($fea)
    {
        $this->feature=$fea;
    }
}
?>
```

Other features can be added as decorations to both components using the $setFea
ture() method. Think of $setFeature() as a *component enhancer* rather than a com-
ponent setter.

Decorator with component methods

The decorator interface extends the component interface. However, as previously noted, it also implements getters/setters for age:

```php
<?php
//Decorator.php
//Decorator participant
abstract class Decorator extends IComponent
{
    public function setAge($ageNow)
    {
        $this->ageGroup=$this->ageGroup;
    }
    public function getAge()
    {
        return $this->ageGroup;
    }
}
?>
```

If you want to add an active error-catching routine using an `else` statement, you can easily do so. However, the current setup would be a "quiet fail," where the object would not be passed.

Concrete decorators

The concrete decorators in this example are quite different from the concrete decorators in the minimalist example. Instead of having a single state, the concrete decorators all contain arrays with multiple property values. Instead of having a single concrete decorator with four different language choices to be used as a concrete decoration, we could have had four separate concrete decorations, each representing a different computer language. However, combining the same choices in an array accomplishes the same goal and maintains loose coupling:

```php
<?php
//ProgramLang.php
//Concrete decorator
class ProgramLang extends Decorator
{
    private $languageNow;

    public function __construct(IComponent $dateNow)
    {
        $this->date = $dateNow;
    }

    private $language=array("php"=>"PHP",
                            "cs"=>"C#",
                            "js"=>"JavaScript",
```

```
                      "as3"=>"ActionScript 3.0");

    public function setFeature($lan)
    {
        $this->languageNow=$this->language[$lan];
    }

    public function getFeature()
    {
        $output=$this->date->getFeature();
        $fmat="<br/>  ";
        $output .="$fmat Preferred programming language: ";
        $output .= $this->languageNow;
        return  $output;
    }
}
?>
```

All of the concrete decorators have the same formatting. An output variable is first assigned the selected element using getFeature( ), and then formatting tags and general concrete component information is concatenated to the output variable:

```
<?php
//Hardware.php
//Concrete decorator
class Hardware extends Decorator
{
    private $hardwareNow;

    public function __construct(IComponent $dateNow)
    {
        $this->date = $dateNow;
    }

    private $box=array("mac"=>"Macintosh",
                       "dell"=>"Dell",
                       "hp"=>"Hewlett-Packard",
                       "lin"=>"Linux");

    public function setFeature($hdw)
    {
        $this->hardwareNow=$this->box[$hdw];
    }

    public function getFeature()
    {
        $output=$this->date->getFeature();
        $fmat="<br/>  ";
        $output .="$fmat Current Hardware: ";
        $output .= $this->hardwareNow;
        return  $output;
    }
}
```

```php
    }
?>
```

Using associative arrays (arrays that use string element keys) makes it a little easier to choose which property of the decorations to select. All of the concrete decorators have a similar style of array for each feature:

```php
<?php
//Food.php
//Concrete decorator
class Food extends Decorator
{
    private $chowNow;

    public function __construct(IComponent $dateNow)
    {
        $this->date = $dateNow;
    }

    private $snacks=array("piz"=>"Pizza",
                    "burg"=>"Burgers",
                    "nach"=>"Nachos",
                    "veg"=>"Veggies");

    public function setFeature($yum)
    {
        $this->chowNow=$this->snacks[$yum];
    }

    public function getFeature()
    {
        $output=$this->date->getFeature();
        $fmat="<br/>  ";
        $output .="$fmat Favorite food: ";
        $output .= $this->chowNow . "<br/>";
        return  $output;
    }
}
?>
```

The concrete decorations all must be easily accessible to the client, and so each of the getter and setter methods are `public`. However, the values set in the different properties (arrays) are `private`, adding a measure of encapsulation in the component decoration process.

The Client

Finally, the Client class requests a component and concrete decorations. After selecting a concrete component through instantiation, the Client sets the age group of interest. The Client sets one of four age groups with the strings "Age Group N" where "N" is a string value from 1–4:

```php
<?php
//Client.php
/*Age groups:
    18-29: Group 1
    30-39: Group 2
    40-49: Group 3
    50+  : Group 4
*/
function __autoload($class_name)
{
    include $class_name . '.php';
}
class Client
{
    //$hotDate is component instance
    private $hotDate;

    public function __construct()
    {
        $this->hotDate=new Female();
        $this->hotDate->setAge("Age Group 4");
        echo $this->hotDate->getAge();
        $this->hotDate=$this->wrapComponent($this->hotDate);
        echo $this->hotDate->getFeature();
    }

    private function wrapComponent(IComponent $component)
    {
        $component=new ProgramLang($component);
        $component->setFeature("php");
        $component=new Hardware($component);
        $component->setFeature("lin");
        $component=new Food($component);
        $component->setFeature("veg");

        return $component;
    }
}
$worker=new Client()
?>
```

After instantiating one of the two concrete components, the Client decorates them by wrapping them in one of three concrete decorators. This whole process is within the wrapComponent() method. As each instance is created, the setFeature() method, using an argument made up of an associative array key, decorates the component. The client generates the following output:

```
Female
Age Group 4
Grrrl programmer features:
    Preferred programming language: PHP
    Current Hardware: Linux
    Favorite food: Veggies
```

As you can see, the decorators are elements from the associative arrays in the concrete decorator classes.

HTML User Interface (UI)

Up to this point in the book, no HTML UI has been included. In Part V, all of the applications include an HTML UI. The reason for not adding a UI thus far is that the focus has been on the fundamentals of the different design patterns. The PHP has not been embedded in an HTML wrapper, and the only HTML generated is that used for general formatting.

At this point, the HTML UI is to show how to connect to a PHP design pattern through the Client class (object). Using the example in the *Developer Dating Service*, you can see that communication between HTML and PHP is the same as you have used with any other HTML→PHP program used in other projects. The only change in the PHP is to allow values to be passed from an HTML form to the Client class. All of the other participants in the pattern remain unchanged.

To get started, take a look at the finished HTML UI in Figure 8-4. As you can see, the page uses radio buttons for all of the data input.

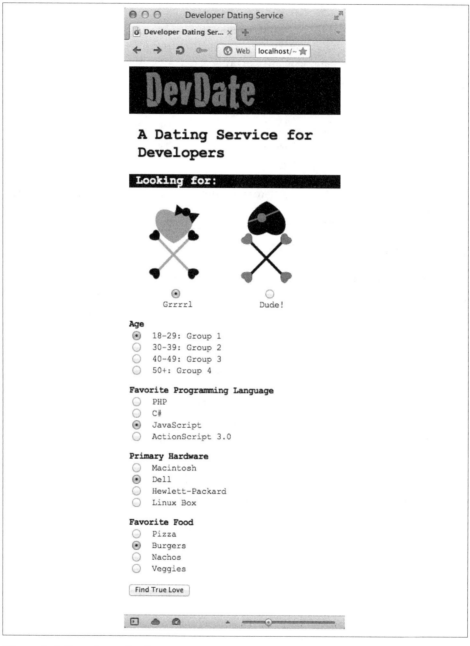

Figure 8-4. Data input for Decorator

The data input is simple, and all that's required are the standard HTML/CSS files for the page. First, the page uses the following CSS file:

```
@charset "UTF-8";
/* CSS Document */
/* devedate.css */
header
{
    font-family:Cracked;
    font-size:72px;
    color:#F00;
    background-color:#000;
}
h2
{
    font-family:"Courier New", Courier, monospace;
    font-size:24px;
}

h3
{
    font-family:"Courier New", Courier, monospace;
    font-size:18px;
    color:#fff;
    background-color:#000;
}

body
{
    font-family:"Courier New", Courier, monospace;
    font-size:14px;
}
#sex
{
    display:table;
}
#fem
{
    display:table-cell;
    width:150px;
    text-align:center;
}
aside
{
    display:table-cell;
    width:150px;
    text-align:center;
}
```

The page is set up for mobile vertical, but it works just as well on a table or desktop system. Next, the HTML for the page is listed in the following code block. It calls a page, *ClientH.php*. The *H* in the class and filename indicates that it is set up to receive HTML data (you may want to add validation code either to the HTML or PHP scripts; it throws errors for any unchecked radio buttons!):

```html
<!doctype html>
<html>
<head>
<meta charset="UTF-8">
<link rel="stylesheet" type="text/css" href="css/devdate.css">
<title>Developer Dating Service</title>
</head>

<body>
<article>
  <header>  DevDate</header>
  <h2> A Dating Service for <br/>
     Developers</h2>
  <h3> Looking for:</h3>
  <form action="ClientH.php" method="post">
    <div id="sex">
      <div id="fem"> <img src="pix/grrrl.png" width="95" height="128"
        alt="grrrl"><br/>
        <input type="radio" name="gender" value="Female">
        <br/>
         Grrrl </div>
      <aside> <img src="pix/dude.png" width="99" height="133" alt="dude"><br/>
        <input type="radio" name="gender" value="Male">
        <br/>
         Dude!
        <p/>
      </aside>
    </div>
    <strong>Age<br/>
    </strong>
    <input type="radio" name="age" value="Age Group 1">
     18-29: Group 1 <br/>
    <input type="radio" name="age" value="Age Group 2">
     30-39: Group 2<br/>
    <input type="radio" name="age" value="Age Group 3">
     40-49: Group 3<br/>
    <input type="radio" name="age" value="Age Group 4">
     50+: Group 4
    <p/>
    <strong>Favorite Programming Language<br/>
    </strong>
    <input type="radio" name="progLang" value="php">
     PHP<br/>
    <input type="radio" name="progLang" value="cs">
     C#<br/>
    <input type="radio" name="progLang" value="js">
     JavaScript<br/>
    <input type="radio" name="progLang" value="as3">
     ActionScript 3.0
    <p/>
    <strong>Primary Hardware<br/>
    </strong>
```

```
        <input type="radio" name="hardware" value="mac">
         Macintosh<br/>
        <input type="radio" name="hardware" value="dell">
         Dell<br/>
        <input type="radio" name="hardware" value="hp">
         Hewlett-Packard<br/>
        <input type="radio" name="hardware" value="lin">
         Linux Box
        <p/>
        <strong>Favorite Food<br/>
        </strong>
        <input type="radio" name="food" value="piz">
         Pizza<br/>
        <input type="radio" name="food" value="burg">
         Burgers<br/>
        <input type="radio" name="food" value="nach">
         Nachos<br/>
        <input type="radio" name="food" value="veg">
         Veggies
        <p/>
        <input type="submit" name="search" value="Find True Love">
    </form>
</article>
</body>
</html>
```

Basically, this page passes data to a PHP page exactly as you would if you were sending data from an HTML page to a MySQL database via PHP. So, even though the data is going to a client class in a Decorator design pattern, passing data is no different than what you're used to doing with any other data to a PHP file.

The Client Class Passing HTML Data

As noted, sending data to a PHP client class from HTML is similar to sending it to a database table. In looking at the ClientH class, you will see that it is just like the Client class except that it uses the data from the *DeveloperDating.html* file:

```
<?php
//ClientH.php
function __autoload($class_name)
{
    include $class_name . '.php';
}
class ClientH
{
    //$hotDate is component instance
    private $hotDate;
    private $progLange;
    private $hardware;
    private $food;
```

```
public function __construct()
{
    $gender=$_POST["gender"];
    $age=$_POST["age"];
    $this->progLang=$_POST["progLang"];
    $this->hardware=$_POST["hardware"];
    $this->food=$_POST["food"];

    $this->hotDate=new $gender();
    $this->hotDate->setAge($age);
    echo $this->hotDate->getAge();
    $this->hotDate=$this->wrapComponent($this->hotDate);
    echo $this->hotDate->getFeature();
}

private function wrapComponent(IComponent $component)
{
    $component=new ProgramLang($component);
    $component->setFeature($this->progLang);
    $component=new Hardware($component);
    $component->setFeature($this->hardware);
    $component=new Food($component);
    $component->setFeature($this->food);

    return $component;
}
}
$worker=new ClientH()
?>
```

Using the $_POST associative array, the radio button variables and values are passed to PHP variables. The gender and age variable were passed within the constructor function, while the component variable ($hotDate) and three decorator variables ($proLang, $hardware, and $food) were all declared as private variables and then used in the place of literals as had been done in the original Client class.

From a Variable Name to an Object Instance

The normal process for instantiating an object instance is to assign a named variable to a class instance. In this book, the convention is to capitalize all class names and use lowercase names for variable class instances, such as the following:

```
$someInstance= new SomeClass();
```

That format works fine as long as you know the name of the class. However, when you have multiple components that must be declared through a variable passed from an HTML page, the name of the class must come through a variable's value. PHP makes the process incredibly easy, especially compared with methods that use some form of an eval function.

The general process for naming and instantiating a class through a variable, as you saw in Chapter 6, is to assign the class name to the variable and then instantiate the class using the variable. For example, suppose you have a class named Nature; an instance can be instantiated dynamically through a variable:

```
$quack = "Nature";
$myNature= new $quack();
```

Now, $myNature is an instance of the Nature class. In the class ClientH, you can see that the $hotDate variable must instantiate one of the two component classes, Female or Male. In selecting a male or female date, the user chooses one of two radio buttons, both named *gender*. The two values are the class names, Female and Male. So, when those values are passed to the PHP variable $gender, they are all set to be instantiated into one or the other of the two concrete component classes. The following line does the instantiation:

```
$this->hotDate=new $gender();
```

Note that the expression includes both the new keyword and adds open and close parentheses at the end of the variable $gender.

Adding a Decoration

Suppose you think it would be a good idea to include a query about the kinds of movies the users enjoy as a measure of compatibility. For example, the categories of action, romance, science fiction, and musicals could be film types that users may enjoy. In order to measure your own understanding of the Decorator design pattern, add a single concrete decorator class that can decorate the selected concrete component with movie preference.

The process is quite easy. In fact, you can copy and paste one of the existing concrete components and rename it Films. Then just change the options for the categories and test it using literal values in the Client class. If that works as desired, update the HTML UI to include a films option and change the ClientH class to pass the request to the rest of the program.

The larger a program gets, the more useful both OOP programming and design patterns from the Structural category become. That's because all of the patterns discussed in Part III are used to change the functionality of existing structures without having to rewrite the existing structure.

PART IV

Behavioral Design Patterns

*Great discoveries and improvements invariably
involve the cooperation of many minds. I may be
given credit for having blazed the trail, but when I
look at the subsequent developments I feel the
credit is due to others rather than to myself.*

—Alexander Graham Bell

*When new turns of behavior cease to appear in the
life of the individual, its behavior ceases to
be intelligent.*

—Thomas Carlyle

*Societies have always been shaped more by the
nature of the media by which men communicate
than by the content of the communication.*

—Marshall McLuhan

Behavioral design patterns make up the plurality of design patterns offered by the Gang of Four. This section covers one class example (Template Method) and one object example (State), but Part V shows more behavioral patterns used with PHP/MySQL examples. All in all, Gamma, Helm, Johnson, and Vlissides provide eleven behavioral patterns:

- Chain of Responsibility
- Command
- Interpreter (class type)
- Iterator

- Mediator
- Memento
- Observer
- State
- Strategy
- Template Method (class type)
- Visitor

The key to understanding behavioral design patterns is communication. The focus shifts from the objects and classes that make up a design pattern to the communication between objects and classes. In the truest form of composition, behavioral patterns are best understood in terms of how objects work together to perform tasks.

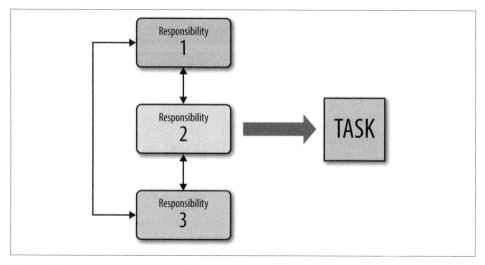

Figure IV.1. Behavioral patterns focus on communication between pattern participants

The emphasis on interaction between the elements that make up a pattern is so important that some class diagrams look identical, such as the State and Strategy patterns. However, because of the way in which the participants communicate and how they handle responsibilities, they are very different.

CHAPTER 9

The Template Method Pattern

It is easy to study the rules of overloading and of templates without noticing that together they are one of the keys to elegant and efficient type-safe containers.

—Bjarne Stroustrup

All the great legends are Templates for human behavior. I would define a myth as a story that has survived.

—John Boorman

I work out the other bits, too, but I need to know what I look like, very early on. And then it's like a template; I'll fill that person out. If I get that out of the way, then I'm all right.

—Dame Judith Dench

What Is the Template Method Pattern?

First of all, you need to differentiate between the *Template Method* as a design pattern and the `templateMethod()`—a class method—used within a Template Method pattern. The `templateMethod()` is a concrete method within an abstract class. It orders the sequence of abstract methods, leaving the implementations up to a concrete class. At its core, the Template Method defines the skeleton of an algorithm in an operation while the exact implementations are left up to the concrete classes.

The good thing about the Template Method is that it is relatively small and easy to implement. A single abstract and concrete class is all you need, as shown in Figure 9-1.

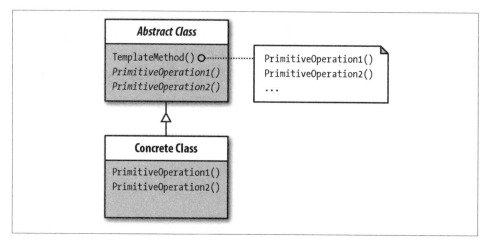

Figure 9-1. Template Method class diagram

One way to think of the template method operation in the abstract class is as *an arranger of primitive operations*. (I will refer to the *Template Method design pattern* with initial caps and the *template method operation* with all lowercase.) Consider the role of a wedding organizer. She has a series of events (operations) that she arranges in a certain order at the reception—the dinner, the cutting of the cake, the first dance, the speeches, and anything else that goes into a wedding reception. The general template that the wedding organizer works from includes the events in a given, logical order, but she leaves it up to the individual bride's family exactly how they want to execute the events. For instance the dinner may vary from a formal dinner to an outdoor barbeque, the dance from waltzes to hip-hop, and the band from a full orchestra to Jacques, the singing accordionist. The events occur in the same order, but they're implemented differently.

When to Use the Template Method

If you have certain steps in an algorithm worked out, but they can be implemented in any number of different ways, then use the Template Method. The Gang of Four note that when the steps in an algorithm are invariant, you can leave up the steps to the subclasses. In this case, use the design pattern for arranging primitive operations (functions/methods) in the abstract class. Then use the subclasses that implement those operations as required by the application.

A little more complex usage is when a common behavior among subclasses needs to be localized in a single class to avoid code duplication. The GoF cite Opdyke's and Johnson's "refactoring to generalize" as the process whereby duplicate code is organized into a Template Method pattern. Duplicate code can happen very quickly where several classes are used to work on the same larger problem.

A final use is in controlling subclass extensions. This involves a "hook" operation that will be discussed in "The Hook in the Template Method Design Pattern" (page 181). The hook controls the extension by allowing extensions only at certain points where the hook operation resides.

Using the Template Method with Images and Captions: A Minimal Example

One of the simple chores you may encounter in PHP programming is setting up images with captions. It's a pretty straightforward algorithm involving nothing more than displaying the image and then displaying the text beneath the image.

Given that only two participants are involved in the Template Method design, this should prove to be one of the easiest patterns to understand, yet it is quite useful at the same time. The abstract class sets up the `templateMethod()` (the actual method) and the concrete class implements it.

The Abstract Class

The abstract class is the key here because it includes both concrete and abstract methods. The template method (the method itself) is always going to be concrete, and its operations are going to be abstract.

To load a picture requires nothing more than an operation to call the URL of the image using an HTML wrapper. Equally simple is an operation to capture text that serves as a caption and place it beneath the image.

The two operations in the form of abstract methods are `addPix($pix)` and `addCaption($cap)`. Both contain a single parameter for an argument with the image's URL information and the caption's string. Properties with protected visibility are set up for encapsulation within the `templateMethod()` function:

```
<?
//AbstractClass.php
abstract class AbstractClass
{
    protected $pix;
    protected $cap;

    public function templateMethod($pixNow,$capNow)
    {
        $this->pix=$pixNow;
        $this->cap=$capNow;
        $this->addPix($this->pix);
        $this->addCaption($this->cap);
    }
```

```
    abstract protected function addPix($pix);
    abstract protected function addCaption($cap);
}
?>
```

Two parameters are added to the template method function so that it can be used for receiving arguments that will be passed on to the protected properties.

The Concrete Class

The concrete class that will use the template method extends the abstract class and implements the primitive operations: addPix() and addCaption(). The algorithm expects them to include code that can be used to display an image and appropriate caption:

```
<?
//ConcreteClass.php
include_once('AbstractClass.php');
class ConcreteClass extends AbstractClass
{
    protected function addPix($pix)
    {
        $this->pix=$pix;
        $this->pix = "pix/" . $this->pix;
        $formatter = "<img src=$this->pix><br/>";
        echo $formatter;
    }
    protected  function addCaption($cap)
    {
        $this->cap=$cap;
        echo "<em>Caption:</em>" . $this->cap . "<br/>";
    }
}
?>
```

Rather than returning an object, the two operations send them to the screen using the echo statement. This is done to keep the example as simple as possible. Both the add Pix() and addCaption() methods are now all set to be used by a client.

The Client

The Gang of Four do not mention the client in discussing this design pattern, but it is just as likely to be the base of a UI connection as to be part of another design pattern. So, the simple Client class here can be considered in any context where a Template Method pattern may be needed:

```
<?
//Client.php
function __autoload($class_name)
{
    include $class_name . '.php';
```

```
    }
    class Client
    {
        function __construct()
        {
            $caption="Modigliani painted elongated faces.";
            $mo=new ConcreteClass();
            $mo->templateMethod("modig.png",$caption);
        }
    }
    $worker=new Client();
    ?>
```

Notice that the $mo variable instantiates the ConcreteClass, but it calls the template
Method(), a concrete operation from the parent class. The parent class (Abstract
Class) calls operations of the subclass through the templateMethod(). Figure 9-2 shows
the output.

Figure 9-2. The picture-then-caption sequence is established by the template method

Essentially, all that the client really needs to supply is the URL to the image and a text
string for the caption.

The Hollywood Principle

The concept of an *inverted control structure* came to be called (and recalled) by the name *the Hollywood Principle*. This principle holds that the parent calls the operations of a subclass and the child does not. (After the screen test, the director tells the young actor, "We'll let you know if you get the part. Don't call us; we'll call you." That's how the inverted control structure came to be called the Hollywood Principle.)

The pattern most associated with the Hollywood Principle is the Template Method because it is implemented in the parent class. Other than the `templateMethod()`, the other operations (methods) in the parent class are abstract and protected. So, even though the client instantiates a concrete class, it calls the method implemented in the parent class. Figure 9-3 may help to illustrate the inverted control structure more clearly.

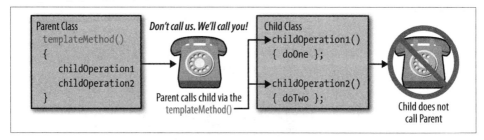

Figure 9-3. The Hollywood Principle

The real question, though, is this: Why is the Hollywood Principle important for OOP and design patterns? In some respects, the question and answer rely on breaking away from sequential and procedural programming thinking. In procedural programming, a key issue is *flow of control*, whereas in OOP, the key issue is *object responsibility*. Because of the focus on flow of control, some explanations use the term *inversion of control* to explain the Hollywood Principle. Inversion of control makes sense from the perspective of procedural programming, but in OOP most of the flow of control is abstracted away through object responsibility and collaboration. That is, rather than thinking about flow of control, you should be thinking about which objects will handle certain responsibilities and how object collaboration can accomplish tasks.

In the context of OOP, the easiest way to think about the Hollywood Principle accurately is in terms of frameworks and possible changes in those frameworks. (I use the term *framework* in this context to depict small structures in a program and not the larger ones that we differentiated from design patterns in Chapter 3. See "Pattern Hatching" by John Vlissides in the February 1996 *C++ Report*.) John Vlissides points out that a template method defines the framework, and subclasses can extend or reimplement the variable parts of the algorithm, but they cannot alter the template method's flow of control. The "call" from the child is to reimplement the parent, and it is that kind of "call" that is not allowed according to the Hollywood Principle. Only the parent can make the "call" to establish or change the framework (order of operations to be launched).

Perhaps a better way of thinking about the Hollywood Principle is in terms of teacher-student relations in a kindergarten class—the *Kindergarten Principle*. The teacher sets up a number of projects for the kids to carry out in a certain order—counting, telling time, vocabulary. The teacher sets the order, but the way it is actually carried out, or implemented by the kids depends on the kids. However, the kids cannot change the order set up by the teacher. In other words, a kid cannot say in the middle of a counting exercise, "I want to do vocabulary now." The structure is ordered:

1. Counting
2. Telling Time
3. Vocabulary

The teacher says, "Sorry, Elmo, we're doing counting now. We'll be doing vocabulary later." The order is invariant as far as the kids are concerned. So the teacher calls the shots, not the other way around. In this context, *inversion of control* doesn't make a lot of sense: the parent sets up the order, and the child carries out the operations in his or her own unique way. That doesn't intuitively seem "inverted." So if you run across *inversion of control* in discussions of the Hollywood Principle, keep in mind that "inversion" makes sense only in the flow of control context of procedural programming.

Using the Template Method with Other Design Patterns

Design patterns do not live in lonely deserts. They live in a community of coded objects, some of which may be other design patterns. To illustrate this, the first example will be used with a Factory Method with the same results—a picture with a caption. Given the fact that the example uses a single image and caption, it may appear to be using an elephant gun to swat a fly. However, the point is to see how two design patterns can work together, and if you understand the interaction between the patterns you can work in far more products. The Template Method orders the algorithms to display an image and caption in a given order, and the Factory Method creates the objects. Figure 9-4 shows the file diagram with the two different patterns delineated by a gray border.

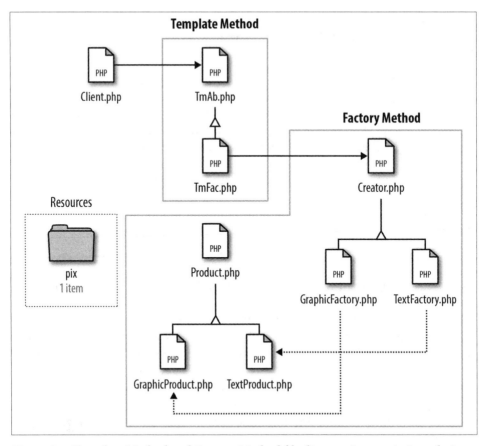

Figure 9-4. Template Method and Factory Method file diagram in associative relation

The reason for using these two patterns in conjunction lies in their separate roles. The Template Method sets up the order of the algorithms (first image, second caption) and the Factory Method creates the image and caption. Looking at this, you might think that the client will have to jump though hoops to make a request; however, the opposite is true.

The Client's Reduced Workload

When the client makes a request, it is through the Template Method. The Template Method has the operations organized so that it automatically passes on the request in the appropriate order:

```
<?
//Client.php
function __autoload($class_name)
{
```

```
        include $class_name . '.php';
    }
class Client
{
    function __construct()
    {
        $mo=new TmFac();
        $mo->templateMethod();
    }
}
$worker=new Client();
?>
```

Most of the `Client` class in this case is made up of error-checking and loading required classes. Just two lines take care of the request:

```
$mo=new TmFac();
$mo->templateMethod();
```

It may seem ironic that after joining two different design patterns the `Client` has less work, but the patterns make it easy. The Template Method has ordered the algorithms that call the factories to create the image and caption. So, all the `Client` has to request is the method that gets the request.

The Template Method Participants

The two classes used to create the Template Method are little changed from the initial minimal example. In some respects, the `TmFac` class acts like a client because it sends the request to the factories in the Factory Method:

```
<?
//TmAb.php
//Abstract Template Method class
abstract class TmAb
{
    protected $pix;
    protected $cap;

    public function templateMethod()
    {
        $this->addPix();
        $this->addCaption();
    }

    protected abstract function addPix();
    protected abstract function addCaption();

}
?>


<?
//TmFac.php
```

```
//Concrete Template Method
//invokes Factory Method
class TmFac extends TmAb
{
    protected function addPix()
    {
        $this->pix=new GraphicFactory();
        echo $this->pix->doFactory();
    }
    protected  function addCaption()
    {
        $this->cap=new TextFactory();
        echo $this->cap->doFactory();
    }
}
?>
```

The templateMethod() operation orders the methods in the TmFac class, and any calls
to the templateMethod() result in calls to the factories in the desired order.

The Factory Method Participants

The Client class has absolutely no communication with the Factory Method. The
Template Method operations have passed on the initial request, but they have not left
any "fingerprints" (so to speak). All Factory Method participants are responding to is
the request from the TmFac object:

```
<?php
//Creator.php
abstract class Creator
{
    protected abstract function factoryMethod();

    public function doFactory()
    {
        $mfg= $this->factoryMethod();
        return $mfg;
    }
}
?>


<?php
//GraphicFactory.php

class GraphicFactory extends Creator
{
    protected function factoryMethod()
    {
        $product=new GraphicProduct();
        return($product->getProperties());
    }
```

```php
}
?>

<?php
//TextFactory.php

class TextFactory extends Creator
{
    protected function factoryMethod()
    {
        $product=new TextProduct();
        return($product->getProperties());
    }
}
?>

<?php
//Product.php
interface Product
{
    public function getProperties();
}
?>

<?php
//GraphicProduct.php

class GraphicProduct implements Product
{
    private $mfgProduct;

    public function getProperties()
    {
        $this->mfgProduct="<img src='pix/modig.png'>";
        return $this->mfgProduct;
    }
}
?>

<?php
//TextProduct.php
class TextProduct implements Product
{
    private $mfgProduct;

    public function getProperties()
    {
        $this->mfgProduct ="<div style='color:#cc0000; font-size:12px;
                        font-family:Verdana, Geneva, sans-serif'>
                        <strong><em>Caption:</em></strong> Modigliani
                        painted elongated faces.</div>";
```

```
        return $this->mfgProduct;
    }
}
?>
```

In looking at Figure 9-5, it is almost identical to Figure 9-2 except that the caption has a different style. That style was generated by the implemented product that was launched by the request to the factory from the `templateMethod()`.

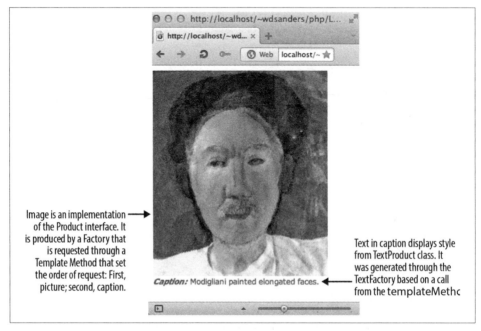

Figure 9-5. Image and caption generated following steps in templateMethod()

The important point about Figure 9-5 is that because the design patterns kept all of the participants (classes and resultant objects) loosely coupled yet connected, the program is flexible enough to return the image and caption through the entire set of classes and interfaces. With a simple image and caption, that feat is unremarkable. However, with more complex algorithms with more steps, Template Method can add a reusable order to any set of responsibilities. Added products or changes in the products will be processed through the same interfaces.

The Hook in the Template Method Design Pattern

Sometimes there may be a step in the template method function that you don't want executed under certain circumstances. For instance, suppose you have a template method that adds up the total cost of an order, adds tax and shipping cost, and then displays the total transaction. However, your customer tells you that if his buyer spends more than $200 on shipped merchandise, the shipping is free. This is where the template method hook comes in.

In the context of the Template Method design pattern, the hook allows a method to be part of a template method, but it does not always have to be used. In other words, it's part of the method, but it contains a hook to deal with exceptions. The child class can add an optional element to the algorithm so that while it is launched within the order established by the template method, it may not do what the template method expects. The hook is the perfect tool for the case of the optional shipping costs.

If you think that this might be in violation of the Hollywood Principle (a subclass monkeying around with the order set by the parent class), you'd be right. The Hollywood Principle does hold that only the parent class can change the framework. The hook is special because even though it implements the methods within the template method, the implemented method has a "back door," so to speak, that deals with exceptions.

To see how the hook works, take a look at a simple example. A company sells GPS devices and maps for trips down the Zambezi River. It also rents boats. The owner decides that if the buyer purchases over $200 in shipped items, the buyer pays no shipping costs. However, this does not include the rental costs of the boats. So he needs a program that will total up the costs of the shipped items, decide whether or not to add shipping costs, and then add the rental costs and display the grand total. Figure 9-6 shows the UI for the business.

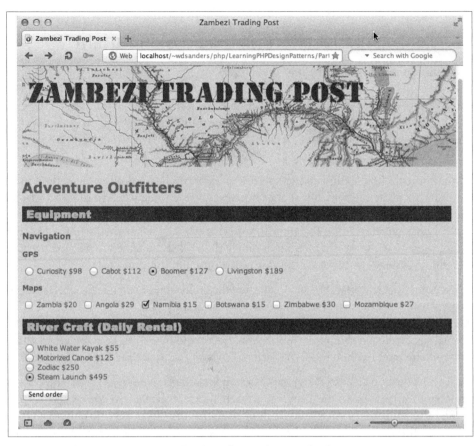

Figure 9-6. UI for PHP that uses hook with template method

The UI HTML code is based on a form for easy data input using radio buttons and check boxes. Each has a value representing the cost of the product or service. The following HTML listing includes an HTML array for the map selection:

```html
<!DOCTYPE html>
<html>
<head>
<meta charset="UTF-8">
<link rel="stylesheet" type="text/css" href="zambezi.css">
<title>Zambezi Trading Post</title>
<body>
<img src="zambezi.png" width="800" height="183" alt="zam">
<h1>Adventure Outfitters</h1>
<form action="Client.php" method="post">
  <h2> Equipment</h2>
  <h3>Navigation</h3>
  <p><strong>GPS</strong></p>
  <input type="radio" name="gps" value="98">
```

```
 Curiosity $98 
<input type="radio" name="gps" value="112">
 Cabot $112 
<input type="radio" name="gps" value="127">
 Boomer $127 
<input type="radio" name="gps" value="189">
 Livingston $189 
<p><strong>Maps</strong></p>
<input type="checkbox" name="map[]" value="20">
 Zambia $20 
<input type="checkbox" name="map[]" value="29">
 Angola $29 
<input type="checkbox" name="map[]" value="15">
 Namibia $15 
<input type="checkbox" name="map[]" value="15">
 Botswana $15 
<input type="checkbox" name="map[]" value="30">
 Zimbabwe $30 
<input type="checkbox" name="map[]" value="27">
 Mozambique $27<br/>
<h2> River Craft (Daily Rental)</h2>
<input type="radio" name="boat" value="55">
 White Water Kayak $55<br/>
<input type="radio" name="boat" value="125">
 Motorized Canoe $125<br/>
<input type="radio" name="boat" value="250">
 Zodiac $250<br/>
<input type="radio" name="boat" value="495">
 Steam Launch $495
<p/>
<input type="submit" name="sender" value="Send order">
</form>
</body>
</html>
```

The CSS that accompanies the HTML page is equally simple:

```
@charset "UTF-8";
/* CSS Document */
/*zambezi.css */
/*D9C68F,F2DAC4,A69586,73635A,592D23*/
body {
    background-color: #f2dac4;
    color: #73635a;
    font-family: Verdana, Geneva, sans-serif;
    font-size: 12px;
}
h1 {
 font-family:"Trebuchet MS", Arial, Helvetica, sans-serif;
 font-size:36px;
}
h2 {
    font-family: "Arial Black", Gadget, sans-serif;
```

```
        font-size: 18px;
        background-color: #592d23;
        color: #d9c68f;
    }
```

As soon as the user clicks the "Send order" button, the PHP `Client` class launches. However, first, take a look at the Template Method pattern employed.

Setting Up the Hook

It may seem ironic to set up the hook method in the template method interface, but even though the child class can change the hook's behavior, it still needs to be placed in the order defined in the template method:

```
<?
//IHook.php
abstract class IHook
{
    protected $purchased;
    protected $hookSpecial;
    protected $shippingHook;
    protected $fullCost;

    public function templateMethod($total,$special)
    {
        $this->purchased=$total;
        $this->hookSpecial=$special;
        $this->addTax();
        $this->addShippingHook();
        $this->displayCost();
    }

    protected abstract function addTax();
    protected abstract function addShippingHook();
    protected abstract function displayCost();
}
?>
```

The three abstract methods—addTax(), addShippingHook(), and displayCost()—are all ordered in the templateMethod() implemented by the abstract class IHook. The hook is placed in the middle; it can be placed anywhere in the template method order. It expects two arguments: a total expenditure and a variable that determines whether the customer gets free shipping or not. These values will have to be provided by the Client class that received the raw data from the HTML document.

Implementing the Hook

Once set up in an order as an abstract method, the child class implements all three methods:

```
<?
//ZambeziCalc.php
class ZambeziCalc extends IHook
{
    protected  function addTax()
    {
        $this->fullCost = $this->purchased + ($this->purchased * .07);
    }
    protected  function addShippingHook()
    {
        if(! $this->hookSpecial)
        {
            $this->fullCost += 12.95;
        }
    }
    protected  function displayCost()
    {
        echo "Your full cost is $this->fullCost";
    }
}
?>
```

The addTax() and displayCost() methods are standard and have a single implementation. However, the addShippingHook() is implemented so that a conditional determines whether a shipping cost is added or not. That's the hook.

The Client and Tripping the Hook

Developers often overlook the importance of Boolean variables because of their binary character. However, these variables are clean and fast in the processing stream, and I find them invaluable for tripping a hook. In any hook operation, something must alert the flow that something different has to happen than the default operation set up when implementing the template method.

Setting the Boolean with comparison operators

Instead of establishing a Boolean's state using conditional statements, using comparison operators is easier and cleaner. The following line in the client sets the Boolean for the hook in the Template Method example of *Zambezi Trading Post*.

```
$this->special = ($this->buyTotal >= 200);
```

It immediately assigns the Boolean, $this->special, a state of *true* or *false*. Zambezi Trading Post offers the special of free shipping for all *shipped purchases* of $200 or more.

Next, looking at the Client class, you can see how the request accesses the hook in the Template Method design pattern.

The Client class

The Client class makes a request based on data received from the HTML form. It must separate the rentals from the equipment purchases so that the special discount can be calculated based only on the equipment purchases. Once the special is established as being true or false, the total is added, which is then subject to tax. Because the variable $special is a Boolean, it is not added to the total. Instead, the $special is passed on as an argument in the templateMethod() method:

```php
<?
//Client.php
function __autoload($class_name)
{
    include $class_name . '.php';
}
class Client
{
    private $buyTotal;
    private $gpsNow;
    private $mapNow;
    private $boatNow;
    private $special;
    private $zamCalc;

    function __construct()
    {
        $this->setHTML();
        $this->setCost();
        $this->zamCalc=new ZambeziCalc();
        $this->zamCalc->templateMethod($this->buyTotal,$this->special);
    }

    private function setHTML()
    {
        $this->gpsNow=$_POST['gps'];
        $this->mapNow=$_POST['map'];
        $this->boatNow=$_POST['boat'];
    }

    private function setCost()
    {
        $this->buyTotal=$this->gpsNow;
        foreach($this->mapNow as $value)
        {
            $this->buyTotal+= $value;
        }
        //Boolean
        $this->special = ($this->buyTotal >= 200);
```

```
        $this->buyTotal += $this->boatNow;
    }
}
$worker=new Client();
?>
```

The equipment totals are determined by the single value in the $gpsNow variable passed from a radio button form. Then a loop adds all values passed in the checkbox array ($mapNow). At this point, the Boolean variable $special is established, as discussed in the previous section. Finally, the $boatNow value that has been passed through a radio button form is added. The program adds the $boatNow value to the $buyTotal value after the setting the $special. The values in the two variables are now ready to be sent to the main program that uses them in the $templateMethod() parameters.

This example has been very simple, the data entry for the user is easy, and most importantly, this design could be reused simply by rewriting the Client. In other words, it's changeable and reusable. This example uses literals for shipping costs and tax rates, but they, too, could be modified with different values for the literals. However, values passed from the client or even calculable rates could be employed instead of literals.

The Small and Mighty Template Method

Learning design patterns is not for the faint of heart, but the Template Method is not only relatively simple, it also contains many lessons. First of all, it is the poster child for illustrating the Hollywood Principle. The notion of "call" in the principle really means "follow the order." Parent (abstract class) establishes the operations and sets their order, and the child class implements the operations. "Don't call us; we'll call you," might be revised to read, "We'll set up the interview, the screen test, and the talent test; you carry them out in the order we set up and in any way you want. Just don't change the order!"

A second important aspect of the Template Method to keep in mind is that it is a design pattern that can be used with other design patterns. You saw how it nicely fit with the Factory Method, and it would fit equally well (and be more helpful to) the Abstract Factory. It is small and tidy, so it can be used as part of or a helper for any number of other patterns.

The best part about the Template Method, though, is that it is easy to learn and has big lessons. Yes, it has many applications, and that's important, too, but concepts and ideas are the most important part of design patterns. Having one you can easily grasp and learn from makes it far more valuable than its compact size would suggest.

CHAPTER 10

The State Design Pattern

> *Could the young but realize how soon they will become mere walking bundles of habits, they would give more heed to their conduct while in the plastic state.*
>
> —William James

> *In each action we must look beyond the action at our past, present, and future state, and at others whom it affects, and see the relations of all those things. And then we shall be very cautious.*
>
> —Blaise Pascal

> *All our final decisions are made in a state of mind that is not going to last.*
>
> —Marcel Proust

What Is the State Pattern?

The State design pattern is one of the most intriguing and useful patterns of those devised by GoF. Games often depend on the State pattern because objects can change states so frequently in games. The purpose of the State pattern is to allow an object to change its behavior when the state changes. Many other simulations, whether they are games or not, depend on the State pattern as well; you will find many uses for it, as this chapter demonstrates. Figure 10-1 shows the basic design pattern in a class diagram.

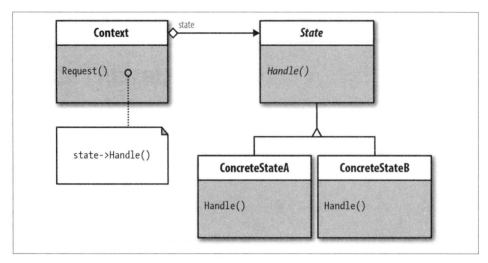

Figure 10-1. State design pattern class diagram

As shown, there's no `Client` class; however, GoF note that the `Context` is the primary interface for the clients. When examining the pattern, think of the `Client` class making its request through the `Context` class. There's a lot to understanding and effectively using the State design pattern, so for now, just take a quick look at the class diagram; the details will be unrolled gradually.

When to Use the State Pattern?

As noted, game and simulator developers use the State pattern to handle different states. Virtually every application in PHP has some state changes, but when an object depends on its state, which must be changed frequently, the State pattern has decided advantages.

One of the problems with frequent state changes in an object is the dependency on conditional statements. In and of themselves, there's nothing wrong with conditional statements, including `switch` statements or those with `else` clauses. Problems arise when the options are so great that they begin to entangle the program or just take up so much time to add or change that they become a burden.

Take a simple example in a simulation or game situation. Suppose you have a 3 × 3 matrix—that's 9 states. Depending on which of the nine cells your object is "in" it will have different options. Consider the matrix in Figure 10-2.

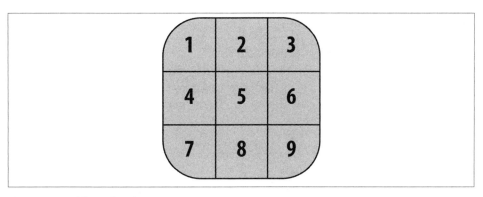

Figure 10-2. Three-by-three matrix

Suppose you create a program that has up/down and left/right movement with no diagonal movement. Other than Cell 5 (in Figure 10-2), where any direction is possible, the other moves require some kind of conditional statement in traditional thinking about how to program. Consider movement from Cell 4, and you might have something like the following:

```
if($this->moveUp())
{
    $this->currentCell=$cell_1;
}
elseif ($this->moveDown())
{
    $this->currentCell=$cell_7;
}
elseif ($this->moveRight())
{
    $this->currentCell=$cell_5;
}
elseif ($this->moveLeft())
{
    $this->currentCell=$errorMove;
}
```

On top of that, the program has to keep track of which cell the object is "in." As you can see, the number of conditional statements (or cases in a switch statement) can grow and entangle just about any program.

With the State design pattern, each state has its own concrete class implemented from a common interface. Instead of looking at the flow of control from the object, the view is from the state that the object holds. The next section, which reviews the state machine, provides you with a better understanding of state-centric thinking.

The State Machine

The state machine is a model that gives focus to different states, the transition from one state to another and the triggers that cause a state to change. The best place to start is with a *statechart*—a chart used instead of a computer flow chart or class diagram. Figure 10-3 shows a simple statechart where a light changes state from *off* to *on*.

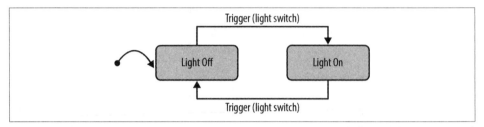

Figure 10-3. Statechart showing lightbulb states

Like class diagrams, statecharts focus on something other than the flow of control. In Figure 10-3, you can see the essentials of the state model:

- States (*light off* and *light on*)
- Transitions (from *light off* → *light on* and from *light on* → *light off*)
- Trigger (light switch)

The states, transitions, and triggers of a light being turned on and off are pretty simple. The transition is instantaneous, and the trigger is a light switch. However, some transitions are more gradual or complex after a trigger has requested a change. For instance, weather triggers the change in the color of tree leaves, and the transition is more gradual. However, going from a state of summer to a state of autumn can be understood using the state model, as can many other situations where states transition from one to another through initiation by a trigger.

Light On, Light Off: The Minimal State Design Pattern

While the concept of a state machine is relatively simple, even the most basic State design pattern can be a challenge. With this in mind, the minimal pattern example in PHP will keep the focus on the steps in creating the pattern. The good news is that if you can do a simple State design pattern, the larger ones turn out to be relatively easy. So take this slowly, and go over the different participants in the pattern.

Context Is King

All State patterns need a participant to keep track of what state the object is in. The matrix in Figure 10-2 is a good image to keep in mind. If the current state is Cell 4, the system needs to know the available transitions to other states. This is the job of the Context class. Bearing in mind that this first example handles only two states, a light state of *off* or *on*, the Context needs to be able to know that the current state is one or the other. Using the statechart in Figure 10-3 as a guide, you can see that the initial state, indicated by a black ball with an arrow attached, is *off*.

In order to have a reference point, first look at the Context class. The following sections go through the context to see the different parts and what role they play:

```php
<?php
//Context.php
class Context
{
    private $offState;
    private $onState;
    private $currentState;

    public function __construct()
    {
        $this->offState=new OffState($this);
        $this->onState=new OnState($this);

        //Beginning state is Off
        $this->currentState=$this->offState;
    }
    //Call State methods--triggers
    public function turnOnLight()
    {
        $this->currentState->turnLightOn();
    }

    public function turnOffLight()
    {
        $this->currentState->turnLightOff();
    }
    //Set current state
    public function setState(IState $state)
    {
        $this->currentState=$state;
    }

    //Get the states
    public function getOnState()
    {
        return $this->onState;
    }
    public function getOffState()
```

```
        {
            return $this->offState;
        }
    }
?>
```

The Context class establishes three properties with private visibility:

```
$offState
$onState
$currentState
```

The first two will be instances of the two states, and the third keeps track of which state the system is in at any given time.

State instances in the Context class

In the constructor function, the Context instantiates two instances of IState implementations—one for the *off* state and one for the *on* state:

```
$this->offState=new OffState($this);
$this->onState=new OnState($this);
```

The instantiation process involves a type of recursion known as *self-referral*. The argument in the parameter of each is written as $this, which is a reference to the Context class itself. The state classes expect an instance of the Context class in its argument, and in order to instantiate a state instance *in the* Context class, it must use $this as the argument.

Because *some state* must be the current state at start-up, the $currentState property is assigned the $offState value. (Think of walking into a room, and the light is off.) It is an instance of the OffState class. In looking at the statechart in Figure 10-3, you can see that the start state is the *off* state, and so the code simply follows the structure in the statechart.

Calling the state methods: Context trigger methods

The Context class has methods that call methods in the state classes. You might think of these methods as *triggers*. They are called to initiate a transition from the current state to a different state. Take, for example, the following method:

```
public function turnOnLight()
{
    $this->currentState->turnLightOn();
}
```

Note that slightly different names are used in the Context method than the state method: turnOnLight versus turnLightOn. The difference is simply to distinguish between a trigger-method in the Context class from the method in the state instance.

Setting the current state

The most important role for the Context class is to keep track of the current state. In this way it provides a correct context or window for the system. Going back to the matrix in Figure 10-2, each move in the matrix depends on the current cell. In Cell 9, the move can be to either Cell 8 or Cell 6 (no diagonal moves allowed). However, the system must know that its current state is Cell 9 in order to know what the options are.

To set a current state, the Context class must somehow be sent information specifying what the current state is. This is done by one of the state classes. As soon as a state is triggered, it sends a message to the Context declaring, "I'm the current state":

```
public function setState(IState $state)
{
    $this->currentState=$state;
}
```

The setState() method expects a state object as an argument (indicated by IState type hinting). When a trigger method fires, it calls a state and its relevant method. The state's method must send a message to the Context that it is now the current state. So the setState() method is called by the most recently triggered state to make it the current state.

The state getters

Finally, the Context class needs a way to get the message sent by the current state. The messages are passed through getter methods. The Context must have getters for each of the states; since this example has two state classes, it just needs two getters. The getter for the OffState is the following:

```
public function getOffState()
{
    return $this->offState;
}
```

And the OnState is the following:

```
public function getOnState()
{
    return $this->onState;
}
```

As you will see in the implemented state classes, these methods are used in setting the current state.

The Context class summary

The Context instantiates instances of all states and sets the default state. It has methods to trigger different states by calling the parallel methods in the concrete states. A setter method keeps track of which state is the current one. To help keep track of the current state, `Context` has getters for each state when calls for changes in state occur.

The States

The `Context` class will make more sense once you see how the concrete state classes implement the `IState` interface. The interface contains only two state methods to implement:

```php
<?php
//IState.php
interface IState
{
    public function turnLightOn();
    public function turnLightOff();
}
?>
```

In the `Context` class, both of the two methods are called as state-change triggers. The important details, though, are all in the implementations of the following two state classes: `OnState` and `OffState`.

OnState

```php
<?php
//OnState.php
class OnState implements IState
{
    private $context;

    public function __construct(Context $contextNow)
    {
        $this->context=$contextNow;
    }
    public function turnLightOn()
    {
        echo "Light is already on-> take no action<br/>";
    }
    public function turnLightOff()
    {
        echo "Lights off!<br/>";
        $this->context->setState($this->context->getOffState());
    }
}
?>
```

OffState

```php
<?php
//OffState.php
class OffState implements IState
```

```
{
    private $context;

    public function __construct(Context $contextNow)
    {
        $this->context=$contextNow;
    }
    public function turnLightOn()
    {
        echo "Lights on! Now I can see!<br/>";
        $this->context->setState($this->context->getOnState());

    }
    public function turnLightOff()
    {
        echo "Light is already off-> take no action<br/>";
    }
}
?>
```

Both the OnState and OffState classes are simple implementations of IState, and the states are indicated by text messages. The state classes hold a reference to the Context class in their constructor functions. Recall that the Context instantiates state instances with a self-reference to the state constructor classes.

The default state is the OffState. It must implement the IState methods turnLight On and turnLightOff. When the Context calls the turnLightOn method it displays "Lights on! Now I can see." Then it establishes the OnState as the current state by sending a message to the Context method, getOnState. However, if the call is to the turnLight Off in the OffState, then all that happens is a message indicating that the light is already off, and no action is taken. It does not reset the current state in the Context because it is already the current state. Basically, if a state is requested to initiate itself, it just does nothing. Likewise, if it is requested to trigger a state that it cannot, it does nothing.

Going back to the nine-cell matrix in Figure 10-2, Cell 3 can legitimately go to Cell 2 or Cell 6. However, in the Cell 3 state, it cannot go up or to the right. So, if it receives an instruction to initiate a state that it cannot, usually the programmer just has a null condition for the unobtainable state.

The Client Request through the Context

The Client makes all requests through the Context. There is absolutely no direct connection between the Client and any of the state classes, including the IState interface. The following Client shows requests that fire all methods in the two state classes:

```
<?php
//Client.php
function __autoload($class_name)
{
```

```
    include $class_name . '.php';
}
class Client
{
    private $context;

    public function __construct()
    {
        $this->context=new Context();
        $this->context->turnOnLight();
        $this->context->turnOnLight();
        $this->context->turnOffLight();
        $this->context->turnOffLight();
    }
}
$worker=new Client();
?>
```

After instantiating a `Context` instance, the initial request is to turn on the light because the default state is for the light to be in the *off* state. The second request is the same, but this should generate a message that the system is already in the requested state and nothing should happen. The following output shows the results of the requests:

```
Lights on! Now I can see!
Light is already on-> take no action
Lights off!
Light is already off-> take no action
```

The *OffState* requests work like the *OnState* requests. If the transition is from one state to another (off→on), the change is initiated. However, if the current state is requested a second time (off→off), it generates a message indicating that nothing is going to happen.

Adding States

An important aspect of any design pattern lies in the ability to make changes easily. The State pattern is no different from other patterns when it comes to ease of update and change. In order to see how added states affect the basic *on/off* states in the minimal example, this next example extends the *on/off* states to a three-way bulb. The new application has double the number of states:

- *Off*
- *On*
- *Brighter*
- *Brightest*

Figure 10-4 shows the updated four-state statechart.

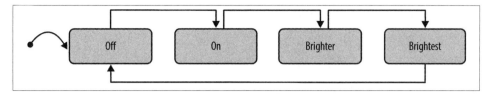

Figure 10-4. Statechart for three-way light

In looking at these four states, the sequence has changed. The *off* state still transitions to the *on* state, but the *on* state cannot transition to the *off* state. Instead, the rules have changed so that the *on* state must transition to the *brighter* state and the *brighter* state, to the *brightest* state. Only from the *brightest* state can the transition be to the *off* state.

Changing the Interface

The first participant to change is the interface, `IState`. It must be assigned methods that can be used to move to the *brighter* and *brightest* states:

```php
<?php
//IState.php
interface IState
{
    public function turnLightOff();
    public function turnLightOn();
    public function turnBrighter();
    public function turnBrightest();
}
?>
```

Now each of the state classes must include all four methods, and they need to be incorporated into the `Context` class.

Changing the States

When added changes come to a State design pattern, they ripple through the entire body of the pattern. However, they are relatively simple to add because the statechart shows the transitions, and in this case each has a single specific transition. Instead of text, each state has a graphic representation of the state. A special image is displayed for an illegal transition. (The *nada.png* image is the illegal visage.)

OffState

```php
<?php
//OffState.php
class OffState implements IState
{
    private $context;
```

```php
    public function __construct(Context $contextNow)
    {
        $this->context=$contextNow;
    }
    public function turnLightOn()
    {
        echo "<img src='lights/on.png'>";
        $this->context->setState($this->context->getOnState());
    }
    public function turnBrighter()
    {
        echo "<img src='lights/nada.png'>";
    }
    public function turnBrightest()
    {
        echo "<img src='lights/nada.png'>";
    }
    public function turnLightOff()
    {
        echo "<img src='lights/nada.png'>";
    }
}
?>
```

OnState

```php
<?php
//OnState.php
class OnState implements IState
{
    private $context;

    public function __construct(Context $contextNow)
    {
        $this->context=$contextNow;
    }
    public function turnLightOn()
    {
        echo "<img src='lights/nada.png'>";
    }
    public function turnBrighter()
    {
        echo "<img src='lights/brighter.png'>";
        $this->context->setState($this->context->getBrighterState());
    }
    public function turnBrightest()
    {
        echo "<img src='lights/nada.png'>";
    }
    public function turnLightOff()
    {
```

```php
        echo "<img src='lights/nada.png'>";
    }
}
?>
```

BrighterState

```php
<?php
//BrighterState.php
class BrighterState implements IState
{
    private $context;

    public function __construct(Context $contextNow)
    {
        $this->context=$contextNow;
    }
    public function turnLightOn()
    {
        echo "<img src='lights/nada.png'>";
    }
    public function turnBrighter()
    {
        echo "<img src='lights/nada.png'>";
    }
    public function turnBrightest()
    {
        echo "<img src='lights/brightest.png'>";
        $this->context->setState($this->context->getBrightestState());
    }
    public function turnLightOff()
    {
        echo "<img src='lights/nada.png'>";
    }
}
?>
```

BrightestState

```php
<?php
//BrightestState.php
class BrightestState implements IState
{
    private $context;

    public function __construct(Context $contextNow)
    {
        $this->context=$contextNow;
    }
    public function turnLightOn()
    {
        echo "<img src='lights/nada.png'>";
    }
```

```php
        public function turnBrighter()
        {
            echo "<img src='lights/nada.png'>";
        }
        public function turnBrightest()
        {
            echo "<img src='lights/nada.png'>";
        }
        public function turnLightOff()
        {
            echo "<img src='lights/off.png'>";
            $this->context->setState($this->context->getOffState());
        }
    }
?>
```

Note that all but one of the methods in each of the states sets up the negative graphic. However, that's exactly the way that three-way lamps work with three-way bulbs. After turning on the lamp, it must cycle through the other two states (*brighter* and *brightest*) before it can be turned off.

Updating the Context Class

The final step is to update the Context class to add the new triggers and include the new states. Likewise, the Context requires added state instances and getters for each of the new states:

```php
<?php
//Context.php
class Context
{
    private $offState;
    private $onState;
    private $brighterState;
    private $brightestState;

    private $currentState;

    public function __construct()
    {
        $this->offState=new OffState($this);
        $this->onState=new OnState($this);
        $this->brighterState=new BrighterState($this);
        $this->brightestState=new BrightestState($this);

        //Beginning state is Off
        $this->currentState=$this->offState;
    }
    //Call State methods
    public function turnOnLight()
    {
```

```
        $this->currentState->turnLightOn();
    }
    public function turnOffLight()
    {
        $this->currentState->turnLightOff();
    }
    public function turnBrighterLight()
    {
        $this->currentState->turnBrighter();
    }

    public function turnBrightestLight()
    {
        $this->currentState->turnBrightest();
    }

    //Set current state
    public function setState(IState $state)
    {
        $this->currentState=$state;
    }

    //Get the states
    public function getOnState()
    {
        return $this->onState;
    }
    public function getOffState()
    {
        return $this->offState;
    }
    public function getBrighterState()
    {
        return $this->brighterState;
    }
    public function getBrightestState()
    {
        return $this->brightestState;
    }
}
?>
```

The added code duplicates the methods and instantiations of the initial states. Whereas the Context class has added code, it's just like the original ones—there's just more of it.

An Updated Client

In the initial example, the Client could request one of two states: *on* or *off*. With two additional states, the Client has more options, but the default state is still *off*; the first request must be to the *on* state. Once the *on* state is established, it can request the *brighter* state and then the *brightest* state before requesting *off* again:

```php
<?php
//Client.php
function __autoload($class_name)
{
    include $class_name . '.php';
}
class Client
{
    private $context;

    public function __construct()
    {
        $this->context=new Context();
        $this->context->turnOnLight();
        $this->context->turnBrighterLight();
        $this->context->turnBrightestLight();
        $this->context->turnOffLight();
        $this->context->turnBrightestLight();
    }
}
$worker=new Client();
?>
```

In the revised `Client`, the requests follow the correct sequence beginning with a transition to the *on* state. However, after cycling through the different states to the *off* state, the `Client` requests a return to the *brightest* state. At this point, the "error light" appears. Figure 10-5 shows the different images resulting from the request sequence.

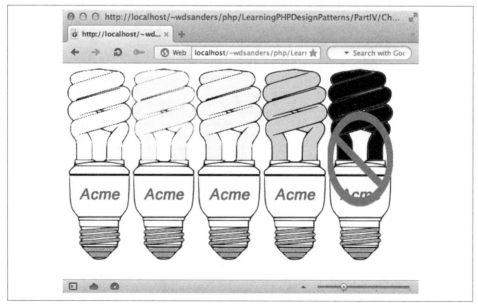

Figure 10-5. Updated State pattern sequence with error display

The first four lightbulbs, from left to right, display the *on*, *brighter*, *brightest*, and *off* states. However, the fifth lightbulb indicates an error in the request. In a typical State pattern implementation, no error message (or image) appears. The request is simply ignored.

The Navigator: More Choices and Cells

Figure 10-2 shows a 3 × 3 matrix of 9 cells. To navigate each cell as though it were a grid position on a map requires a set of rules for movement. Consider four simple moves or *transitions*:

- Up
- Down
- Left
- Right

Given those moves, the rules imply no diagonal movement between cells. Further, the rules will specify that movement from one cell to the next can be only one cell at a time.

In "When to Use the State Pattern?" (page 190), a series of conditional statements showed one possible approach to navigating through a matrix. However, even with a 3 × 3 matrix, such a solution can become quickly entangled in a series of conditions and/or else clauses. This example shows how to treat navigation as a series of different states.

Setting Up a Matrix Statechart

The first step in making a navigation system using the State design pattern is to work up a statechart as was done with the changing light states. Figure 10-6 represents the matrix that will be used along with the rules for changing states (moving from one cell to the next).

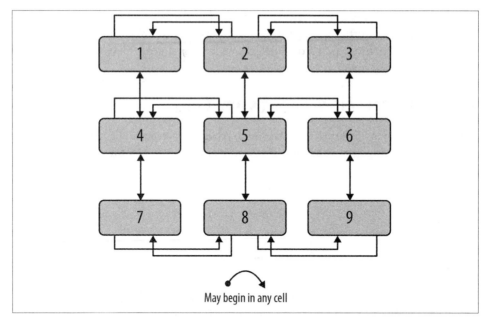

Figure 10-6. Statechart for navigation of matrix

Other than being a little crowded with transition arrows, the same logic that applies to the *on/off* states of a light switch also applies here. Take, for example, Cell 2 with the rules for changing states. It has the following movement options:

- Up (cannot move up)
- Down (to Cell 5)
- Left (to Cell 1)
- Right (to Cell 3)

In looking at any single cell, the options are very clear, and thinking about how to program movement or changes in state should begin to make more sense. Unlike the *on/off* example where the starting point is *off*, the starting point can be in any cell, as indicated by the label with the start arrow in the statechart.

Setting Up the Interface

The state interface, IMatrix, in this example reflects the idea of the different movements and not the name of the state. Rather than having state-like names, each is given a transition or movement name:

```
<?php
//IMatrix.php
//State interface
```

```
interface IMatrix
{
    public function goUp();
    public function goDown();
    public function goLeft();
    public function goRight();
}
?>
```

Even though this implementation of the State design pattern has nine states, one for each of the nine cells, a single state needs only up to four transitions.

The Context

With four transition or move methods in the states, the context must have methods to call the transition methods as well as instantiations of each state. This is exactly like the example with only two states—just with more methods and instantiations:

```
<?php
//Context.php
class Context
{
    private $cell1;
    private $cell2;
    private $cell3;
    private $cell4;
    private $cell5;
    private $cell6;
    private $cell7;
    private $cell8;
    private $cell9;
    private $currentState;

    public function __construct()
    {
        $this->cell1=new Cell1State($this);
        $this->cell2=new Cell2State($this);
        $this->cell3=new Cell3State($this);
        $this->cell4=new Cell4State($this);
        $this->cell5=new Cell5State($this);
        $this->cell6=new Cell6State($this);
        $this->cell7=new Cell7State($this);
        $this->cell8=new Cell8State($this);
        $this->cell9=new Cell9State($this);

        //Beginning state is up to developer
        $this->currentState=$this->cell5;
    }
    //Call State methods
    public function doUp()
    {
        $this->currentState->goUp();
```

```php
    }
    public function doDown()
    {
        $this->currentState->goDown();
    }
    public function doLeft()
    {
        $this->currentState->goLeft();
    }

    public function doRight()
    {
        $this->currentState->goRight();
    }

    //Set current state
    public function setState(IMatrix $state)
    {
        $this->currentState=$state;
    }

    //Get the states
    public function getCell1State()
    {
        return $this->cell1;
    }
    public function getCell2State()
    {
        return $this->cell2;
    }
    public function getCell3State()
    {
        return $this->cell3;
    }
    public function getCell4State()
    {
        return $this->cell4;
    }
    public function getCell5State()
    {
        return $this->cell5;
    }
    public function getCell6State()
    {
        return $this->cell6;
    }
    public function getCell7State()
    {
        return $this->cell7;
    }
    public function getCell8State()
    {
```

```
        return $this->cell8;
    }
    public function getCell9State()
    {
        return $this->cell9;
    }
}
?>
```

Most of the Context is devoted to creating getter methods for each of the nine state classes.

The States

The nine states represent different cells on the 3 × 3 matrix. To display each cell uniquely, graphic images have been labeled with different numbers and colors. In this way, the pathway through the matrix is clearer.

Each of the nine state classes has the required four methods needed to implement the IMatrix interface. In the previous State examples, when a choice was not possible (such as going from the *on* state to the *brightest* state in the three-way light), instead of displaying an illegal call, comment lines indicate an illegal move in the code.

Cell1State

```php
<?php
//Cell1State.php
class Cell1State implements IMatrix
{
    private $context;

    public function __construct(Context $contextNow)
    {
        $this->context=$contextNow;
    }
    public function goLeft()
    {
        //Illegal move
    }
    public function goRight()
    {
        echo "<img src='cells/two.png'>";
        $this->context->setState($this->context->getCell2State());
    }
    public function goUp()
    {
        //Illegal move

    }
    public function goDown()
    {
```

```php
        echo "<img src='cells/four.png'>";
        $this->context->setState($this->context->getCell4State());
    }
}
?>
```

Cell2State

```php
<?php
//Cell2State.php
class Cell2State implements IMatrix
{
    private $context;

    public function __construct(Context $contextNow)
    {
        $this->context=$contextNow;
    }
    public function goLeft()
    {
        echo "<img src='cells/one.png'>";
        $this->context->setState($this->context->getCell1State());
    }
    public function goRight()
    {
        echo "<img src='cells/three.png'>";
        $this->context->setState($this->context->getCell3State());
    }
    public function goUp()
    {
        //Illegal move
    }
    public function goDown()
    {
        echo "<img src='cells/five.png'>";
        $this->context->setState($this->context->getCell5State());
    }
}
?>
```

Cell3State

```php
<?php
//Cell31State.php
class Cell3State implements IMatrix
{
    private $context;

    public function __construct(Context $contextNow)
    {
        $this->context=$contextNow;
    }
    public function goLeft()
```

```php
    {
        echo "<img src='cells/two.png'>";
        $this->context->setState($this->context->getCell2State());
    }
    public function goRight()
    {
        //Illegal move
    }
    public function goUp()
    {
        //Illegal move

    }
    public function goDown()
    {
        echo "<img src='cells/six.png'>";
        $this->context->setState($this->context->getCell6State());
    }
}
?>
```

Cell4State

```php
<?php
//Cell4State.php
class Cell4State implements IMatrix
{
    private $context;

    public function __construct(Context $contextNow)
    {
        $this->context=$contextNow;
    }
    public function goLeft()
    {
        //Illegal move
    }
    public function goRight()
    {
        echo "<img src='cells/five.png'>";
        $this->context->setState($this->context->getCell5State());
    }

    public function goUp()
    {
        echo "<img src='cells/one.png'>";
        $this->context->setState($this->context->getCell1State());
    }
    public function goDown()
    {
        echo "<img src='cells/seven.png'>";
        $this->context->setState($this->context->getCell7State());
```

```php
        }
    }
    ?>
```

Cell5State

```php
<?php
//Cell5State.php
class Cell5State implements IMatrix
{
    private $context;

    public function __construct(Context $contextNow)
    {
        $this->context=$contextNow;
    }
    public function goLeft()
    {
        echo "<img src='cells/four.png'>";
        $this->context->setState($this->context->getCell4State());
    }
    public function goRight()
    {
        echo "<img src='cells/six.png'>";
        $this->context->setState($this->context->getCell6State());
    }

    public function goUp()
    {
        echo "<img src='cells/two.png'>";
        $this->context->setState($this->context->getCell2State());
    }
    public function goDown()
    {
        echo "<img src='cells/eight.png'>";
        $this->context->setState($this->context->getCell8State());
    }
}
?>
```

Cell6State

```php
<?php
//Cell6State.php
class Cell6State implements IMatrix
{
    private $context;

    public function __construct(Context $contextNow)
    {
        $this->context=$contextNow;
    }
```

```php
    public function goLeft()
    {
        echo "<img src='cells/five.png'>";
        $this->context->setState($this->context->getCell5State());
    }
    public function goRight()
    {
        //Illegal move
    }

    public function goUp()
    {
        echo "<img src='cells/three.png'>";
        $this->context->setState($this->context->getCell3State());

    }
    public function goDown()
    {
        echo "<img src='cells/nine.png'>";
        $this->context->setState($this->context->getCell9State());
    }
}
?>
```

Cell7State

```php
<?php
//Cell71State.php
class Cell7State implements IMatrix
{
    private $context;

    public function __construct(Context $contextNow)
    {
        $this->context=$contextNow;
    }
    public function goLeft()
    {
        //Illegal move
    }
    public function goRight()
    {
        echo "<img src='cells/eight.png'>";
        $this->context->setState($this->context->getCell8State());
    }

    public function goUp()
    {
        echo "<img src='cells/four.png'>";
        $this->context->setState($this->context->getCell4State());
    }
    public function goDown()
```

```php
        {
            //Illegal move
        }
    }
    ?>
```

Cell8State

```php
<?php
//Cell81State.php
class Cell8State implements IMatrix
{
    private $context;

    public function __construct(Context $contextNow)
    {
        $this->context=$contextNow;
    }
    public function goLeft()
    {
        echo "<img src='cells/seven.png'>";
        $this->context->setState($this->context->getCell7State());
    }
    public function goRight()
    {
        echo "<img src='cells/nine.png'>";
        $this->context->setState($this->context->getCell9State());
    }

    public function goUp()
    {
        echo "<img src='cells/five.png'>";
        $this->context->setState($this->context->getCell5State());
    }
    public function goDown()
    {
        //Illegal move
    }
}
?>
```

Cell9State

```php
<?php
//Cell9State.php
class Cell9State implements IMatrix
{
    private $context;

    public function __construct(Context $contextNow)
    {
        $this->context=$contextNow;
    }
    public function goLeft()
    {
        echo "<img src='cells/eight.png'>";
        $this->context->setState($this->context->getCell8State());
    }
    public function goRight()
    {
        //Illegal move
    }
    public function goUp()
    {
        echo "<img src='cells/six.png'>";
        $this->context->setState($this->context->getCell6State());
    }
    public function goDown()
    {
        //Illegal move
    }
}
?>
```

The real trick to using State design patterns effectively is to imagine what the physical reality or simulation looks like. For example, if you imagine that each cell in the matrix is a different room in a house, the set of options are different for each room. Some rooms have to be entered by first entering a hallway or even another room.

The Client Picks a Path

To help visualize moving from state to state, Figure 10-7 shows a path the Client takes; in looking at the Client code, try to visualize the states in terms of moving through the matrix.

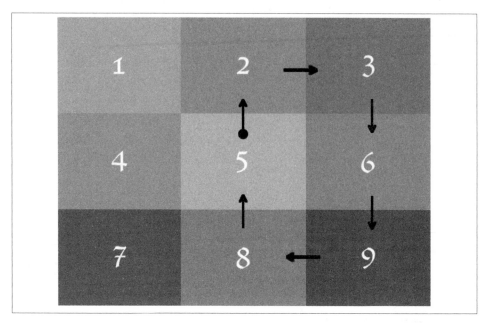

Figure 10-7. Path through states

Beginning in Cell 5, the path takes the following moves:

1. Move up

2. Move right

3. Move down

4. Move down

5. Move left

6. Move up

The Client follows those moves (transitions in state) to create the indicated path. Setting Cell 5 as the default in the Context class, the Client makes the same moves:

```php
<?php
//Client.php
function __autoload($class_name)
{
    include $class_name . '.php';
}
class Client
{
    private $context;

    public function __construct()
    {
```

```
        $this->context=new Context();
        $this->context->doUp();
        $this->context->doRight();
        $this->context->doDown();
        echo "<br/>";
        $this->context->doDown();
        $this->context->doLeft();
        $this->context->doUp();


    }
}
$worker=new Client();
?>
```

After moving through three cells, the Client throws in a line break (<br/>) so that the cells do not run off the side of the browser screen. Figure 10-8 shows how the program displays the path.

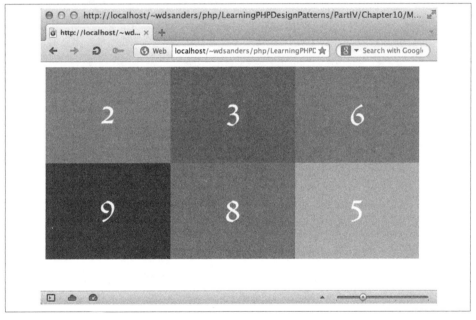

Figure 10-8. Six states the Client "moves" through

Compare Figure 10-8 to Figure 10-7, and you can better see (left to right and top to bottom) how the program followed the path laid out through the matrix.

The State Pattern and PHP

Many see the State design pattern as one primarily for simulation and games. To no small extent that vision of the State pattern is true, but the State model (State Engine) and State design pattern have many applications in PHP. As PHP tackles larger projects, including large hunks of Facebook and WordPress, more demands for added features and current states will develop. Grady Booch (*http://ibm.co/yCL6se*) has suggested that Facebook will have increasing challenges keeping its site updated and working as it expands at an exponential rate and outgrows a roomfull of programmers. The expandable State pattern would be one of the ways to handle a situation of continual change and growth.

The extent to which PHP developers create programs with multiple states will determine the range of uses for the State pattern. So while many uses exist for state machines in the gaming and simulation world, there are an equal number if not more areas where the state model applies. Wherever a set of finite states are available to the user of a PHP program, there will be a State design pattern available to the developer.

PART V

MySQL and PHP Design Patterns

We must combine the toughness of the serpent with
the softness of the dove, a tough mind and a
tender heart.

—Martin Luther King, Jr.

All the interests of my reason, speculative as well
as practical, combine in the three following
questions: 1. What can I know? 2. What ought I to
do? 3. What may I hope?

—Immanuel Kant

When bad men combine, the good must associate;
else they will fall one by one, an unpitied sacrifice
in a contemptible struggle.

—Edmund Burke

The Role of MySQL in PHP Design Patterns

While some very advanced MySQL programmers use design patterns with relational databases, the four chapters in Part V use PHP design patterns employed in conjunction with MySQL. The MySQL example code in Part V uses simple MySQL statements. So you need not brush up on your JOIN statements or any other relational database code used with MySQL and PHP in the following four chapters.

However, the use of MySQL is so ubiquitous with PHP that not having a section on using OOP structures and design patterns with MySQL would be a serious oversight. Besides, this last section provides a way to add some more design patterns in PHP. They include the following:

- Proxy
- Strategy
- Chain of Responsibility
- Observer

None of these patterns are the exclusive domain of a combined PHP–MySQL application, and the patterns can be used perfectly well with PHP on its own. Further, in one of the Chain of Responsibility examples, you can see how more than one design pattern can be used together in a single application.

You will also find a combination interface and class that should take care of connections using `mysqli`. This little duo is employed throughout Part V, and once you substitute your own connection information—host, username, password, and database—you can use it for any MySQL connection you want.

While you will find no MySQL design patterns *per se* in Part V, you will find reusable structures that can be used with other PHP projects that employ MySQL. As experienced programmers know, making even small changes in PHP or MySQL code can wreak havoc on a program where both are present. However, you will find the well-structured design patterns handle changes with aplomb, even in a MySQL environment.

CHAPTER 11

A Universal Class for Connections and a Proxy Pattern for Security

It is art that makes life, makes interest, makes importance... and I know of no substitute whatever for the force and beauty of its process.

—Henry James

Substitute "damn" every time you're inclined to write "very"; your editor will delete it and the writing will be just as it should be.

—Mark Twain

The work of science is to substitute facts for appearances, and demonstrations for impressions.

—John Ruskin

A Simple Interface and Class for MySQL

In Chapter 2, you saw one example of how PHP allows interfaces to store constants that can be used by classes that implement the interface. One set of constants that can be stored in the interface is that required for connecting to a MySQL database. The routine using the PHP `mysqli` extension provides some variations for connection, but all variations need the host, username, password, and database information. Once the routine is set in a class, it should be available for general reuse whenever a program requires a MySQL connection. Figure 11-1 shows the class diagram for this arrangement.

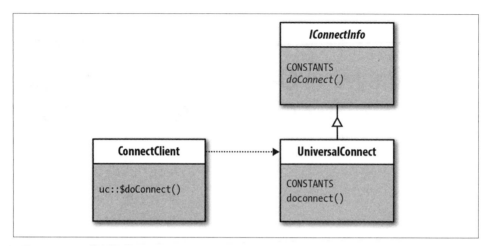

Figure 11-1. Universal MySQL class diagram

The connection information is independent of the client because the concrete information is stored in constants in the interface. The UniversalConnect class uses the Scope Resolution Operator to access the data stored in the constants in the interface.

The Pregnant Interface

In design patterns, interfaces allow developers to create loosely bound objects and classes, but in this case, the interface is used to store data—MySQL connection data. So, far from being an abstract structure for organizing operations, this interface has concrete data the classes that implement the interface can use.

```php
<?php
//Filename: IConnectInfo.php
interface IConnectInfo
{
    const HOST ="localhost";
    const UNAME ="phpWorker";
    const PW ="easyWay";
    const DBNAME = "dpPatt";

    public function doConnect();
}

?>
```

This interface is easily isolated and changed to include any host you want. By using mysqli, the four elements are available for it to employ to make a connection to the desired database. By substituting an interface for a set of values defined in a class, less time is consumed in development because a simple yet necessary part of the program has been set aside and can be implemented by any number of programs.

Universal MySQL Connection Class and Static Variables

All IConnectInfo interface implementations access the connection values using the Scope Resolution Operator. In the context of the way in which the values are passed from the interface to an implementing class and employed, assigning variables a private static status has the speed advantage of a static variable and the encapsulation of a private visibility:

```php
<?php
include_once('IConnectInfo.php');

class UniversalConnect implements IConnectInfo
{
    private static $server=IConnectInfo::HOST;
    private static $currentDB= IConnectInfo::DBNAME;
    private static $user= IConnectInfo::UNAME;
    private static $pass= IConnectInfo::PW;
    private static $hookup;

    public function doConnect()
    {
        self::$hookup=mysqli_connect(self::$server, self::$user, self::$pass,
                    self::$currentDB);
        if(self::$hookup)
        {
            //Remove slashes in following line for debugging
            //echo "Successful connection to MySQL:";
        }
        elseif (mysqli_connect_error(self::$hookup))
        {
            echo('Here is why it failed: ' . mysqli_connect_error());
        }
        return self::$hookup;
    }
}
?>
```

In addition to assigning the connection variables static status, the mysqli variable ($hookup) is static as well in the UniversalConnect class. This enables it to be used in a larger static context when requested by a client class.

Are Global Variables Always Evil?

I tend to avoid global variables wherever possible. A global variable may well be involved in breaking encapsulation—running amok and causing all kinds of mischief in a program. In larger programs, this is especially troublesome as you try tracking down all of the little buggers. In some respects, static variables share many of the characteristics of global variables, and unless I have a good reason, I tend not to use them. Lately, I've had a lot of good reasons to use them because of speed issues in changing programming environments, but I still use them judiciously. Likewise, when a class must be instantiated again and again, static variables can help cut down on instantiations.

As some may have noticed, this book does not include an example of the Singleton design pattern. In no small part, this is due to the fact that, if implemented correctly, Singleton design patterns can act like global variables. Plenty of wrongly implemented Singleton design patterns have been developed, and they tend to be harmless, but correctly implemented Singletons can cause global variable type problems. One developer, Miško Hevery, refers to Singletons as pathological liars (see *http://bit.ly/cI6mll*). Even Erich Gamma, lead author of *Design Patterns*, favors dropping the Singleton as a design pattern (see *http://bit.ly/3Lg5IN*). The general reason for Singleton avoidance is their capacity to act like global variables.

So while I do not think that the use of the static variables in this example has the potential for causing problems, if you're concerned about the possible effect of global variables, you can remove the `static` keyword from all of the code and use the `$this->` format for the variables with `private` visibility.

Perhaps the biggest advantage of using static variables is the capacity to use their values without having to instantiate the `UniversalConnect` class every time a different part of the program must create a new connection. For example, data entry requires a new connection every time new data are entered in a table through an online HTML form. That means a new instantiation with every data entry. Using static variables avoids constant reinstantiation.

Easy Client

The client in this case is any program that needs a connection to MySQL. In a typical application, the client would simply be any concrete class that requires a MySQL connection. Other than an `include_once()` operation to access the `UniversalConnect` class, the connection routine takes only a single line:

```php
<?php
include_once('UniversalConnect.php');

class ConnectClient
```

```
{
    private $hookup;

    public function __construct()
    {
        //One line for entire connection operation
        $this->hookup=UniversalConnect::doConnect();
    }
}

$worker=new ConnectClient();
?>
```

By having a simple connection operation set up through a single class and interface, development time can be cut considerably. Changes are easy because all of the information is stored in constants. To change a host, user, password, or database name requires only a change to the value of the constants in the interface. Nothing has to be done either to the UniversalConnect class or the program that uses the UniversalConnect class.

The Protection Proxy for Login

One of the Structural category design patterns is the Proxy. The Gang of Four specify four types of Proxy patterns:

Remote proxy

> When a proxy object is in one address space and the real object is in another, the proxy is remote. Besides using a remote proxy as a firewall, the remote proxy can be used for online games where the same object is needed in different places at the same time.

Virtual proxy

> A virtual proxy may cache information about a real subject so that access to the real subject can be postponed. Sometimes high security logins use a virtual proxy for the login before the real object handles the login data.

Protection proxy

> The protection proxy keeps the request away from the real subject until the request is verified by the protection proxy. The real subject is the target of the request, such as access to database information. Many protection proxies have different levels of access, depending on the user's login information; instead of having a single real subject, the real subject may be multiple and restricted.

A smart reference

> When the program requires something more than what GoF call a "bare pointer," the Proxy can act as a smart reference (or smart pointer) that performs additional

actions when an object is referenced. For instance, data from a database may be first loaded by the Proxy participant acting as a smart reference.

The Proxy patterns have two primary participants: a *proxy subject* and a *real subject*. Clients submit requests through the Subject interface to the Proxy, but access to the RealSubject is possible only if a request first goes through the Proxy. Figure 11-2 shows the class diagram of the Proxy design pattern.

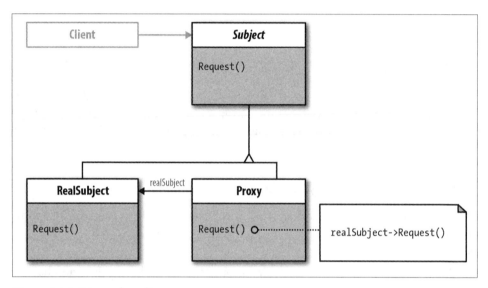

Figure 11-2. Proxy class diagram

Both the Proxy and RealSubject participants implement the Subject interface, but the Proxy implements it in the role of a gatekeeper or an encryption module. If the request is cleared by the Proxy, the Proxy then calls the RealSubject to provide the user with the content of the request.

Setting Up Login Registration

To create a Proxy for a login that requires registration, this program first sets up a table with username and password fields—and nothing else. This is a simple example that can be expanded, but the focus will be on the Proxy design pattern. The following PHP script creates the table that stores the user information:

```php
<?php
include_once('UniversalConnect.php');
class CreateTable
{
    private $tableMaster;
    private $hookup;
```

```
    public function __construct()
    {
        $this->tableMaster="proxyLog";
        $this->hookup=UniversalConnect::doConnect();

        $drop = "DROP TABLE IF EXISTS $this->tableMaster";

        if($this->hookup->query($drop) === true)
        {
            printf("Old table %s has been dropped.<br/>",$this->tableMaster);
        }

        $sql = "CREATE TABLE $this->tableMaster (uname NVARCHAR(15),
                pw NVARCHAR(120)";

        if($this->hookup->query($sql) === true)
        {
            echo "Table $this->tableMaster has been created successfully.<br/>";
        }
        $this->hookup->close();
    }
}
$worker=new CreateTable();
?>
```

The class is pretty standard for creating a table storing a username and password. The number of characters provided for the password, NVARCHAR (120), reflects the capacity to use hashed passwords up to 120 characters. To enter data, the following PHP accepts data sent from an HTML form:

```
<?php
include_once('UniversalConnect.php');
class HashRegister
{
    public function __construct()
    {
        $this->tableMaster="proxyLog";
        $this->hookup=UniversalConnect::doConnect();
        $username=$this->hookup->real_escape_string(trim($_POST['uname']));
        $pwNow=$this->hookup->real_escape_string(trim($_POST['pw']));

        $sql = "INSERT INTO $this->tableMaster (uname,pw) VALUES ('$username',
                md5('$pwNow'))";

        if($this->hookup->query($sql))
        {
            echo "Registration completed:";
        }

        elseif ( ($result = $this->hookup->query($sql))===false )
        {
            printf("Invalid query: %s <br/> Whole query: %s <br/>",
```

```
                    $this->hookup->error, $sql);
            exit();
        }
        $this->hookup->close();
    }
}
$worker=new HashRegister();
?>
```

The MD5 function returns the hash as a 32-character hexadecimal number. The md5() function represents an older but simpler hash function used only for purposes of illustration of where encryption might take place on setting up a registration password that would later be used with a Proxy login.

The following HTML5 script is used for registration—adding a username and password:

```
<!DOCTYPE HTML>
<html>
<head>
<link rel="stylesheet" href="proxy.css">
<meta http-equiv="Content-Type" content="text/html; charset=UTF-8">
<title>Username/Password Registration</title>
</head>
<body>
<header>Registration</header>
<section>
  <article id="entry">
    <form action="HashRegister.php" method="post">
      Username: (15 Characters Max-No spaces)<br/>
      <input type="text" name="uname" maxlength="15">
      <br/>
      Password: (10 Characters Max-No spaces)<br/>
      <input type="password" name="pw" maxlength="10">
      <br/>
      <input type="submit" value="Register">
    </form>
  </article>
</section>
</body>
</html>
```

Finally, a CSS file, used by some of the other files, is straightforward:

```
@charset "UTF-8";
/* CSS Document */
/*EFECCA,046380,002F2F */

body {
    margin-left:20px;
    font-family:Verdana, Geneva, sans-serif;
    background-color:#EFECCA;
}
header {
```

```
        font-family: "Arial Black", Gadget, sans-serif;
        font-size:24px;
        color:#002F2F;
}
#entry {
        font-size:11;
        color:#046380;
}
.subhead
{
        font-size:16px;
        font-family:Verdana, Geneva, sans-serif;
}
```

Figure 11-3 shows what the user sees during the registration process. (The HTML files are all separated for the sake of clarity in understanding the different elements that go into the setup and execution of the login into a site using a Proxy design pattern. The login registration and login itself could easily be included in a single HTML5 page with multiple forms; one for registration and one for login.)

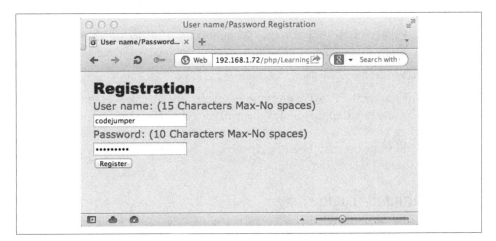

Figure 11-3. Registration screen

Once a user has registered, a small "confirmation" message displays a completion message, as shown in Figure 11-4.

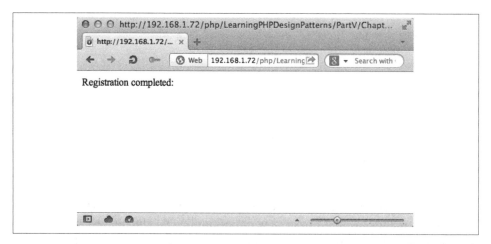

Figure 11-4. Registration confirmation

The confirmation message is short and could have been embedded in HTML code with an option to now log in, but as noted, everything has been modularized for better clarity.

In the two PHP files that use the `UniversalConnect` class to link to the MySQL database, we're able to do so using a single line, which avoids a good deal of code smog:

```
$this->hookup=UniversalConnect::doConnect();
```

To prepare for testing the Proxy pattern implementation, "register" several users with passwords. The next section that builds the proxy login application uses the `proxyLog` table to check to see if the username and password are available and correct. So before continuing, add some usernames and passwords to the `proxyLog` table with the `Regis tration.html` and `InsertData` class.

Implementing the Login Proxy

In looking at the participants in the Proxy file diagram in Figure 11-5, the names of the classes (and their files) closely follows the participant names in the design pattern.

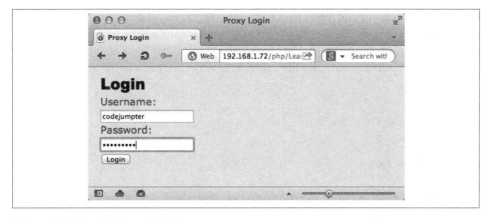

Figure 11-5. Login Proxy file diagram

The Proxy class calls the MySQL database to make sure that the username and password are matches, and if they are, the request is passed to the RealSubject class. So while the IConnectInfo interface and the UniversalConnect class are not part of the design pattern, they play an important component of the gatekeeper role.

The login form and the Client

The user places the login information into a form in the HTML file. As soon as the user enters the data and clicks the Submit button, the information is sent to the Client:

```
<!DOCTYPE HTML>
<html>
<head>
<meta http-equiv="Content-Type" content="text/html; charset=UTF-8">
<title>Proxy Login</title>
<link rel="stylesheet" href="proxy.css">
</head>
<body>
<header>Login</header>
<section>
  <article id="entry">
    <form action="Client.php" method="post">
      Username: <br/>
      <input type="text" name="uname" >
      <br/>
      Password: <br/>
      <input type="password" name="pw" maxlength="10">
      <br/>
      <input type="submit" value="Login">
    </form>
  </article>
</section>
</body>
</html>
```

In the initial development, the HTML form sent the data directly to the Proxy class, but on reconsideration, the Client is a good place to encapsulate the password and username. It also trims and filters the data from the HTML form. The Client uses a private method with type hinting to pass the data from the HTML form to the login method in the Proxy class:

```php
<?php
include_once("Proxy.php");
class Client
{
    private $proxy;
    private $un;
    private $pw;

    public function __construct()
    {
        $this->tableMaster="proxyLog";
        $this->hookup=UniversalConnect::doConnect();
        $this->un=$this->hookup->real_escape_string(trim($_POST['uname']));
        $this->pw=$this->hookup->real_escape_string(trim($_POST['pw']));
        $this->getIface($this->proxy=new Proxy());
    }

    private function getIface(ISubject $proxy)
    {
            $proxy->login($this->un,$this->pw);
    }
}
$worker=new Client();
?>
```

Because the username and password are unwrapped into a private variable and dispatched to the Proxy class in a private method (getIface), they are effectively encapsulated before being compared for validity in the Proxy class.

The Proxy at work

When passed to the Proxy class, the data sent from the HTML form via the Client must be compared to stored data in a MySQL table. Because the Proxy and RealSubject classes share a common interface, each must implement the ISubject interface:

```php
<?php
interface ISubject
{
    function request();
}
?>
```

The single method, request, can be implemented in many different ways. For the Proxy, it is a way to pass on the original request to the RealSubject class if the username

---

and password are validated. In other words, the `Proxy` determines whether the `Real Subject` method, `request`, is to be called at all.

In designing the Proxy, little was done other than informing the user that the password and username are invalid. Other available options are to return the user to the login page or the registration page:

```php
<?php
include_once("ISubject.php");
include_once('RealSubject.php');
include_once('UniversalConnect.php');
class Proxy implements ISubject
{
    private $tableMaster;
    private $hookup;
    private $logGood;
    private $realSubject;

    public function login($uNow,$pNow)
    {
        //Filtered from Client; hash the password
        $uname=$uNow;
        $pw=md5($pNow);
        $this->logGood=false;
        //Choose table and connect
        $this->tableMaster="proxyLog";
        $this->hookup=UniversalConnect::doConnect();

        //Create MySQL statement
        $sql = "SELECT pw FROM $this->tableMaster WHERE uname='$uname'";

        if($result=$this->hookup->query($sql))
        {
            $row=$result->fetch_array(MYSQLI_ASSOC);
            if($row['pw']==$pw)
            {
                $this->logGood=true;
            }
        $result->close();
        }
        elseif ( ($result = $this->hookup->query($sql))===false )
        {
            printf("Failed: %s <br/>", $this->hookup->error);
            exit();
        }
        $this->hookup->close();

        if($this->logGood)
        {
            $this->request();
        }
        else
```

```
        {
            echo "Username and/or Password not on record.";
        }
    }
    public function request()
    {
        $this->realSubject=new RealSubject();
        $this->realSubject->request();
    }
}

?>
```

Most of the work is done by the login method. It receives the password and username, hashes the password with the md5() function, opens the database, and queries the table. If it finds a matching pair (username and password), it sets the $logGood variable to true. It then summons the request method if $logGood is true; otherwise, it simply leaves a message.

The Proxy request method calls the RealSubject request method. In the case of the Proxy pattern, the surrogate for the real subject (the target of the request) is the Proxy class, and so its job is to run interference for the real subject, not to duplicate the request method of the real subject.

The real subject

The "star" of the Proxy design pattern is the proxy participant. However, what the user wants is whatever is in the real subject, and so the only thing important to the user is the real subject. The good news is that it can be virtually anything. For this example, it is a page with some OOP and design pattern pointers:

```
<?php
include_once('ISubject.php');

class RealSubject implements ISubject
{
    public function request()
    {
    $practice=<<<REQUEST
<!DOCTYPE html>
<html>
    <head>
    <meta charset="UTF-8">
    <link rel='stylesheet' type='text/css' href='proxy.css' />
    </head>
    <body>
    <header>PHP Tip Sheet:<br>
      <span class='subhead'>For OOP Developers</span></header>
    <ol>
        <li>Program to the interface and not the implementation.</li>
        <li>Encapsulate your objects.</li>
```

```
            <li>Favor composition over class inheritance.</li>
            <li>A class should only have a single responsibility.</li>
        </ol>
    </body>
</html>
REQUEST;
echo $practice;
    }
  }
?>
```

Its only method is one required when implementing the ISubject interface—re
quest. The request method simply generates some HTML to display an ordered list.
It could be anything, and as for its position in the pattern, it's the caboose and has no
backward impact.

From the user's perspective, all of the classes and code are transparent. Figure 11-6 shows
what the user first sees at login in the HTML5 page.

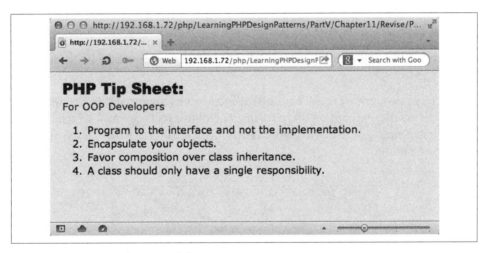

Figure 11-6. HTML5 login module

The login sends the request to the Client class, which takes the login data from the
HTML5 form and forwards the request to the Proxy through the Proxy login method.
Of course, the user never sees any of this. All she sees is the RealSubject output, as
shown in Figure 11-7.

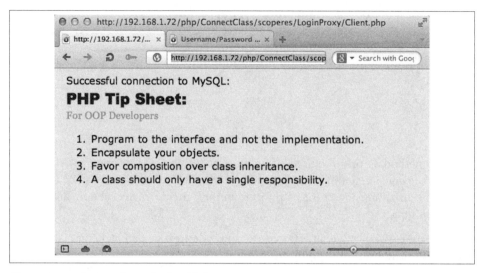

Figure 11-7. Output from the RealSubject

Of course, the contents of the RealSubject class is all the user wanted to see in the first place, and she has no idea that the initial request had to successfully go through the Client and Proxy classes.

If the request does not work out because the incorrect username and/or password was entered or the user has not registered, some alternative message must be sent. In this case, a simple message like that in Figure 11-8 informs the user that the entered materials could not be found.

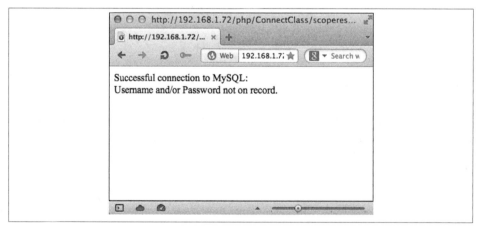

Figure 11-8. Message from Proxy that the request is not found

Typically, a message to the user would suggest registration or taking more care in logging in. Further, it would most likely link to a page where the user has the option to register or try logging in again. However, this example has been kept to a minimum for the sake of clarity. Once you're comfortable with using the Proxy design pattern implemented as a protection proxy, you can make the necessary modifications to create a seamless registration and login. After all, the purpose of any website is to make access easy for the users, and the proxy simply ensures that the users with the correct privileges can use it.

The Proxy and Real-World Security

The Proxy pattern by itself, especially as illustrated in this chapter's example, is certainly not enough for real-world site security. It is even less secure if a financial transaction may be involved. However, if a Proxy module hands off a request to a high security module, it maintains the Proxy design pattern. In fact, you can think of the proxy participant in the pattern to be a place where a true high security operation takes place before the user goes to the real subject. In this example, the md5() function shows where a password hash can be generated, but MD5 is not a very high security encryption. You can add far more security for your site. For example, in a credit card financial processing context, the proxy would send the request to a credit card processing company's module to take care of the financial matters, and if the return from the processing module indicates that the transaction is successful, it would pass on the request to the real subject, which itself would then make the product or service available to the user.

However, under no circumstance should you think that the Proxy design pattern, with PHP or any other programming language, is a high security design. Instead, it stands as a general model for security with the details of that security handled by a different module within or outside of the Proxy. Figure 11-9 illustrates the Proxy role in real-world high security.

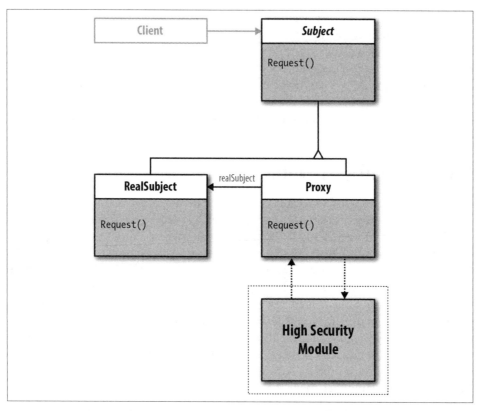

Figure 11-9. Adding a high security module to a Proxy pattern

As far as the user is concerned, all requests go directly to the real subject. The proxy module can be a simple password check, or it can be used to call a high security module to process sensitive materials.

CHAPTER 12

The Flexibility of the Strategy Design Pattern

Victorious warriors win first and then go to war,
while defeated warriors go to war first and then
seek to win.

—Sun Tzu

In preparing for battle I have always found that
plans are useless, but planning is indispensable.

—Dwight D. Eisenhower

All I had done was to improve on their strategy,
and it was the beginning of a very important lesson
in life—that anytime you find someone more
successful than you are, especially when you're
both engaged in the same business—you know
they're doing something that you aren't.

—Malcolm X

Encapsulating Algorithms

One of the ongoing tasks in using PHP with MySQL is writing algorithms for the different kinds of requests made of a MySQL application. Typical requests include creating tables or entering, selecting, changing, and deleting data. The algorithms for these different requests are simple or complex depending on both the complexity of the request and of the table.

One of the main principles of design patterns is to encapsulate what varies. With several different algorithms for different kinds of requests sent to a PHP class that handles these MySQL requests, the variation is clearly the algorithms. The variations may be small or great, but using the Strategy design pattern, we can greatly simplify the process.

Generally, with design patterns, the question is "What causes redesign?" Then, we proceed to avoid those things that force redesign. But what if we instead think of a way to make changes without redesign? By encapsulating what varies, programmers first decide what will vary in a program and then encapsulate those features. When a design requires change, the encapsulated elements can be changed without affecting the rest of the system. Since different MySQL tasks require different algorithms, the algorithms (tasks) can be encapsulated, and the Strategy design pattern applied.

Differentiating the Strategy from the State Design Pattern

To get started, take a look at Figure 12-1. It shows the class diagram for the Strategy design pattern.

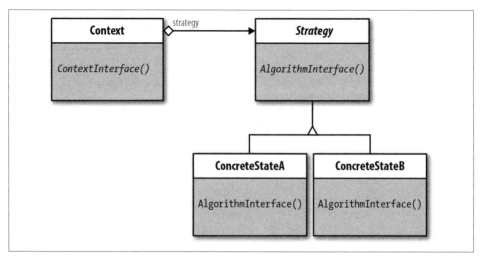

Figure 12-1. Class diagram of Strategy design pattern

Now go back to Chapter 10 and look at Figure 10-1. The pattern participants are organized in a very similar fashion to what you see in Figure 12-1. The Context participant has an aggregate relationship with an interface in both designs. With the State pattern it is the State interface, and with the Strategy pattern it is the Strategy interface. Otherwise they appear identical.

To understand the differences, you need to see how the different Context participants behave in relationship to the Strategy and State interfaces and their concrete implementations. Table 12-1 summarizes these differences.

Table 12-1. Context and variation differences between State and Strategy design patterns

Pattern	What Varies?	Context
State	State	Maintains an instance of the current state of the subclass that defines the current state.
Strategy	Algorithm	Configured with concrete strategy object—an encapsulated algorithm.

As you saw in Chapter 10, the Context kept a variable holding the current concrete state. The concrete states provide methods for going to another state from the current state as recorded in a Context variable.

However, the Context participant in the Strategy pattern has no ongoing record of the current strategy in use. It has no reason to because unlike changing states, generally changing algorithms is not dependent on the current one in use. Obviously, you have situations where one algorithm should be used before another, such as inserting data into a table before attempting to retrieve it. Nevertheless, that does not prevent the algorithm from being used to *attempt* to retrieve data from an empty table. In the State pattern, though, it is easy to have a state that can go to only certain states and not others. In the three-way light example in Chapter 10, a light state in the second *on* state cannot go to either the first *on* state or the *off* state. It can go only to the third *on* state. (See Figure 10-5 in Chapter 10.) Such is not the case with most algorithms.

No Conditional Statements, Please

One of the many features of both the State and Strategy design patterns is that the Context participants avoid conditional statements. If you look at the examples in Chapter 10, you'll notice that none have conditional statements. In the "When to Use the State Pattern?" (page 190) section in Chapter 10, you will find pseudocode that illustrates the difficulty in moving from one cell to the next using conditional statements. (Never mind what it would take when new states are added to or changed in an existing set of states!)

Design patterns certainly do not advocate never using conditional or case statements, but in some patterns, such as the State and Strategy, they can make maintenance difficult. If a single strategy (encapsulated algorithm) is changed and it requires changing a whole set of conditional or case statements, there's a greater chance that errors can be introduced. Further, in using either pattern, introducing conditional or case statements in the client participant is acceptable because all that the client does is make requests. Further, in the encapsulated algorithms (concrete strategies), carrying out a task may require a conditional or case statement. Likewise, in data output and error checking using `mysqli`, a conditional statement is often essential. Strategies eliminate conditional statements for selecting desired behavior. The different tasks are handled by the different concrete strategies, and because the client requests concrete strategies through the context, it must be aware of the available strategies. This does not mean that conditionals cannot be part of the client's selection process. It means that conditionals are not part of the context.

A Family of Algorithms

One of the less detailed elements in GoF's *Design Patterns* is the notion of a *family of algorithms*. Developers are left to define a family of algorithms, but GoF does not specify the exact meaning of "family" in the context of design patterns. However, in the book *Head First Design Patterns*, Eric and Elizabeth Freeman provide a simple yet useful concept—*a set of behaviors*. Any project that relies on a certain set of behaviors can be cast into a Strategy design pattern by encapsulating the behaviors into strategies. That is, the behaviors require some kind of algorithm to make them functional. By encapsulating them into concrete strategies, they can be used, reused, and modified.

This chapter's "family" consists of the behaviors typically required in work with a MySQL table. Data are entered, changed, retrieved, and deleted. Those behaviors involving data operations then become the "family" that can be cast into a strategy for each family member. The strategies require slightly different algorithms in conjunction with the MySQL commands and the PHP `mysqli` class. By putting these operations into separate concrete classes that implement a common interface, they can be incorporated as part of a Strategy design pattern.

A Minimalist Strategy Pattern

In order to see the general pattern using a MySQL connection, this first example uses no table but instead sets up the pattern for later incorporation of the details in each strategy. Because the HTML form cannot pass selected parameters to a PHP class or file, this example uses several small PHP trigger scripts. The trigger scripts call different methods from a single client that in turn calls the requested concrete strategy through the context.

Figure 12-2 shows the file diagram for this implementation. The HTML file has separate forms for each strategy that is passed through a PHP trigger script to methods in the `Client`. The `Client` passes on the request through the `Context` to a concrete strategy. The connection helpers are an interface and class to connect to a MySQL database.

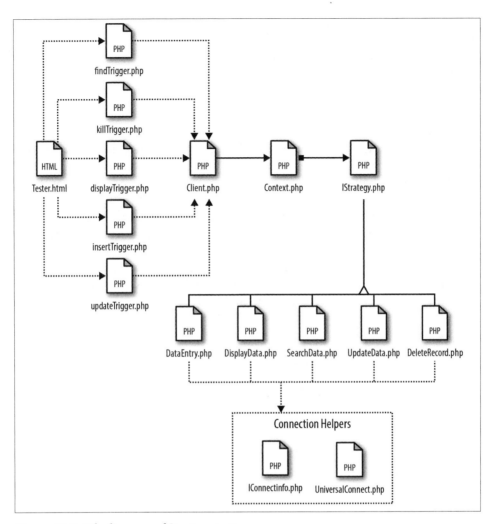

Figure 12-2. File diagram of Strategy pattern

For those developers who have considerable experience dealing with MySQL databases, Figure 12-2 may appear to be an overengineered approach to a task. However, the purpose of design patterns is to make the objects available for change and reuse. Each of the concrete strategies is encapsulated so that any changes (maintaining the implemented interfaces) will not crash the system. Even from the perspective of this minimal strategy, it should be easy to see how the behaviors in the concrete strategies are open to a wide range of implementations.

The Client and the Trigger Scripts

The Client class makes requests through the Context, creating a concrete strategy. The request for the different strategies is accomplished with a set of methods. The following two lines are key in the request:

```
$context=new Context(new ConcreteStrategy());
$context->algorithm();
```

Each Client method provides the name of the concrete strategy to implement, and algorithm() is a Context method implemented in the concrete strategies. This process reveals how *polymorphism* works. Each request for the concrete method's algorithm is through a Context instance, and so the requests for all of them look exactly alike: $context->algorithm(). However, the Client instantiates the Context with a concrete strategy as an argument. That argument allows the Context to use the requested concrete strategy by implementing the concrete strategy's implementation of the algorithm() method. In this way, the Strategy pattern lets the algorithm vary independently from the clients that use it. Instead of having several different client classes, several different trigger scripts use the same client in the following example:

```php
<?php
class Client
{
    public function insertData()
    {
        $context=new Context(new DataEntry());
        $context->algorithm();
    }

    public function findData()
    {
        $context=new Context(new SearchData());
        $context->algorithm();
    }

    public function showAll()
    {
        $context=new Context(new DisplayData());
        $context->algorithm();
    }

    public function changeData()
    {
        $context=new Context(new UpdateData());
        $context->algorithm();
    }

    public function killer()
    {
        $context=new Context(new DeleteRecord());
```

```php
        $context->algorithm();
    }
}
?>
```

In order to fire the methods for the different concrete strategies (encapsulated algorithms), the HTML calls one of the following PHP trigger scripts:

```php
<?php
//insertTrigger.php
function __autoload($class_name)
{
    include $class_name . '.php';
}
$trigger=new Client();
$trigger->insertData();
?>
-------------
<?php
//displayTrigger.php
function __autoload($class_name)
{
    include $class_name . '.php';
}
$trigger=new Client();
$trigger->showAll();
?>
-------------
<?php
//findTrigger.php
function __autoload($class_name)
{
    include $class_name . '.php';
}
$trigger=new Client();
$trigger->findData();
?>
-------------
<?php
//updateTrigger.php
function __autoload($class_name)
{
    include $class_name . '.php';
}
$trigger=new Client();
$trigger->changeData();
?>
-------------
<?php
//killTrigger.php
function __autoload($class_name)
{
    include $class_name . '.php';
```

```
}
$trigger=new Client();
$trigger->killer();
?>
```

The form in the HTML document calls each PHP trigger separately. The request from the trigger script is passed on to the client, which uses one method for each request. In Strategy design patterns, the client typically creates and passes a concrete object to the context. However, the request origins lie in the HTML document:

```
<!DOCTYPE html>
<html>
<head>
<meta charset="UTF-8">
<title>Test</title>
</head>
<body>
Insert<br />
<form name="insert" action="insertTrigger.php" method="post">
  <input type="text" name="data">
  <br />
  <input type="submit" value="Insert">
</form>
<br />
Find Data
<form name="find" action="findTrigger.php" method="post">
  <input type="text" name="data">
  <br />
  <input type="submit" value="Find">
</form>
<br />
Display All Data
<form name="display" action="displayTrigger.php" method="post">
  <input type="submit" value="Show all data">
</form>
<br />
Update Data
<form name="change" action="updateTrigger.php" method="post">
  <input type="text" name="data">
  <br />
  <input type="submit" value="Change data in record">
</form>
<br />
Delete Record
<form name="killer" action="killTrigger.php" method="post">
  <input type="text" name="data">
  <br />
  <input type="submit" value="Delete Record">
</form>
</body>
</html>
```

One of the tricky elements in this arrangement is protecting the $_POST data by using the mysqli->real_escape_string() method for extracting the data values sent from the HTML document. It would be possible to include an extra variable in all posts to indicate a concrete strategy request method that the client will use and then make the selection without using a gaggle of trigger scripts. The MySQL connection could be made in the client, making it possible to extract the data, close the connection, and then pass it on to the concrete strategy, where a second connection could be opened to process the request through the appropriate strategy. However, this example attempts to keep the focus on design patterns and not abandoning all security issues. One result is the separate trigger scripts for fulfilling a request.

The Context Class and Strategy Interface

In the State design, the Context class acts as a "track keeper"; it keeps track of the current state. In the Strategy design, the Context has a much different function. It serves to separate a request from a concrete strategy, thereby allowing the strategy and request to act independently of one another. It represents another form of loose binding between request and consequence. At the same time, it facilitates a request from the Client.

The Context is not an interface (of either the abstract class or interface variety), but it is aggregated with the Strategy interface. The Gang of Four specify the following characteristics:

- It is configured with a concrete strategy object. (See how the Client class instantiates Context in "The Client and the Trigger Scripts" (page 244).)
- It maintains a reference to a Strategy object.
- It may define an interface that lets the Strategy access its data.

In the following listing, you can see these features of a Context class:

```php
<?php
class Context
{
    private $strategy;

    public function __construct(IStrategy $strategy)
    {
        $this->strategy = $strategy;
    }

    public function algorithm()
    {
        $this->strategy->algorithm();
    }
}
?>
```

First, the constructor function expects an implementation of IStrategy as a parameter. Second, it maintains a reference to a Strategy object through an encapsulated (private visibility) property, $strategy. The $strategy property receives its instance from the constructor parameter that will be an instance of a concrete strategy. Third, the algo rithm() method implements IStrategy method, also named algorithm() as implemented by the concrete strategy selected through the Client. Because the Context and IStrategy make up an *aggregation*, the Context has certain features of an abstract class or interface. In fact, a Context may be best understood in the aggregation. In looking at the Strategy interface, IStrategy, you can see the single method to be implemented is algorithm():

```php
<?php
interface IStrategy
{
    public function algorithm();
}
?>
```

Each concrete strategy can implement the method in any fashion required.

The Concrete Strategies

The encapsulated family of algorithms that makes up the concrete strategies provides a mockup of possible strategies. The point in this minimalist example is to see how the different participants in the Strategy design pattern work in concert. In this section, you will see a fully implemented example.

The five concrete strategies include the following classes:

- DataEntry
- DisplayData
- SearchData
- UpdateData
- DeleteData

Each of these concrete strategies represents typical algorithms used with PHP and MySQL.

DataEntry

This first strategy mockup represents entering data into a table:

```php
<?php
class DataEntry implements IStrategy
//DataEntry.php
{
    public function algorithm()
```

```php
    {
        $hookup=UniversalConnect::doConnect();
        $test = $hookup->real_escape_string($_POST['data']);
        echo "This data has been entered: " . $test . "<br/>";
    }
}
?>
```

DisplayData

The $_POST['data'] is not used in this example because the algorithm displays only the string "Here's all the data!!" which was assigned to the variable $test as a string literal:

```php
<?php
//DisplayData.php
class DisplayData implements IStrategy
{
    public function algorithm()
    {
        $hookup=UniversalConnect::doConnect();
        $test = "Here's all the data!!";
        echo $test . "<br/>";
    }
}
?>
```

SearchData

Here the search term is in the $_POST['data'] and passed to the $test variable:

```php
<?php
//SearchData.php
class SearchData implements IStrategy
{
    public function algorithm()
    {
        $hookup=UniversalConnect::doConnect();
        $test = $hookup->real_escape_string($_POST['data']);
        echo "Here's what you were looking for " . $test . "<br/>";
    }
}
?>
```

UpdateData

The "new" data is in the $_POST['data'] and passed to the $test variable. In an actual implementation, the name of the field would likely be included as well:

```php
<?php
//UpdateData.php
class UpdateData implements IStrategy
```

```
{
    public function algorithm()
    {
        $hookup=UniversalConnect::doConnect();
        $test = $hookup->real_escape_string($_POST['data']);
        echo "Your new data is now " . $test . "<br/>";
    }
}
?>
```

DeleteRecord

Finally, using a unique identifier passed in $_POST['data'] and stored in $test would be used to remove a record from a table:

```
<?php
//DeleteRecord.php
class DeleteRecord implements IStrategy
{
    public function algorithm()
    {
        $hookup=UniversalConnect::doConnect();
        $test = $hookup->real_escape_string($_POST['data']);
        echo "The record " . $test . "has been deleted.<br/>";
    }
}
?>
```

Connection interface and class

All of the concrete strategies implement the same connection object (as seen in other chapters). The following interface would include names used by the actual program:

```
<?php
//Filename: IConnectInfo.php
interface IConnectInfo
{
    const HOST ="localhost";
    const UNAME ="alpha";
    const PW ="beta";
    const DBNAME = "gamma";

    public function doConnect();
}
?>
```

The following connection class implements the IConnectInfo interface:

```
<?php
include_once('IConnectInfo.php');

class UniversalConnect implements IConnectInfo
{
```

```
        private static $server=IConnectInfo::HOST;
        private static $currentDB= IConnectInfo::DBNAME;
        private static $user= IConnectInfo::UNAME;
        private static $pass= IConnectInfo::PW;
        private static $hookup;

        public function doConnect()
        {
            self::$hookup=mysqli_connect(self::$server, self::$user, self::$pass,
                        self::$currentDB);
            if(self::$hookup)
            {
                echo "Successful connection to MySQL:<br/>";
            }
            elseif (mysqli_connect_error(self::$hookup))
            {
                echo('Here is why it failed: '  . mysqli_connect_error());
            }
            return self::$hookup;
        }
    }
    ?>
```

Using a connection class and separate interface allows for easy reuse and change. The only change is the values of the constants in the interface.

Expanded Strategy Pattern with Data Security and Parameterized Algorithms

In the minimalist example in the previous section, you were able to see all of the basic elements of a Strategy design pattern in PHP using a MySQL database. To make a more robust example, this next example adds functionality to the different strategies. It also adds a helper class to deal with a secure movement of data from the HTML client to the MySQL database. This means that the client is able to make secure requests using data passed through the `mysqli->real_escape_string($_POST['data'])` function. The Client class could handle the security itself, but that would give it an added responsibility beyond making the requests.

A Data Security Helper Class

Using the `mysqli->real_escape_string($_POST['data'])` function to pass data securely between the HTML form and the PHP class requires a MySQL connection, but once the connection has been opened and the data securely passed, it can be closed again to free up resources used by the connection.

Anticipating the different concrete strategies, the helper class has unique methods for securing data for each of the concrete strategies. A single method passes an array back to the Client containing the required data for the request. Figure 12-3 diagrams the relationship of the helper class to the Strategy.

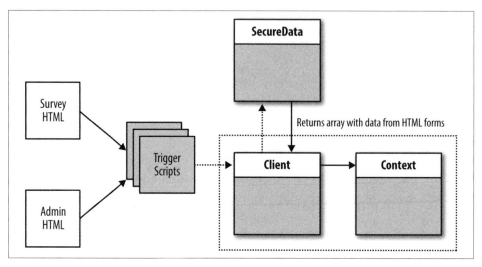

Figure 12-3. Adding a helper class for data security

The rest of the Strategy pattern is not shown in Figure 12-3 after the Context class, but it follows the standard class diagram shown in Figure 12-1. Also, the same MySQL helper classes that are used for database requests are used with the SecureData class to create the MySQL connection.

The SecureData class has methods for each of the concrete strategies that rely on data from the HTML forms. The DisplayAll concrete strategy requests that all data be displayed, and so it needs no special data passed from the HTML form:

```php
<?php
//Helper class
//SecureData.php
class SecureData
{
    private $changeField;
    private $company;
    private $devdes;
    private $device;
    private $disappear;
    private $field;
    private $hookup;
    private $lang;
    private $newData;
    private $oldData;
    private $plat;
    private $style;
```

```php
private $term;
//$dataPack will be an array
private $dataPack;

public function enterData()
{
    $this->hookup=UniversalConnect::doConnect();
    $this->company=$this->hookup->real_escape_string($_POST['company']);
    $this->devdes=$this->hookup->real_escape_string($_POST['devdes']);
    $this->lang= $this->hookup->real_escape_string($_POST['lang']);
    $this->plat= $this->hookup->real_escape_string($_POST['plat']);
    $this->style=$this->hookup->real_escape_string($_POST['style']);
    $this->device=$this->hookup->real_escape_string($_POST['device']);
    $this->dataPack=array(
        $this->company,
        $this->devdes,
        $this->lang,
        $this->plat,
        $this->style,
        $this->device
    );

    $this->hookup->close();
}

public function conductSearch()
{
    $this->hookup=UniversalConnect::doConnect();
    $this->field=$this->hookup->real_escape_string($_POST['field']);
    $this->term=$this->hookup->real_escape_string($_POST['term']);
    $this->dataPack=array(
        $this->field,
        $this->term
        );
    $this->hookup->close();
}

public function makeChange()
{
    $this->hookup=UniversalConnect::doConnect();
    $this->changeField=$this->hookup->real_escape_string($_POST['update']);
    $this->oldData=$this->hookup->real_escape_string($_POST['old']);
    $this->newData=$this->hookup->real_escape_string($_POST['new']);
    $this->dataPack=array(
        $this->changeField,
        $this->oldData,
        $this->newData
        );
    $this->hookup->close();
}

public function removeRecord()
```

```
    {
        $this->hookup=UniversalConnect::doConnect();
        $this->disappear=$this->hookup->real_escape_string($_POST['delete']);
        $this->dataPack=array($this->disappear);
        $this->hookup->close();
    }

    //Returns secure data as array to requesting Client
    public function setEntry()
    {
        return $this->dataPack;
    }
}
?>
```

All of the methods except for setEntry() generate an array named dataPack. The setEntry() method returns the current contents of dataPack. Depending on the request, the SecureData class generates values placed into the array, which is passed back to the Client and becomes part of a request to a concrete strategy through the algorithm() method.

Adding a Parameter to an Algorithm Method

A second added feature is a change in the Strategy algorithm method. By adding an array as a parameter to the function, it is far more flexible in what it can handle. Each call to the algorithm function contains an array made up of data passed from the HTML form:

```
<?php
interface IStrategy
{
    const TABLENOW ="survey";
    public function algorithm(Array $dataPack);
}
?>
```

Likewise, a constant, TABLENOW, has been added to the interface. Because every concrete strategy uses the same table in this implementation, using PHP's capability of passing on constants from an interface allows a loose and reusable code. Obviously if different tables were to be used for the different concrete strategies, the table references would have to be assigned in the individual concrete strategies. Type hinting in the parameter forces an array to be used as an argument.

The Survey Table

The following script is used to create a table for the survey. Larger or smaller tables can be used with the Strategy design by altering the size of the array used in the concrete strategies:

```php
<?php
include_once('UniversalConnect.php');
class CreateTable
{
    private $tableMaster;
    private $hookup;

    public function __construct()
    {
        $this->tableMaster="survey";
        $this->hookup=UniversalConnect::doConnect();

        $drop = "DROP TABLE IF EXISTS $this->tableMaster";

        if($this->hookup->query($drop) === true)
        {
            printf("Old table %s has been dropped.<br/>",$this->tableMaster);
        }

        $sql = "CREATE TABLE $this->tableMaster (
            id SERIAL,
            company        NVARCHAR(40),
            devdes         NVARCHAR(10),
            lang           NVARCHAR(15),
            plat           NVARCHAR(15),
            style          NVARCHAR(20),
            device         NVARCHAR(10),
            PRIMARY KEY (id))";

        if($this->hookup->query($sql) === true)
        {
            printf("Table $this->tableMaster has been created successfully.
                <br/>");
        }
        $this->hookup->close();
    }
}
$worker=new CreateTable();
?>
```

This particular table-creation class is used during the development and debugging cycle. Once you have your table the way you want it and want it installed on different systems, you can remove the following section:

```php
$drop = "DROP TABLE IF EXISTS $this->tableMaster";

if($this->hookup->query($drop) === true)
{
    printf("Old table %s has been dropped.<br/>",$this->tableMaster);
}
```

and change the following code:

```
$sql = "CREATE TABLE $this->tableMaster (
```

to the following:

```
$sql = "CREATE TABLE IF NOT EXISTS $this->tableMaster (
```

In this way, the class will not remove any existing tables that may have data already stored in them.

The same `UniversalConnect` class is employed as with all of the other MySQL connections in this chapter.

Data Entry Modules

Given the job of the `SecureData` helper class and the revised `IStrategy` interface to include a parameter for the `algorithm()` method, `Client` can more easily make requests based on methods for the various requests from the HTML forms. Before going on, take a look at the requests originating in the HTML forms. Two forms are used: one for user input of survey data and one for viewing the data stored in a MySQL table. All are very simple and represent generic HTML forms. Both forms share a single CSS file:

```css
@charset "UTF-8";
/*survey.css */
/* CSS Document */
/*B2B2B2,B2A1A1,666666,8FB299*/
body
{
    background-color:#B2B2B2;
    color:#666666;
    font-family:Verdana, Geneva, sans-serif
}

h2
{
    font-family:"Arial Black", Gadget, sans-serif;
    color:#666666
}

h3
{
    font-family:"Trebuchet MS", Arial, Helvetica, sans-serif;
    background-color:#8FB299;
    color:#666666
}

th
{
    text-align:left;
    background-color:#8FB299;
```

```
      color:#666666
   }
```

The CSS is set for minimum differentiation.

First, the survey is a simple text entry plus several selections from radio forms:

```
<!DOCTYPE html>
<html>
<head>
<link rel="stylesheet" href="survey.css">
<meta charset="UTF-8">
<title>Programmer Profile Survey</title>
</head>
<body>
<h2>Programmer Survey</h2>
<form name="survey" action="insertTrigger.php" method="post">
  <input type="text" name="company">
   Company Name<br />
  <h3> Primary Role</h3>
  <input type="radio" name="devdes" value="developer">
   Developer<br />
  <input type="radio" name="devdes" value="designer">
   Designer<br />
  <h3> Primary Programming Language</h3>
  <input type="radio" name="lang" value="PHP">
   PHP<br />
  <input type="radio" name="lang" value="C#/ASP.NET">
   C# ASP.NET<br />
  <input type="radio" name="lang" value="PERL">
   PERL<br />
  <input type="radio" name="lang" value="JavaScript">
   JavaScript<br />
  <input type="radio" name="lang" value="ActionScript 3.0">
   ActionScript 3.0<br />
  <h3> Primary Development/Design Platform</h3>
  <input type="radio" name="plat" value="WinPC">
   Windows PC<br />
  <input type="radio" name="plat" value="Mac">
   Apple Macintosh<br />
  <input type="radio" name="plat" value="Linux">
   Linux<br />
  <h3> Primary Programming Style</h3>
  <input type="radio" name="style" value="sequential">
   Sequential<br />
  <input type="radio" name="style" value="procedural">
   Procedural<br />
  <input type="radio" name="style" value="OOP">
   Object Oriented Programming<br />
  <input type="radio" name="style" value="design patterns">
   Design Patterns
  <p />
  <h3> Primary Platform Development/Design</h3>
```

```
<input type="radio" name="device" value="Desktop">
 Desktop<br />
<input type="radio" name="device" value="Tablet">
 Tablet<br />
<input type="radio" name="device" value="Smartphone">
 Smartphone
<p />
<input type="submit" value="Create Profile" name="sender">
</form>
</body>
</html>
```

Figure 12-4 shows the survey opened in a tablet device.

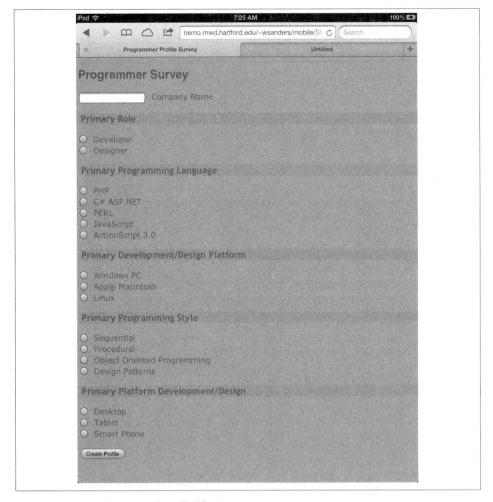

Figure 12-4. UI for survey handled by Strategy pattern

A second HTML document provides an administrative tool for examining the table. Again, it is quite simple and used primarily for following the data from its origins in an HTML form through a Strategy design pattern:

```html
<!DOCTYPE html>
<html>
<head>
<link rel="stylesheet" href="survey.css">
<meta charset="UTF-8">
<title>Administrative Module</title>
</head>

<body>
<h2>Administrative Module</h2>
<h3> Display all data</h3>
<form name="allData" action="displayTrigger.php" method="post">
  <input type="submit" value="Display Data" name="display">
</form>
<form name="search" action="findTrigger.php" method="post">
  <h3> Search Field</h3>
  <input type="radio" name="field" value="id">
   ID<br />
  <input type="radio" name="field" value="company">
   Company<br />
  <input type="radio" name="field" value="devdes">
   Designer/Developer<br />
  <input type="radio" name="field" value="lang">
   Computer Language<br />
  <input type="radio" name="field" value="plat">
   Development Platform<br />
  <input type="radio" name="field" value="style">
   Programming Style<br />
  <input type="radio" name="field" value="device">
   Target Device
  <p />
  <input type="text" name="term">
   Term to find
  <p />
  <input type="submit" value="Search" name="searcher">
</form>
<form name="search" action="changeTrigger.php" method="post">
  <h3> Change Field</h3>
  <input type="radio" name="update" value="id">
   ID <br />
  <input type="radio" name="update" value="company">
   Company<br />
  <input type="radio" name="update" value="devdes">
   Designer/Developer<br />
  <input type="radio" name="update" value="lang">
   Computer Language<br />
  <input type="radio" name="update" value="plat">
   Development Platform<br />
```

```
<input type="radio" name="update" value="style">
 Programming Style<br />
<input type="radio" name="update" value="device">
 Target Device
<p />
<input type="text" name="old">
 Old Value
<p />
<input type="text" name="new">
 New Value
<p />
<input type="submit" value="Change Value" name="changer">
</form>
<h3> Delete Record</h3>
<form name="killer" action="killTrigger.php" method="post">
  <input type="text" name="delete" size=3>
   Number of Record to Delete
  <p />
  <input type="submit" value="Permanently Delete Record" name="doa">
</form>
</body>
</html>
```

Figure 12-5 shows the UI displayed on a tablet device.

Figure 12-5. Administrative module UI on tablet device

Both UIs use a mobile layout of a single column that can be adjusted for viewing on mobile phones with Internet capabilities.

Each button in the two HTML documents represents a separate form. Each form calls a trigger file that in turn instantiates the Client class and the appropriate method required to carry out the requested task.

The Client Calls for Help

The Client has no constructor function, but instead it has several methods available for different requests. The methods are similar to the minimalist example, but they do more with the help of a SecureData helper class discussed previously, in "A Data Security Helper Class" (page 251).

First, review what the SecureData class does, and then take a look at the Client:

```php
<?php
//Client.php
class Client
{
    public function insertData()
    {
        $secure=new SecureData();
        $context=new Context(new DataEntry());
        $secure->enterData();
        $context->algorithm($secure->setEntry());
    }

    public function findData()
    {
        $secure=new SecureData();
        $context=new Context(new SearchData());
        $secure->conductSearch();
        $context->algorithm($secure->setEntry());
    }

    public function showAll()
    {
        $dummy=array(0);
        $context=new Context(new DisplayAll());
        $context->algorithm($dummy);
    }

    public function changeData()
    {
        $secure=new SecureData();
        $context=new Context(new UpdateData());
        $secure->makeChange();
        $context->algorithm($secure->setEntry());
    }
```

```
    public function killer()
    {
        $secure=new SecureData();
        $context=new Context(new DeleteRecord());
        $secure->removeRecord();
        $context->algorithm($secure->setEntry());
    }
}
?>
```

With the exception of the showAll() method, all of the methods in the Client first instantiate the SecureData class. Then the methods create a context object, using the concrete method as a parameter. Next, the SecureData object calls the appropriate method related to the concrete strategy to create the required array. Finally, the Client method calls the Context->algorithm() using the array, $secure->setEntry() returned from the SecureData class as an argument. The array contents depend on user input sent from the HTML form and the type of strategy requested.

The Gang of Four point out that all concrete strategy classes share the same interface whether they are used or not. Therefore all concrete strategy classes must implement the method in the Strategy interface (the algorithm() method in IStrategy). However, not all concrete strategies may need the algorithm and certainly not in the same way.

To some extent, you can see this in the showAll() method in the Client class. Instead of using an array returned from the SecureData class, it creates a dummy array containing it and uses it as a parameter in the Context->algorithm(). This is one way to meet the requirements of the IStrategy interface to include an array as a parameter.

The Minor but Major Change in Context Class

Compared to the minimalist example in the first part of this chapter, the Context class is little changed other than adding a parameter to the algorithm() method required by the updated IStrategy interface. Because of the aggregate relationship between the Context class and IStrategy, the Context class must hold a reference to IStrategy. As in the minimalist example, the Context is created with a concrete strategy object. That part is unchanged. However, it also includes a method that instantiates the concrete strategy's implementation of the algorithm() method:

```
<?php
class Context
{
    private $strategy;
    private $dataPack;

    public function __construct(IStrategy $strategy)
    {
        $this->strategy = $strategy;
    }
```

```php
    public function algorithm(Array $dataPack)
    {
        $this->dataPack=$dataPack;
        $this->strategy->algorithm($this->dataPack);
    }
}
?>
```

The name of the Context class method is also "algorithm" and requires an array parameter. The common algorithm name is to emphasize the aggregate relationship between the context and strategy participants. If this is confusing, you might want to rename the method contextAl gorithm to differentiate it from the IStrategy algorithm() method.

The Context also includes an additional property, $dataPack, reflecting the name of the array that is being passed through the Context algorithm() method. It is then passed to the concrete strategy's algorithm() method.

The Concrete Strategies

The whole purpose of passing data through an array to the concrete strategies is to allow the different strategies to respond to different requests. It gives flexibility to the design because of the wide range of data that can be passed with an array. As you can see in the following concrete strategy classes, each implements the IStrategy algorithm() method using the data passed through the methods array parameter.

All of the concrete classes use the same UniversalConnect class as used in the mini-malist strategy example. The table name is stored as a constant (TABLENOW) in the IS trategy interface.

DataEntry

Of all of the concrete strategies, the DataEntry class uses the largest array. That's because it must insert all of the data from the HTML survey:

```php
<?php
class DataEntry implements IStrategy
//DataEntry.php
{
    private $tableMaster;
    private $dataPack;
    private $hookup;
    private $sql;

    public function algorithm(Array $dataPack)
    {
```

```php
$this->dataPack=$dataPack;
$comval=$this->dataPack[0];
$devdesval=$this->dataPack[1];
$langval=$this->dataPack[2];
$platval=$this->dataPack[3];
$styleval=$this->dataPack[4];
$deviceval=$this->dataPack[5];

$this->tableMaster=IStrategy::TABLENOW;
$this->hookup=UniversalConnect::doConnect();
$this->sql = "INSERT INTO $this->tableMaster
(
    company,
    devdes,
    lang,
    plat,
    style,
    device
)
VALUES
(
    '$comval',
    '$devdesval',
    '$langval',
    '$platval',
    '$styleval',
    '$deviceval'
)";

if($this->hookup->query($this->sql))
{
    printf("Successful data entry for table: $this->tableMaster <br/>");
}
elseif ( ($result = $this->hookup->query($this->sql))===false )
{
    printf("Invalid query: %s <br/> Whole query: %s <br/>",
                        $this->hookup->error, $this->sql);
    exit();
}

$this->hookup->close();
        }
    }
    ?>
```

The only conditional statements are those used in standard MySQL statements. The general algorithm that makes up the core of the class uses none.

DisplayAll

This is the class that is passed a dummy array. As you can see, it simply uses a general algorithm for sending data from the table to the screen:

```php
<?php
//DisplayAll.php
class DisplayAll implements IStrategy
{
    private    $tableMaster;
    private $hookup;

    public function algorithm(Array $dataPack)
    {
        $this->tableMaster=IStrategy::TABLENOW;
        $this->hookup=UniversalConnect::doConnect();

        //Create Query Statement
        $sql ="SELECT * FROM $this->tableMaster";
        //Conditional statement in MySQL command
        if ($result = $this->hookup->query($sql))
        {
            printf("Select returned %d rows.<p />", $result->num_rows);

            echo "<link rel='stylesheet' href='survey.css'>";
            echo "<table>";

             while ($finfo = mysqli_fetch_field($result))
            {
                echo "<th> {$finfo->name}</th>";
            }
            echo "</tr>\n";

            while($row=mysqli_fetch_row($result))
            {
                echo "<tr>";
                foreach($row as $cell)
                {
                    echo "<td>$cell</td>";
                }
                echo "</tr>";
            }
            echo"</table>";
            $result->close();
        }
    $this->hookup->close();
    }
}
?>
```

A table aids in the data display but is by no means optimized. Rather, with the focus on implementing the design pattern, the format is kept simple. Figure 12-6 shows the output.

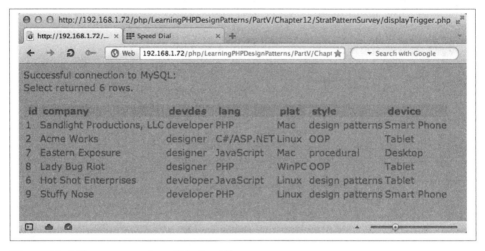

Figure 12-6. Data output from DisplayAll concrete strategy

SearchData

The search algorithm selects a specified value from a specified field. The field name and search value are passed through the array as an argument in the `algorithm()` method. A match results in the record being displayed, while nothing is displayed when there's no match:

```php
<?php
//SearchData.php
class SearchData implements IStrategy
{
    private $tableMaster;
    private $dataPack;
    private $hookup;
    private $sql;

    public function algorithm(Array $dataPack)
    {
        $this->tableMaster=IStrategy::TABLENOW;
        $this->hookup=UniversalConnect::doConnect();
        $this->dataPack=$dataPack;
        $field=$this->dataPack[0];
        $term=$this->dataPack[1];
        $this->sql = "SELECT * FROM $this->tableMaster WHERE $field='$term'";
        //Conditional statement in MySQL query for data output
        if ($result = $this->hookup->query($this->sql))
        {
```

```php
            echo "<link rel='stylesheet' href='survey.css'>";
            echo "<table>";
            while($row=mysqli_fetch_row($result))
            {
                echo "<br />";
                echo "<tr>";
                foreach($row as $cell)
                {
                    echo "<td>$cell</td>";
                }
                echo "</tr>";
            }
            echo "</table>";
            $result->close();
        }
        $this->hookup->close();

        }
    }
?>
```

A more sophisticated algorithm and display design can be easily substituted. If more data is required, it is a simple matter to change the data generated in the HTML document and placed into an array in the SecureData class. This can be done without affecting any other components of the program, and this is in no small part the *sine qua non* of design patterns overall. Figure 12-7 shows a search for "designer" in the Designer/Developer field.

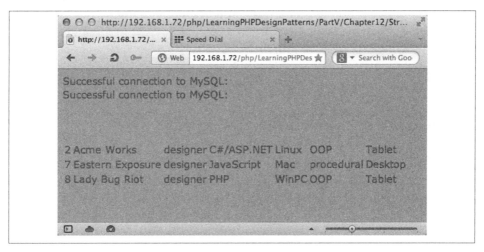

Figure 12-7. Output displays all hits for "designer"

UpdateData

To change the value in a current field, this implementation requires only three elements: the name of the field, the old value, and the new value. The algorithm is flexible, and like all other concrete strategies, this one can be modified to reflect requirements:

```php
<?php
//UpdateData.php
class UpdateData implements IStrategy
{
    private $tableMaster;
    private $dataPack;
    private $hookup;
    private $sql;

    public function algorithm(Array $dataPack)
    {
        $this->tableMaster=IStrategy::TABLENOW;
        $this->hookup=UniversalConnect::doConnect();
        $this->dataPack=$dataPack;
        $changeField=$this->dataPack[0];
        $oldData=$this->dataPack[1];
        $newData=$this->dataPack[2];
        $this->sql = "UPDATE $this->tableMaster SET $changeField='$newData'
                    WHERE $changeField='$oldData'";
        //Conditional statement in MySQL query for error checking
        if ($result = $this->hookup->query($this->sql))
        {
            echo "$changeField changed from $oldData to: $newData";
        }
        else
        {
            echo "Change failed: " . $hookup->error;
        }
    }
}
?>
```

The output informs the user that a change has been made.

DeleteRecord

The final concrete strategy removes a record and requires only a single element in an array to pass on the record number to delete. Because the table has been created with an automatic numbering system, the identification number is an integer:

```php
<?php
//DeleteRecord.php
class DeleteRecord implements IStrategy
{
    private $tableMaster;
    private $dataPack;
```

```php
        private $hookup;
        private $sql;

        public function algorithm(Array $dataPack)
        {
            $this->tableMaster=IStrategy::TABLENOW;
            $this->hookup=UniversalConnect::doConnect();
            $this->dataPack=$dataPack;
            $destroy=$this->dataPack[0];
            $destroy= intval($destroy);

            $this->sql = "DELETE FROM $this->tableMaster  WHERE id='$destroy'";
            //Conditional statement in MySQL query for error checking
            if ($result = $this->hookup->query($this->sql))
            {
                echo "Record #$destroy removed from table: $this->tableMaster";
            }
            else
            {
                echo "Removal failed: " . $hookup->error;
            }
        }
    }
}
?>
```

The class and accompanying concrete strategy are simple, and those who want to add a more robust algorithm can do so without disrupting the rest of the program.

The Flexible Strategy Pattern

The Strategy pattern is so flexible that not only can changing the algorithm change one implementation, but also the pattern itself has more than one implementation. On the one hand, this chapter showed how the minimalist version of the Strategy design pattern could call up different algorithms that worked independent of data outside of the concrete strategy. On the other hand, the second example used parameters that passed secure data to the concrete strategies.

The Gang of Four point out that one approach is to have the Context pass data in parameters to Strategy operations. That is exactly what the second example did. This approach takes the data to the strategy, whereas keeping the Context and Strategy decoupled may also pass data to the Strategy that it does not need. The approach to this dilemma was to use an array to add flexibility in what was passed to the Strategy. This included an empty array.

The particular type of Strategy implementation depends on the needs of the particular algorithm and what it requires. Some implementations of the Strategy involve storing a reference to its context, which eliminates the need to pass anything. However, in so doing, it more tightly couples the Context and Strategy.

A further issue to consider is the number of objects the Strategy pattern generates in the form of concrete strategies. As you've seen in the examples, quite a few objects (classes) are built to handle the different requests made in a simple MySQL survey run by PHP. More could be built. However, that may not be as big a problem in view of the advantages in reuse and change of the pattern. Design patterns are built for speed in managing an application, but not executing code. A developer with a well-organized Strategy pattern can easily optimize and reoptimize the encapsulated algorithms without it falling in around his head. So the speed is in the reuse and change time, and the cost of additional objects is a small expense.

CHAPTER 13

The Chain of Responsibility Design Pattern

*Most people do not really want freedom, because
freedom involves responsibility, and most people
are frightened of responsibility.*

—Sigmund Freud

*We are made wise not by the recollection of our
past, but by the responsibility for our future.*

—George Bernard Shaw

*By imposing too great a responsibility, or rather,
all responsibility, on yourself, you crush yourself.*

—Franz Kafka

The buck stops here.

—Harry S. Truman

Passing the Buck

The Chain of Responsibility design pattern separates the sender of a request from the receiver. This avoids coupling of the requester and receiver. Further, the pattern allows a request to be passed along a chain to several different objects that have an opportunity to handle the request. The sender doesn't need to know which object handles the request, and the object doesn't need to know who sent the request. There's no coupling between the two.

The advantages of the Chain of Responsibility is that any object can send the request to the objects that handle it, and the objects that handle a request can be changed so that more or different objects can be incorporated to deal with requests. So changes can be made in both the requester and request handlers without disrupting a larger system. Figure 13-1 shows the class diagram for the Chain of Responsibility pattern.

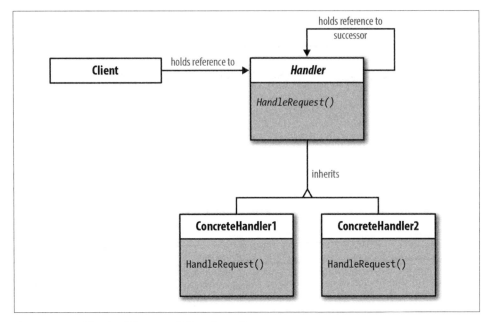

Figure 13-1. Chain of Responsibility class diagram

Note that the Client is an integral part of the program. In fact, it can be a quite hard-working part of the arrangement because not only can it be used to initiate the request, it can initiate the successors implemented in the concrete handlers. One approach is to establish the successor methods in the Handler interface and implement them in the concrete handlers. Then when the Client initiates a request, at the same time it can establish the chain and determine the order of succession.

Some may look at the Chain of Responsibility Pattern and think "this is nothing but a big switch statement." In some respects it is, but in most it is not. It does examine a request to determine whether it matches one of several case conditions. However, while a switch statement is fixed, a Chain of Responsibility has its successor defined by each concrete handler. Because of that arrangement, you could have any number of responses stored in a MySQL database table and then have several different Help Desks using the same table *and* the same PHP Chain of Responsibility. Because each concrete handler includes a method for specifying its own successor, the Client defines the order when it assigns successors through concrete handler objects.

Further, because the Client starts the request chain, it can start it anywhere the developer decides. Suppose that concrete request handlers 4, 10, 15, and 30 have exactly what you want for a new Help Desk. All you need to do is to specify handler 4 as the first in the chain, and then specify 10 as it successor, 15 as 10's successor and 30 as 15's successor. You have incredible flexibility that you will not find in a switch statement.

The Chain of Responsibility in a MySQL Help Desk

The first implementation of the Chain of Responsibility is a Help Desk where users choose from a series of possible help topics. It is a simple implementation both in terms of the PHP design pattern and the use of MySQL as a text data-storage system. Basically, the user selects a query from a set of radio buttons to launch a request, and the structure searches through a chain of responses. When the correct response is located, the object retrieves the response from a MySQL table and displays it on the screen.

Building and Loading the Response Table

The first order of business is to build a table where text responses may be stored. The MySQL in this chapter uses the same connection classes and interface as shown in Chapter 11. They are reproduced here for convenience. First the interface:

```php
<?php
//Filename: IConnectInfo.php
interface IConnectInfo
{
    const HOST ="localhost";
    const UNAME ="phpWorker";
    const PW ="easyWay";
    const DBNAME = "dpPatt";

    public function doConnect();
}

?>
```

Of course, you will use your own connection information. Now, the connection class that implements the interface:

```php
<?php
include_once('IConnectInfo.php');

class UniversalConnect implements IConnectInfo
{
    private static $server=IConnectInfo::HOST;
    private static $currentDB= IConnectInfo::DBNAME;
    private static $user= IConnectInfo::UNAME;
    private static $pass= IConnectInfo::PW;
    private static $hookup;

    public function doConnect()
    {
        self::$hookup=mysqli_connect(self::$server, self::$user, self::$pass,
                    self::$currentDB);
        if(self::$hookup)
        {
            //You may wish to remove this message
```

```php
            echo "Successful connection to MySQL:<br/>";
        }
        elseif (mysqli_connect_error(self::$hookup))
        {
            echo('Here is why it failed: '  . mysqli_connect_error());
        }
        return self::$hookup;
    }
}
?>
```

The connection interface and class are used with every MySQL connection required in this chapter.

The response table requires only an ID, a field to indicate a chain object, and a field for holding the text that will provide the "help" in the Help Desk:

```php
<?php
include_once('../UniversalConnect.php');
class CreateTable
{
    private $tableMaster;
    private $hookup;

    public function __construct()
    {
        $this->tableMaster="helpdesk";
        $this->hookup=UniversalConnect::doConnect();

        $drop = "DROP TABLE IF EXISTS $this->tableMaster";

        if($this->hookup->query($drop) === true)
        {
            printf("Old table %s has been dropped.<br/>",$this->tableMaster);
        }

        $sql = "CREATE TABLE $this->tableMaster (id INT NOT NULL AUTO_INCREMENT,
                chain VARCHAR(3), response TEXT, PRIMARY KEY (id))";

        if($this->hookup->query($sql) === true)
        {
            printf("Table $this->tableMaster has been created successfully.
                    <br/>");
        }
        $this->hookup->close();
    }
}

$worker=new CreateTable();
?>
```

Adding the automatic id field is done as a precaution for possible table editing, but you can omit it if you like. Also, the above format that first deletes a table and then creates a new one is a process used in development. It speeds up the process and ensures that old table versions are removed before proceeding. Once you have the table debugged, you can use the MySQL command and remove the code that first deletes the table:

```
CREATE TABLE IF NOT EXISTS
```

(Of course you can create it using MySQL administrative tools!)

In order for this table to be useful, it needs to be filled with responses to the queries, and so it needs a data entry module made up from a PHP class and an HTML form. The help materials must also be updated, so it requires data update as well as data entry. First the HTML:

```html
<!DOCTYPE html>
<html>
<head>
<meta charset="UTF-8">
<link href="help.css" rel="stylesheet" type="text/css" >
<title>Help Desk Data Entry and Update</title>
</head>
<body>
<h2>Help Desk Data Entry</h2>
<form action="InsertData.php" method="post" name="dataentry">
  Enter Query Chain Value (q1...qx)<br/>
  <input type="text" name="chain" size="3">
  <p/>
  Enter Help Information<br/>
  <textarea name="response" rows="8" cols="24"></textarea>
  <p/>
  <input type="submit" value="Enter data into table" name="send">
</form>
<h2>Update Information</h2>
<form action="UpdateData.php" method="post" name="dataupdate">
  Enter Query Chain Value (q1...qx)<br/>
  <input type="text" name="chain" size="3">
  <p/>
  Enter Help Information<br/>
  <textarea name="response" rows="8" cols="24"></textarea>
  <p/>
  <input type="submit" value="Update table" name="update">
</form>
</body>
</html>
```

The InsertData and UpdateData classes take the data sent from the HTML form and store it in the helpdesk table.

InsertData.php

```php
<?php
include_once('UniversalConnect.php');
class InsertData
{
    private $tableMaster;
    private $hookup;

    public function __construct()
    {

        //Name table and connect
        $this->tableMaster="helpdesk";
        $this->hookup=UniversalConnect::doConnect();
        //From HTML form
        $chain=$this->hookup->real_escape_string($_POST['chain']);
        $response=$this->hookup->real_escape_string($_POST['response']);

        //Create MySQL statement
        $sql = "INSERT INTO $this->tableMaster (chain,response) VALUES
                ('$chain','$response')";

        if($this->hookup->query($sql))
        {
            printf("Chain query: %s <br/>Response %s <br/> have been inserted
                into %s.",$chain,$response,$this->tableMaster);
        }
        //%s is a string from parameter
        elseif ( ($result = $this->hookup->query($sql))===false )
        {
            printf("Invalid query: %s <br/> Whole query: %s <br/>",
                $this->hookup->error, $sql);
          exit();
        }
        $this->hookup->close();
    }
}
$worker=new InsertData();
?>
```

UpdateData.php

```php
<?php
include_once('UniversalConnect.php');
class UpdateData
{
    private $tableMaster;
    private $hookup;

    public function __construct()
    {

        //Name table and connect
        $this->tableMaster="helpdesk";
        $this->hookup=UniversalConnect::doConnect();
        //From HTML form
        $chain=$this->hookup->real_escape_string($_POST['chain']);
        $response=$this->hookup->real_escape_string($_POST['response']);

        //Create MySQL statement
        $sql = "UPDATE $this->tableMaster SET response='$response' WHERE chain=
                '$chain'";

        if($this->hookup->query($sql))
        {
            printf("Chain query: %s <br/>Response %s <br/> have been changed and
                set into %s.",$chain,$response,$this->tableMaster);
        }
        //%s is a string from parameter
        elseif ( ($result = $this->hookup->query($sql))===false )
        {
            printf("Invalid query: %s <br/> Whole query: %s <br/>",
                $this->hookup->error, $sql);
          exit();
        }
        $this->hookup->close();
    }
}
$worker=new UpdateData();
?>
```

Entering or updating data in the table for the Chain of Responsibility help desk requires a simple form. Figure 13-2 shows what the data entry/update administrative tool looks like.

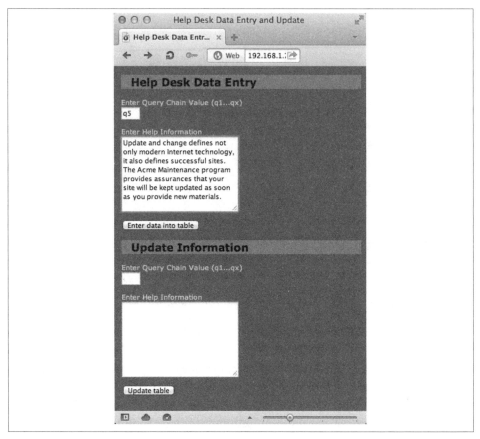

Figure 13-2. Data entry for the responses

Only the application administrator enters help data, and the user has no access to the data entry form. The Query Chain Value in Figure 13-2 is an identifier for the request, or help, the user may be seeking. The way this particular program is organized is that the request identifies the query with a value from q1 to q($number\ of\ queries$). In this example, the "help desk" has only five queries (q1 to q5.) However, you can have as many or few as you want. Further, if you want to add more once you have completed the program, you can use the Help Desk Data Entry Module to add them. Then, just add more concrete handlers that make up the Chain of Responsibility pattern. With the update module, the help desk has a mini content management system (CMS).

The Help Desk Chain of Responsibility

Once you've entered the data for responding to requests, the Chain of Responsibility can be used to provide a program not only for retrieving information but also for ordering the sequence of the chain. Figure 13-3 shows the class diagram for the Help Desk application.

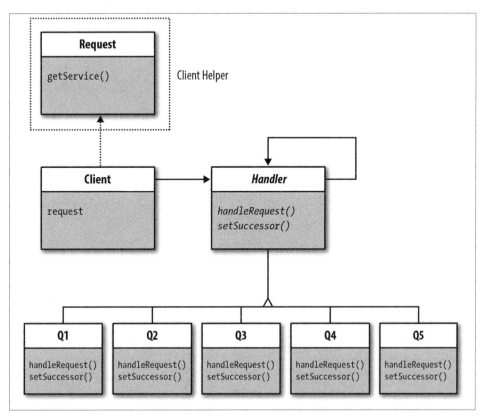

Figure 13-3. Help Desk class diagram

In this implementation of the Chain of Responsibility, a request originates with the Client using a helper class (Request) to send the request to the first concrete handler. The Client sets the sequence of the chain in any way required because it sets the sequence. After calling the first of the concrete handler classes (Q1 through Q5), the concrete handlers take care of the rest, either handling the query or passing it on to the next handler class.

HTML Data Entry, Client and Request Participants

The data entry form is an HTML document with five radio buttons representing different requests for "Help." Each one is identified with a value that identifies the question, ranging from q1 to q5:

```
<!DOCTYPE html>
<html>
<head>
<meta charset="UTF-8">
<link href="help.css" rel="stylesheet" type="text/css" >
<title>Help Desk</title>
</head>
<body>
<img src="logo/acmelogo.png" width="143" height="143"/>
<form action="Client.php" method="post">
  <h2>Acme Help Desk</h2>
  <p/>
  <input type="radio" name="help" value="q1" />
    Website Design and Development<br/>
  <input type="radio" name="help" value="q2" />
    What about just adding a database on existing website?<br/>
  <input type="radio" name="help" value="q3" />
    Can Acme help with UX and UI?<br/>
  <input type="radio" name="help" value="q4" />
    Does Acme also provide graphic design?<br/>
  <input type="radio" name="help" value="q5" />
    What is a site maintenance contract?<br/>
  <p/>
  <input type="submit" name="sendNow" value="Click here for selected help" />
</form>
</body>
</html>
```

A CSS stylesheet provides a "company" style (of course, you can make it any style desired). Save the file as *help.css*:

```
@charset "UTF-8";
/* CSS Document */
body
{
    background-color:#6A6A61;
    color:#DDDCC5;
    font-family:Verdana, Arial, Helvetica, sans-serif;
    font-size:11px;
    margin-left:12px;
}

h2
{
    background-color:#958976;
    color:#1D2326;
    font-family:Tahoma, Geneva, sans-serif
    font-size:18px;
    margin-left:0px;
    text-indent:1em;
}
```

The idea here is to create a simple way for the user to select and the developer to create a request that will enter into a Chain of Responsibility flow. Figure 13-4 shows the UI that users employ to make help selections.

Figure 13-4. User interface for data entry

The Client class processes the request sent from the HTML form. It accepts the request from a $_POST variable and stores it in a variable, $queryNow. Then the Client instantiates instances of each of the concrete responses (handlers) it will use in the chain. Once the object variables are instantiated, the Client then sets up the successor for each of the concrete handlers using the setSuccessor() method. So now the chain is "loaded" with the sequence order:

```php
<?php
function __autoload($class_name)
{
    include $class_name . '.php';
}
class Client
{
    private $queryNow;

    public function __construct()
    {
        if (isset($_POST['sendNow']))
        {
            {
```

```
            $this->queryNow  = $_POST['help'];
        }
        $q1 = new Q1();
        $q2 = new Q2();
        $q3 = new Q3();
        $q4 = new Q4();
        $q5 = new Q5();

//Set successors
            $q1->setSuccessor($q2);
            $q2->setSuccessor($q3);
            $q3->setSuccessor($q4);
            $q4->setSuccessor($q5);

            // Generate and process load requests
            $loadup = new Request($this->queryNow);
//Set beginning of chain
            $q1->handleRequest ($loadup);
    }
}
$makeRequest = new Client();
?>
```

Once the concrete handlers have been instantiated and each (except the end of the chain) has been given a successor, the `Client` is ready to make a request. To aid in the request, the `Client` uses a helper class, `Request`:

```php
<?php
class Request
{
    private $value;

    public function __construct($service)
    {
        $this->value=$service;
    }

    public function getService()
    {
        return $this->value;
    }
}
?>
```

The `Request` class provides an object that can be passed along the chain with a method for retrieving the request.

Handler interface and concrete handlers

The interface for the Chain of Responsibility is an abstract class. In this implementation, it is made up of two abstract methods and a number of properties used by the concrete handlers:

```php
<?php
    abstract class Handler
    {
        protected $successor;
        protected $hookup;
        protected $tableMaster;
        protected $sql;
        protected $handle;
        abstract public function handleRequest($request);
        abstract public function setSuccessor($nextService);


    }
?>
```

Each of the concrete handlers has methods for handling requests and setting successors. The handling requests methods in this example are quite simple. The handleRe quest() method passes the request as an argument. (This is initially done by the Cli ent to start the chain—light a fuse, so to speak.) If the $handle variable matches the $request passed from the Client (via the Request helper), the query is handled by the concrete handler. Otherwise, it passes the request to the successor in the chain:

```php
<?php
class Q1 extends Handler
{
    public function setSuccessor($nextService)
    {
        $this->successor=$nextService;
    }

    public function handleRequest ($request)
    {
        $this->handle="q1";
        if ($request->getService() == $this->handle)
        {
                $this->tableMaster="helpdesk";
            $this->hookup=UniversalConnect::doConnect();
            $this->sql = "SELECT response FROM $this->tableMaster WHERE chain=
                        '$this->handle'";

            if($result=$this->hookup->query($this->sql))
            {
                $row = $result->fetch_assoc();
                echo $row["response"];
            }
            $this->hookup->close();
        }
        else if ($this->successor != NULL)
        {
                $this->successor->handleRequest ($request);
        }
    }
}
```

```
}
?>
```

The way this Chain of Responsibility has been designed, only five help requests are available to the user, and so the handler at the end of the chain has a NULL successor—that is, no successor is defined by the client. This ensures that all requests have handlers and no possible request goes unhandled.

Automated Chain of Responsibility and Factory Method

This next example shows how the Chain of Responsibility can work in conjunction with a Factory Method. Rather than having a UI make a request, the Chain of Responsibility instead uses a date function to act as a "request." This illustrates the flexibility of the Chain of Responsibility. In turn, the concrete handlers in the program call a Factory Method application to load the requested text and images. Figure 13-5 shows the general relationship between the two design patterns in this application.

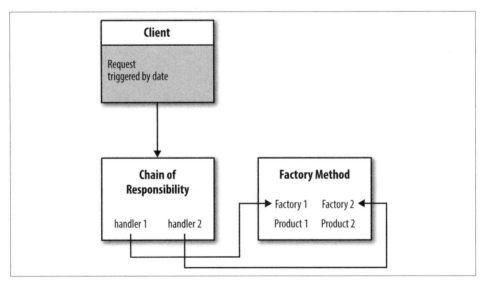

Figure 13-5. Chain of Responsibility handles requests through Factory Method

In practice, many developers use combinations of design patterns depending on the application needs. The Factory Method is commonly used with other patterns for making product requests.

This particular application is a weekly extra-credit assignment for students learning about world hunger. Beginning with a map that has had the major names of cities, rivers, oceans, and other identifying characteristics removed, a photo and a text write-up are added to the page. Students identify the correct country plus hunger, literacy, and gender breakdown, and return the answers for credit.

The Chain of Responsibility and Date-Driven Requests

Linking to an address for this application automatically launches a client through an *index.php* file. The `Client` then places the current date into a variable, `$queryNow`, which is passed to a `Request` helper class. Going through the Chain of Responsibility, the query finds the concrete handler that acts as a client to the Factory Method, which creates and displays the materials.

Why the Date Functions Changed: Temporal Tower of Babel

If you've ever created a worldwide date-sensitive application in PHP, you may be aware that some odd time zone rules apply (or don't apply). With PHP 5.4, the date object requires you to look up the time zone code at *php.net/manual/en/timezones.php* and place it in as a string literal in a variable to set the default time zone. For example, the following code is used in the `Client` to get the request variable set:

```
$tz= 'America/New_York';
date_default_timezone_set($tz);
$this->queryNow=getdate();
```

The time zone is set for the East Coast of the United States. Some countries, like India, have time zones that have half-hour offsets from UTC. China has a single time zone from Kashgar in the west to Beijing in the east, a distance of around 3,400 km (2,100 miles) that would easily span four time zones in the United States. To set your time zone from "Europe/Minsk" to "Australia/Tasmania" you'll need to look up the time zone identifier. (If you live in Indiana, expect to find eight time identifiers—"America/Indiana/Knox"—and both "America/Indiana/Indianapolis" and "America/Indianapolis"!) It's time to learn geography.

First, to establish an automatic takeoff, the following "trigger" file launches the `Client` and is saved as *index.php*:

```
<?php
//index.php
//trigger file
//This file can be replaced by
//wrapping this code around
//Client class
function __autoload($class_name)
{
    include $class_name . '.php';
}
```

```php
$worker=new Client();
?>
```

The Client also takes care of setting up the succession list in addition to creating a request from a date:

```php
<?php
//index.php acts as trigger
class Client
{
    private $queryNow;
    private $dateNow;

    public function __construct()
    {
        //Get the date in selected time zone
        //See php.net/manual/en/timezones.php
        $tz= 'America/New_York';
        date_default_timezone_set($tz);
        $this->queryNow=getdate();

            $d1 = new D1();
            $d2 = new D2();
            $d3 = new D3();
            $d4 = new D4();
            $d5 = new D5();
            $d6 = new D6();
            $d7 = new D7();
            $d8 = new D8();
            $d9 = new D9();
            $d10 = new D10();
            $d11 = new D11();
            $d12 = new D12();
            $d13 = new D13();
            $d14 = new D14();
            $d15 = new D15();

            $d1->setSuccessor($d2);
            $d2->setSuccessor($d3);
            $d3->setSuccessor($d4);
            $d4->setSuccessor($d5);
            $d5->setSuccessor($d6);
            $d6->setSuccessor($d7);
            $d7->setSuccessor($d8);
            $d8->setSuccessor($d9);
            $d9->setSuccessor($d10);
            $d10->setSuccessor($d11);
            $d11->setSuccessor($d12);
            $d12->setSuccessor($d13);
            $d13->setSuccessor($d14);
            $d14->setSuccessor($d15);
```

```php
            // Generate and process load requests
            $loadup = new Request($this->queryNow);
            $d1->handleRequest ($loadup);
        }
    }
?>
```

The classes D1 through D15 are the concrete handlers for the different dates set up in succession. If the first one (D1) doesn't match the request date, it keeps going until it finds the right date. The Request class is the same as used in the first example of the Chain of Responsibility and is used as a Client helper class:

```php
<?php
class Request
{
    private $value;

    public function __construct($service)
    {
        $this->value=$service;
    }

    public function getService()
    {
        return $this->value;
    }
}
?>
```

The handler participant is again an abstract class serving as an interface. It has the same methods but contains added properties for the date-request:

```php
<?php
    abstract class Handler
    {
        protected $hungerFactory;
        protected $successor;
        protected $monthNow;
        protected $dayNow;
        protected $handleNow;
        abstract public function handleRequest($request);
        abstract public function setSuccessor($nextService);
    }
?>
```

In turn, the concrete handlers that implement the concrete handling of requests have date ranges used to determine whether the concrete handler is the right one for the current job:

```php
<?php
class D1 extends Handler
{
    public function setSuccessor($nextService)
```

```
{
    $this->successor=$nextService;
}

public function handleRequest ($request)
{
    $dateCheck= $request->getService();
    $this->monthNow=intval($dateCheck['mon']);
    $this->dayNow=intval($dateCheck['mday']);

    //$this->handleNow is a Boolean based on
    //a Boolean expression with date ranges
    $this->handleNow=($this->monthNow == 9 && $this->dayNow >=15) &&
            ($this->monthNow == 9 && $this->dayNow <=22);

    if ($this->handleNow)
    {
            $this->hungerFactory=new HungerFactory();
        echo $this->hungerFactory->feedFactory(new C1());
    }
    else if ($this->successor != NULL)
    {
            $this->successor->handleRequest ($request);
    }
}
}
?>
```

Using a Boolean variable ($handleNow) and Boolean expression, the handler queries $handleNow, and if true, it is directed to a Factory Method that loads the necessary materials. At this point, the Chain of Responsibility concrete handler (D1 through D15) is a client making a request from the Factory Method. Figure 13-6 shows how the two patterns work together.

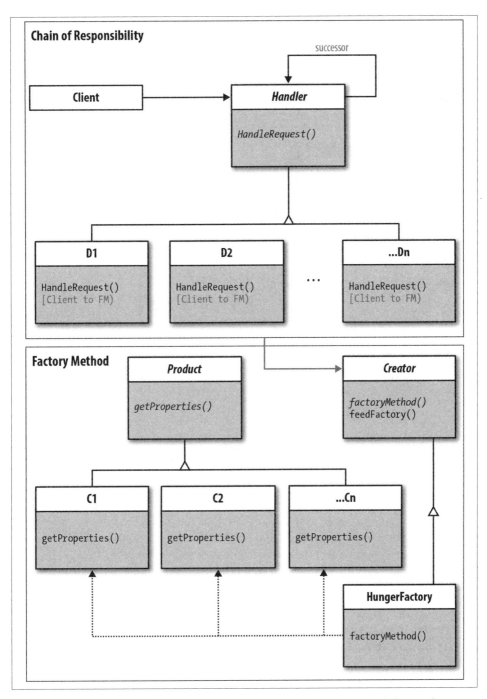

Figure 13-6. Class diagram showing link between Chain of Responsibility and Factory Method

The code at the linking point is in the Dn series of objects. The code that makes the request is no different from any client request:

```
$this->hungerFactory=new HungerFactory();
echo $this->hungerFactory->feedFactory(new C1());
```

This following section examines the role of the Factory Method design pattern called by the Chain of Responsibility concrete handler.

Factory Method Finishes Job

The Factory Method pattern works in a similar manner as one of the examples in Chapter 5 (see Figure 5-6) with slight differences. The fact that the request originated in the concrete handler rather than a class named "Client" makes no difference at all. As indicated in Figure 13-6, the handleRequest() method acts as a client.

The Creator and HungerFactory

Having identified the source of the client, the first step is to construct the Creator abstract class that acts as an interface for the Factory Method design:

```php
<?php
//Creator.php
abstract class Creator
{
    protected $countryProduct;
    protected abstract function factoryMethod(Product $product);

    public function feedFactory(Product $productNow)
    {
        $this->countryProduct=$productNow;
        $mfg= $this->factoryMethod($this->countryProduct);
        return $mfg;
    }
}
?>
```

Both the factoryMethod() function and the feedFactory() method use type hinting to ensure that the argument contains the Product interface. However, because the feed Factory() function is not abstract, all concrete implementations of the Creator automatically include it.

As you saw in Chapter 5, some implementations of the Factory Method use separate factories (concrete creators) for the different products. However, when the products are similar, the concrete creator can handle any number of different concrete products:

```php
<?php
//HungerFactory.php
class HungerFactory extends Creator
{
    private $country;
```

```php
    protected function factoryMethod(Product $product)
    {
        $this->country=$product;
        return($this->country->getProperties());
    }
}
?>
```

The `factoryMethod()` implementation is parameterized to accept a concrete product instance. In the concrete handlers (the clients for the factory), the parameter is determined in the Chain of Responsibility and sent to the Factory Method. The individual concrete products meet the original request sent through the Chain of Responsibility.

The product and individual countries

The end result displays a web page with a photo image, a map, and a short write-up. It is used in a class where students are studying world hunger and must identify the name of the country, the infant mortality rate, and gender equality based on differential literacy rates.

The `Product` interface has a single method, `getProperties()` used by the `HungerFactory` to get the requested product. The concrete product classes (C1 to C15) display the required parts:

```php
<?php
class C1 implements Product
{
    private $mfgProduct;
    private $formatHelper;
    private $countryNow;

    public function getProperties()
    {
        //Loads text writeup from external text file
        $this->countryNow = file_get_contents("../hunger/c01/clue.txt");

        $this->formatHelper=new FormatHelper();
        $this->mfgProduct=$this->formatHelper->addTop();
        //Load images
        $this->mfgProduct.="<img src='../hunger/c01/map.gif'  width='300'
                        height='322'>";
        $this->mfgProduct .="<img class='pixLeft' src='../hunger/c01/pic.jpg'
                        width='200' height='400'>";
        $this->mfgProduct .="<p>$this->countryNow</p>";
        $this->mfgProduct .=$this->formatHelper->closeUp();
        return $this->mfgProduct;
    }
}
?>
```

After putting together the product, it is returned to the client, which in this case is the concrete handler from the Chain of Responsibility segment of the application. Figure 13-7 shows the final product.

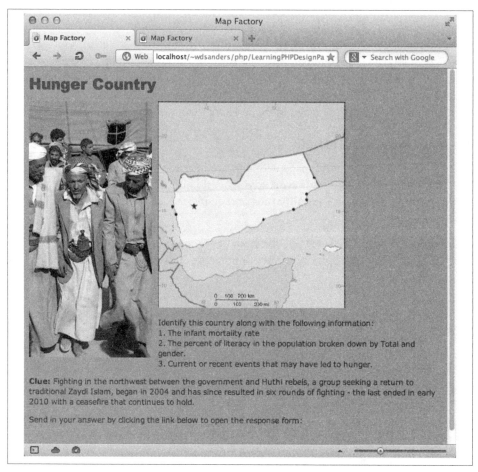

Figure 13-7. The concrete product display

The parts that make up the graphics and text are kept in a separate folder.

Helpers, resources, and style

The concrete product objects have external style sheets, folders for text and graphic files, and a helper class for formatting. Figure 13-8 shows the general arrangement vis-à-vis the general application.

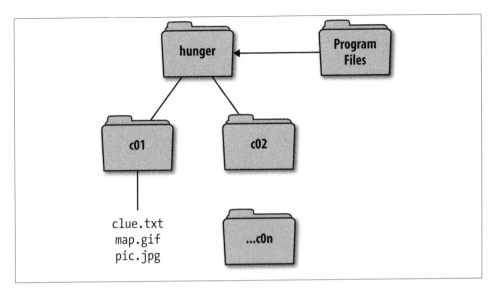

Figure 13-8. Resources

The main resource folder is named *hunger*. In it are files named *c01* through *c15*. Each of those folders, in turn, contain three files with identical names in all folders: *clue.txt*, *map.gif*, and *pic.jpg*. I can change the contents of any of the files without disrupting the program in any way. The only caveat is if the dimensions of the graphics change, the dimensions in the corresponding concrete product must change to match them.

The FormatHelper class reduces the amount of HTML used to create the output:

```php
<?php
class FormatHelper
{
    private $topper;
    private $bottom;

    public function addTop()
    {
        $this->topper="<!DOCTYPE html><html><head>
        <link rel='stylesheet' type='text/css' href='products.css'/>
        <meta charset='UTF-8'>
        <title>Map Factory</title>
        </head>
        <body>
        <header>Hunger Country </header>";
    }

    public function closeUp()
    {
        $this->bottom="<br/><a href='Answer.html' target='_blank'>Click for
                    Credit</a>";
```

```
        $this->bottom.="</body></html>";
    }
}
?>
```

Finally, the external style sheet (`products.css`) has to help bring the final product together so that it clearly communicates the information for the students:

```css
@charset "UTF-8";
/*C9DBF2,3B3E40,D9C6B0,8C7A70,BFACA4 */
/* CSS Document */
img
{
    padding: 10px 5px 0px 0px;
}

.pixRight
{
    float:right; margin: 0px 0px 5px 5px;
}

.pixLeft
{
    float:left; margin: 0px 5px 5px 0px;
}

header
{
    color:#900;
    font-size:24px;
    font-family:"Arial Black", Gadget, sans-serif;
}

body
{
    font-family:Verdana, Geneva, sans-serif;
    font-size:12px;
    background-color:#BFACA4;
    color:#3B3E40;
}

a
{
    text-decoration:none;
    color:#C9DBF2;
    font-weight:bold;
}

h1
{
    font-family:"Arial Black", Gadget, sans-serif;
    font-size:18px;
    background-color:#C9DBF2;
```

```
    color:#3B3E40;
}
```

With all those parts, good organization is important, and in the long run, it is extremely easy to change and add new material to this application.

Ease of Update

The most important feature of design patterns is that they allow the developer to make changes and add new materials without the whole thing falling down like a house of cards. Often, developers will attempt to save programming time for short-term goals, but in the long run, they end up having to refactor entire programs to make simple changes.

The hunger application in the previous section is a good example of how reuse and change is important. Because of the date timing, the application has to be changed every new term, but that's easy because all of the date queries are done in the D series (D1 to D15) classes as part of the Chain of Responsibility pattern. Likewise, the concrete products are easy to change because as long as the graphic dimensions are observed, all that needs to be changed are the new images. The names are constant (for example, *clue.txt*, *map.gif*) and so the developer does not have to worry about what the program is looking for in a given folder. If new materials are added, a new class for each addition must be added and a new folder for the resources needs to be added as well.

For whatever reason, the developer may decide to place the chain in a different order. This can be done simply by changing the succession in the original client. Nothing else needs to be changed. Whatever the plan, it is far easier to make changes using these design patterns than to attempt to compact code into the fewest lines possible. What may work in the short term decidedly does not in the long term.

CHAPTER 14

Building a Multidevice CMS with the Observer Pattern

If there were observers on Mars, they would
probably be amazed that we have survived
this long.

—Noam Chomsky

In dream consciousness... we make things happen
by wishing them, because we are not only the
observer of what we experience but also the creator.

—Pir Vilayat Khan

Knowledge is what we get when an observer,
preferably a scientifically trained observer,
provides us with a copy of reality that we can
all recognize.

—Christopher Lasch

Built-In Observer Interfaces

One of the many treats found within PHP 5.1.0 and up is a set of interfaces that can be used with the Observer design pattern. This chapter will look at an Observer pattern beginning from scratch without any built-in features, but to get started we'll have a short overview of the `SplObserver` interface along with the `SplSubject` and the `SplObject Storage` interfaces that make building an Observer pattern with PHP a snap. "SPL" is shorthand for *Standard PHP Library* and consists of a collection of interfaces and classes used to solve standard problems.

However, before we get ahead of ourselves, you need some idea of what the Observer pattern is and what it does. Fortunately, its class diagram is quite detailed, and many of the features prized in the Model-View-Controller (MVC) pattern can be found in the

Observer. (You might even think of the pattern as an alternative to the MVC.) At the root of the Observer are Subject and Observer interfaces. The Subject holds a given state and the observers "subscribe" to the subject to be informed of the current state. You can think of it as a blog with many subscribers—one set of information is routinely updated for a variety of users who subscribe or regularly read the blog. Each time the blog is changed (its state changes), all of the subscribers "are informed." Figure 14-1 shows the Observer class diagram.

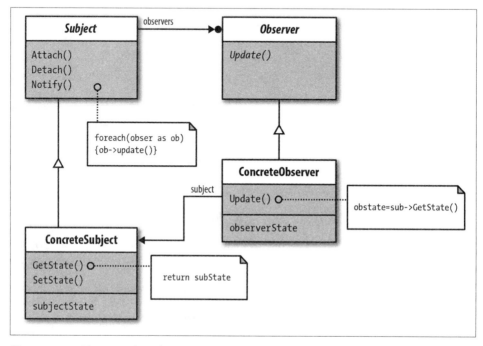

Figure 14-1. Observer class diagram

One of the more interesting and possibly perplexing features of this pattern is the Subject's methods. While the italicized title *"Subject"* title indicates an interface (an abstract class in this case), abstract methods are italicized as well. However, as you can see in Figure 14-1, none of the methods are italicized. It is clear which methods Subject generates, and the Notify() method even has pseudocode to help out. You will find several different implementations of the Observer pattern, and even the one built into PHP has its own spin.

When to Use the Observer Pattern

The Observer pattern was designed so that a single object could keep track of a state and when the state changed, all of the subscribing objects would be informed. In situations where you need consistency in one state but may have several different views of a given state, the Observer pattern is both appropriate and helpful. You can maintain consistency while keeping down the number of objects that must create a given state on their own.

The Observer pattern makes intuitive sense. Why should more than one object do the work to create or keep track of a given state? If one object can do the job and then inform others that may use the state, it makes a lot more sense.

One ongoing issue for PHP developers and designers is taking one set of data in the form of text, numbers, and graphics and formatting them for different devices for web presentation. Mobile devices ranging from smartphones to tablets of varying sizes, and nonmobile devices like desktop computers and laptops all need different design configurations. However, they need the same data. Figure 14-2 illustrates this relationship.

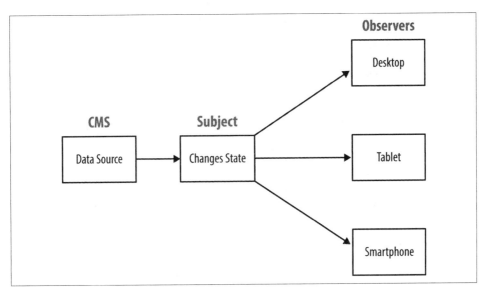

Figure 14-2. Observer pattern used with CMS

Connected to a content management system (CMS), the Observer design pattern is a way to make sure that all configurations are presenting the same materials. Each observer can use the identical data, and all the developer and designer have to concern themselves with is setting up the content for the different devices and getting the data information to the Subject participant.

Using SPL with the Observer Pattern

The three SPL interfaces/classes that can be employed usefully with the Observer design pattern are the following:

- SplSubject
- SplObserver
- SplObjectStorage

A quick review of each shows its structure in relationship to the Observer design pattern. Figure 14-3 gives a quick conceptual layout.

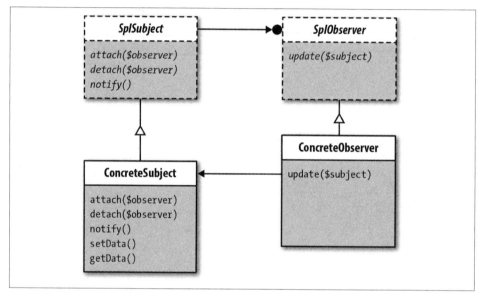

Figure 14-3. Observer class diagram with SPL elements

Compare the SPL Observer class diagram in Figure 14-3 with the GoF version in Figure 14-1. All of the same parts are there, but the SPL diagram has more abstractions.

SplSubject

The SplSubject interface has three abstract methods similar to the ones found in the original Observer class diagram. However, SplSubject is an interface, whereas the most likely implementation of the original Subject participant is an abstract class because its methods are not abstract.

The *PHP Manual* lists the methods for SplSubject as the following:

```
abstract public void attach ( SplObserver $observer )
abstract public void detach ( SplObserver $observer )
abstract public void notify ( void )
```

The void term simply means that the methods do not return anything. In a standard PHP interface, the function keyword would be included as well. Here's what it would look like if you created the interface yourself:

```
public function attach(SplObserver $observer);
public function detach(SplObserver $observer);
public function notify();
```

The SplSubject interface can be implemented without having to create a Subject interface or abstract class. Importantly, the interface specifies that the data type of the $observer must be a SplObserver object in both the attach() and detach() methods parameters.

SplObserver

The SplObserver interface has a single method, update(). It is presented as the following:

```
abstract public void update ( SplSubject $subject )
```

In standard PHP interface formatting, that would be:

```
public function update(SplSubject $subject);
```

The update() method is crucial to the Observer pattern because it gets the latest changes in the Subject state to the observer instance. However, the original GoF version does not include a parameter for a Subject data type, and in further PHP Observer implementations in this chapter, you will see implementations that do not include such parameters and the implications of doing so.

SplObjectStorage

The SplObjectStorage class has no inherent relationship to the Observer design pattern, but it is a handy way to attach and detach observer instances from a subject instance. While the SplObjectStorage class is described as providing a map from objects to data or, by ignoring data, an object set, I like to think of it as an array with built-in attach() and detach() methods. This class provides a simple way of attaching and detaching observers from a subject object sending out state-change notifications.

The SPL Concrete Subject

The subject needs to attach and detach observers and to notify subscribers (attached observers) of the change. A private variable $observers encapsulates the property. In this implementation, the $observers property is instantiated as a SplObjectStorage object. Think of it as something like an array. Then, individual $observer instances are *attached* as SplObserver objects (The storage unit is $observers that stores individual $observer instances.) Figure 14-4 shows this arrangement.

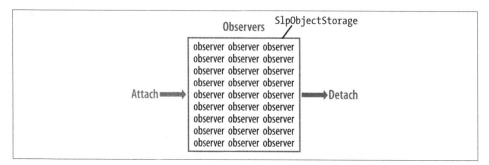

Figure 14-4. Concrete observer instances in SplObjectStorage, Observers

What makes the SplObjectStorage valuable is its built-in attach() and detach() methods, which make it easy to program which observer instances will "subscribe" and "unsubscribe" to update notifications:

```
<?
class ConcreteSubject implements SplSubject
{
    private $observers;
    private $data;

    public function setObservers()
    {
        $this->observers=new SplObjectStorage();
    }

    public function attach(SplObserver $observer)
    {
        $this->observers->attach($observer);
    }

    public function detach(SplObserver $observer)
    {
        $this->observers->detach($observer);
    }

    public function notify()
    {
        foreach ($this->observers as $observer) {

            $observer->update($this);
        }
    }
}
```

```
    public function setData($dataNow)
    {
        $this->data=$dataNow;
    }

    public function getData()
    {
        return $this->data;
    }
}
?>
```

Getter and setter methods are not part of the SplSubject interface, but they are part of the design pattern and so need to be added. The setter method, setData(), includes a parameter for any kind of data to be added. The getter method, getData(), stores the current subject state and is used by the concrete observer to update observer data.

The setObservers() method is added as well. Rather than setting the SplObjectStor age() instance in a constructor function that would require a new instance of the ConcreteSubject class or placing it inside the setData() method, the separate setOb servers() method provides a looser coupling and allows for the possibility of more than one set of observers.

The SPL Concrete Observer

The concrete observer is both simple and possibly complex. In this example, it fulfills the single function of updating attached observer instances. The update() method is implemented with code hinting using the SplSubject interface as a method parameter. This forces the developer to include an SplSubject instance in all update() calls:

```
<?
class ConcreteObserver implements SplObserver
{
    public function update(SplSubject $subject)
    {
        echo $subject->getData() . "<br />";
    }
}
?>
```

Given that concrete observers need only a single update() method, it is not too difficult to see that concrete observers can be made up of more robust classes or even parts of other design patterns. Further on in this chapter, while developing a CMS using an Observer pattern, you will see far more useful observers.

The SPL Client

The "SPL" Client class is just a standard client. The client makes several requests to concrete subjects and observers based on SPL interfaces but implements no SPL classes or interfaces itself.

In this example, the Client creates a single subject instance and three concrete observer instances. Then it sets a new state using the setData() method and attaches the three observers to the subject. Finally, it calls the concrete subject instance notify() method to send the current state to the subscribing observers:

```php
<?php
//Client
function __autoload($class_name)
{
    include $class_name . '.php';
}
//
class Client
{
    public function __construct()
    {
        echo "<p>Create three new concrete observers, a new concrete subject:
            </p>";
        $ob1 = new ConcreteObserver();
        $ob2 = new ConcreteObserver();
        $ob3 = new ConcreteObserver();

        $subject = new ConcreteSubject();
        $subject->setObservers();
        $subject->setData("Here's your data!");
        $subject->attach($ob1);
        $subject->attach($ob2);
        $subject->attach($ob3);

        $subject->notify();

        echo "<p>Detach observer ob3. Now only ob1 and ob2 are notified:</p>";
        $subject->detach($ob3);
        $subject->notify();

        echo "<p>Reset data and reattach ob3 and detach ob2--only ob 1 and 3 are
            notified:</p>";
        $subject->setData("More data that only ob1 and ob3 need.");
        $subject->attach($ob3);
        $subject->detach($ob2);
        $subject->notify();
    }
}
```

```
$worker=new Client();
?>
```

The output from the `Client` is as follows:

```
Create three new concrete observers, a new concrete subject:
Here's your data!
Here's your data!
Here's your data!

Detach observer ob3. Now only ob1 and ob2 are notified:

Here's your data!
Here's your data!

Reset data and reattach ob3 and detach ob2--only ob 1 and 3 are notified:

More data that only ob1 and ob3 need.
More data that only ob1 and ob3 need.
```

One possible source of confusion may exist in differentiating the `ConcreteSubject` `->attach()` and `ConcreteSubject->detach()` methods from the `SplObjectStorage` `->attach()` and `SplObjectStorage->detach()` methods. The `ConcreteSubject` class wraps the `SplObjectStorage` `attach()` and `detach()` methods in its own `attach()` and `detach()` methods. The following pseudocode shows a class version of how the `ConcreteSubject` created its attach/detach methods:

```
public function attach(SplObserver $observer)
    {
        SplObjectStorage->attach($observer);
    }

public function detach(SplObserver $observer)
    {
        SplObjectStorage->detach($observer);
    }
```

Changing the concrete subject class attach/detach methods to some other name would probably be equally confusing, so just understand that built-in SPL attach/detach methods are used to create `ConcreteSubject` attach/detach methods.

Free Range PHP and the Observer Pattern

Moving now from some of the few SPL interfaces in PHP designed specifically for a design pattern to using non-SPL participants, you can get an alternative view of the Observer closer to the original structure as shown in Figure 14-1. The main differences are the following:

- The `Subject` participant is an abstract class instead of an interface.

- The notify() method is implemented in the Subject instead of in the concrete subject.
- The concrete subject uses an array object instead of an SplObjectStorage object to store observer instances.

The observer participants are virtually identical to the SPL ones except that the Subject is an abstract class (instead of an interface) that includes a concrete notify() method. Only slight implementation differences, such as including a $currentState property in the concrete observer, are found.

The Abstract Subject Class and ConcreteSubject Implementation

Unlike the SPL implementation where the Subject participant is an interface and all methods are abstract, this implementation is close to the original by GoF and employs implemented attach/detach methods. The attach/detach methods include an Observer interface as a parameter that is structurally the same as using the SplObserver as a parameter in the SPL example:

```php
<?php
//Subject.php
abstract class Subject
{
    protected $stateNow;
    protected $observers=array();

    public function attachObser(Observer $obser)
    {
        array_push($this->observers,$obser);
    }

    public function detachObser(Observer $obser)
    {
        $position=0;
        foreach($this->observers as $viewer)
        {
            ++$position;
            if($viewer==$obser)
            {
                array_splice($this->observers,($position),1);
            }
        }
    }

    protected function notify()
    {
        foreach($this->observers as $viewer)
        {
            $viewer->update($this);
        }
```

```php
        }
    }
?>
```

The notify() method is concrete as well, and is inherited and used by the Subject child classes. As a result, the concrete subject does not have to implement attachObser(), detachObser(), or notify(), but it uses the methods without any additional code in the ConcreteSubject:

```php
<?php
//ConcreteSubject.php
class ConcreteSubject extends Subject
{
    public function setState($stateSet)
    {
        $this->stateNow=$stateSet;
        $this->notify();
    }

    public function getState()
    {
        return $this->stateNow;
    }
}
?>
```

As you can see in the detachObser() method, multiple observers must be notified by iterating through the $observers array. Of course, you can use the SplObjectStor age class even though you're not using the SPL subject and observer. In that way, you could use a SplObjectStorage object for holding the attached observers instead of an array. In addition, you could also use the attach/detach methods built into the SplOb jectStorage class.

Observer and Multiple Concrete Observers

Up to this point, a single concrete observer has been used with an observer interface. In this implementation, the Observer pattern uses more than a single observer type. In the most rudimentary way, the multiple concrete observers represent displays that will be shown on a desktop computer, an Internet-connected tablet, and a smartphone. The subject generates a single graphic URL, and the different observers use that data to generate the graphic provided in the same subject state.

The Observer is an interface with a single method, update(). It is virtually identical to the SplObserver:

```php
<?php
//Observer.php
interface Observer
{
    function update(Subject $subject);
```

```php
}
?>
```

The abstract method update() awaits the child classes to provide it with a specific implementation. In the following implementations of the concrete observer, the differences are minor but important for development, now and later.

ConcreteObserverDT (Desktop implementation)

```php
<?php
//ConcreteObserverDT.php
class ConcreteObserverDT implements Observer
{
    private $currentState;

    public function update(Subject $subject)
    {
        $this->currentState=$subject->getState();
        echo "<img src='desktop/$this->currentState'><br />";
    }
}
?>
```

ConcreteObserverTablet (Tablet implementation)

```php
<?php
//ConcreteObserverTablet.php
class ConcreteObserverTablet implements Observer
{
    private $currentState;

    public function update(Subject $subject)
    {
        $this->currentState=$subject->getState();
        echo "<img src='tablet/$this->currentState'><br />";
    }
}
?>
```

ConcreteObserverPhone (Smartphone implementation)

```php
<?php
//ConcreteObserverPhone.php
class ConcreteObserverPhone implements Observer
{
    private $currentState;

    public function update(Subject $subject)
    {
        $this->currentState=$subject->getState();
        echo "<img src='phone/$this->currentState'><br />";
    }
```

```
}
?>
```

As you can see, the differences lie in the directory where the image can be found. For example, the table implementation uses the following line:

```
echo "<img src='tablet/$this->currentState'><br />";
```

The others use directories named after the particular type of device that's in use because whatever message the subscribed-to subject generates as a current state is going to be the same to all subscribers. In this particular implementation, the current state of the ConcreteSubject is an image URL, and the wrapper for the image is an HTML line using the <img> tag.

The Client

The Client in this context is most likely to come from a source that recognizes a device as one of three types: desktop, tablet, or phone. For the purposes of illustration, the following client calls up all three to illustrate how they would appear in different sizes:

```
<?php
//Client.php
function __autoload($class_name)
{
    include $class_name . '.php';
}
class Client
{
    public function __construct()
    {
        $sub=new ConcreteSubject();

        $ob1=new ConcreteObserverPhone();
        $ob2=new ConcreteObserverTablet();
        $ob3=new ConcreteObserverDT();

        $sub->attachObser($ob1);
        $sub->attachObser($ob2);
        $sub->attachObser($ob3);
        $sub->setState("decoCar.png");
    }
}
$worker=new Client();
?>
```

A single concrete subject and three instances of three different concrete observers make up the set of instances. All three observer instances use the same subject source for data. Using the concrete subject's setState() method, the Client sets the current state that will be used by all observers. Figure 14-5 shows the results in a tablet device.

Figure 14-5. Different concrete observers generate different sized images from the same concrete subject state

As the gradations in mobile and desktop devices become finer, a good site may need more sets of bitmap graphics to optimize user experience. Likewise, more CSS files may be required to optimize text viewing on an array of devices. However, by having a single data source and multiple subscribers, keeping track of the current desired state is much easier using a single concrete subject with multiple subscribers.

Making a Simple CMS

The "CMS" being built will use a MySQL database to store data used for a simple database. A summary of the design pattern is stored in a MySQL text field, and finally, the URL to a graphic is to be stored in a third field. The table will also include an automatically generated field for a unique numbered record stored as an integer.

The Observer pattern will be used to get the information from the table and send it to selected observers. The single data set stored in an array goes out to observers viewed by a desktop computer, a tablet, or a smartphone. An HTML selection form provides the user with selections of available patterns generated as web pages through PHP. The phone viewing uses jQuery Mobile to optimize viewer experience. The tablet view and desktop view are in two columns, while the phone view is a single column.

CMS Utilities

To get started, create a MySQL table and a module to enter and update the data for the web pages. First, create the table using the connection utility interface and class that has been employed throughout the book. They are listed first.

CMS table

```php
<?php
//Filename: IConnectInfo.php
interface IConnectInfo
{
    const HOST ="localhost";
    const UNAME ="uname";
    const PW ="password";
    const DBNAME = "dataBase";

    public function doConnect();
}

?>
```

The output to alert the user to a successful connection is commented out, since this same connection class is used with other MySQL connections that make up the program:

```php
<?php
include_once('IConnectInfo.php');
```

```php
class UniversalConnect implements IConnectInfo
{
    private static $server=IConnectInfo::HOST;
    private static $currentDB= IConnectInfo::DBNAME;
    private static $user= IConnectInfo::UNAME;
    private static $pass= IConnectInfo::PW;
    private static $hookup;

    public function doConnect()
    {
        self::$hookup=mysqli_connect(self::$server, self::$user, self::$pass,
                    self::$currentDB);
        if(self::$hookup)
        {
            //comments for debugging
        }
        elseif (mysqli_connect_error(self::$hookup))
        {
            echo('Here is why it failed: '  . mysqli_connect_error());
        }
        return self::$hookup;
    }
}
?
```

The following code creates the table:

```php
<?php
include_once('UniversalConnect.php');
class CreateTable
{
    private $tableMaster;
    private $hookup;

    public function __construct()
    {
        $this->tableMaster="cms";
        $this->hookup=UniversalConnect::doConnect();

        $drop = "DROP TABLE IF EXISTS $this->tableMaster";

        if($this->hookup->query($drop) === true)
        {
            printf("Old table %s has been dropped.<br/>",$this->tableMaster);
        }

        $sql = "CREATE TABLE $this->tableMaster (
            id          SERIAL,
            dpHeader    NVARCHAR(50),
            textBlock   TEXT,
            imageURL    NVARCHAR(60),
                        PRIMARY KEY (id))";
```

```
            if($this->hookup->query($sql) === true)
            {
                printf("Table $this->tableMaster has been created successfully.
                    <br/>");
            }
            $this->hookup->close();
        }
    }
    $worker=new CreateTable();
    ?>
```

Once the table is in place, you will need to add data to it that will be used in the little design pattern web pages.

CMS data entry and update

The CMS table stores the required data used for the web pages. The UI, *Admin.html*, is a simple HTML document calling up PHP classes to enter and update the text write-ups:

```
<!doctype html>
<!-- Admin.html -->
<html>
<head>
<meta charset="UTF-8">
<link rel="stylesheet" type="text/css" href="desktop.css">
<title>CMS Admin Module</title>
</head>
<body>
<h1>CMS Administrative Module</h1>
<h2>Data Entry</h2>
<form action="DataEntry.php" method="post">
  <input type="text" name="dpHeader">
   Design pattern name<br />
  Write up for design pattern:<br />
  <textarea name="textBlock" cols="48" rows="16"></textarea>
  <p />
  <input type="text" name="imageURL">
   Graphic URL
  <p />
  <input type="submit" name="entry" value="Enter Page Data">
</form>
<h2>Data Update</h2>
<form action="DataUpdate.php" method="post">
  <input type="text" name="dpUpdate">
   Design pattern name to update<br />
  New write-up for design pattern:<br />
  <textarea name="newData" cols="48" rows="16"></textarea>
  <p />
  <input type="submit" name="update" value="Update Page Data">
</form>
```

```
    </body>
    </html>
```

The data input simply enters the appropriate data into the three fields where the header, body text, and image go in each page.

```php
<?php
//DataEntry.php
include_once('UniversalConnect.php');
class DataEntry
{
    private $tableMaster;
    private $hookup;
    private $sql;

    public function __construct()
    {
        $this->tableMaster="cms";
        $this->hookup=UniversalConnect::doConnect();

        if ( $_POST['dpHeader'] )
        $dpHeader=$this->hookup->real_escape_string($_POST['dpHeader']);
        if ( $_POST['textBlock'] )
        $textBlock=$this->hookup->real_escape_string($_POST['textBlock']);
        if ( $_POST['imageURL'] )
        $imageURL=$this->hookup->real_escape_string($_POST['imageURL']);

        $this->sql = "INSERT INTO $this->tableMaster
            (dpHeader,textBlock,imageURL) VALUES
            ('$dpHeader','$textBlock','$imageURL')";

        if($this->hookup->query($this->sql))
        {
            printf("Successful data entry for table: $this->tableMaster <br/>");
        }
        elseif ( ($result = $this->hookup->query($this->sql))===false )
        {
            printf("Invalid query: %s <br/> Whole query: %s <br/>",
                    $this->hookup->error, $this->sql);
            exit();
        }
        $this->hookup->close();
    }
}
$worker=new DataEntry();
?>
```

The second administrative tool for the CMS is an update for the content write-up about a design pattern. One of the problems users encounter with long, detailed write-ups is space. Even with a single column, the write-ups seem to always need tweaking, and so this tool allows for all the tweaking a web administrator could want.

```php
<?php
//DataUpdate.php
include_once('UniversalConnect.php');
class DataUpdate
{
    private $tableMaster;
    private $hookup;
    private $sql;

    public function __construct()
    {
        $this->tableMaster="cms";
        $this->hookup=UniversalConnect::doConnect();

        if ( isset($_POST['dpUpdate']) )
        $dpHeader=$this->hookup->real_escape_string($_POST['dpUpdate']);
        if ( $_POST['newData'] )
        $newData=$this->hookup->real_escape_string($_POST['newData']);

        $changeField="textBlock";
        $this->sql = "UPDATE $this->tableMaster SET $changeField='$newData'
                    WHERE dpHeader='$dpHeader'";

        if ($result = $this->hookup->query($this->sql))
        {
            echo "$changeField changed to:<br /> $newData";
        }
        else
        {
            echo "Change failed: " . $hookup->error;
        }
    }
}
$worker=new DataUpdate();
?>
```

Finally, the CSS for viewers using desktop computers is set for two columns—one for the graphic and one for the write-up—but it works well for the single-column administrative UI as well:

```css
//CSS
@charset "UTF-8";
/* desktop.css */
/* CSS Document */
/* 595241,B8AE9C,FFFFFF,ACCFCC,8A0917 */
body
{
    font-family:Verdana, Geneva, sans-serif;
    background-color:#ffffff;
    color:#595241;
    padding-right:10px;
}
```

```
h1
{
    font-family:"Arial Black", Gadget, sans-serif;
    text-align:center;
    color:#8A0917;
    background-color:#ACCFCC;
}

img
{
    padding-right:10px;
    float:left;
}
```

The CSS file, *desktop.css*, is also used with requests recognized as nonmobile, so future references should use the same file.

The Multiple Device Observer

From the previous examples in this chapter, you should be familiar with the basic structure of the Observer pattern. Given that the CMS portion of the plan stores and updates data for web pages, this part of the project retrieves the data and places them on those pages configured for different viewing devices: smartphone, tablet, or desktop. In order to get an overview of the entire project and the role of the Observer design pattern, Figure 14-6 shows a file diagram with all of the different objects and related parts.

The project is divided into three groups: the HTML UI, the PHP Observer pattern, and Helper objects. The rest of this section explains how the parts work together. The following shows the sequence of the object communications:

1. User requests web page through HTML UI.
2. Request is forwarded to SniffClient, which determines the viewer device.
3. Concrete observer instance is created based on viewer device.
4. Concrete subject instance attaches observer (determined by device).
5. Current state from MySQL data is set by page selected by user by the ConcreteSubject class.
6. Subscribing (attached) observers receive data from concrete subject.
7. The concrete observer takes the state information from the concrete subject and displays page on screen.

Of course, all of the requests are transparent to the user.

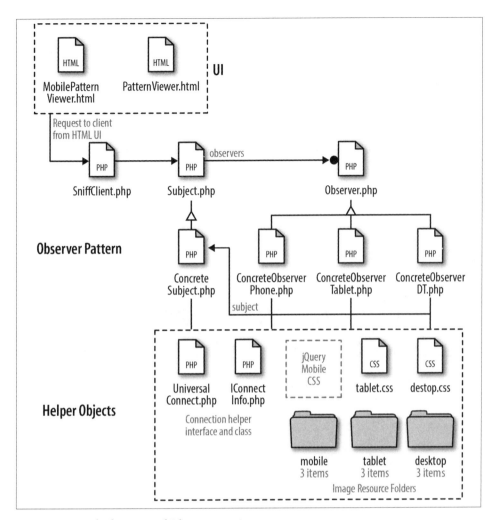

Figure 14-6. File diagram of Observer project

Two HTML UI documents

In order to avoid typing errors in requesting a page (a design pattern), the design patterns are selected using radio buttons:

```
<!doctype html>
<html>
<head>
<meta charset="UTF-8">
<link rel="stylesheet" type="text/css" href="desktop.css">
<title>Design Pattern Summary Viewer</title>
</head>
<body>
```

```
<h1>Select Pattern</h1>
<h2>Available Patterns</h2>
<form action="SniffClient.php" method="post">
  <input type="radio" name="dp" id="tm" value="Template Method"  />
  <label for="tm">Template Method</label>
  <br/>
  <input type="radio" name="dp" id="bld" value="Builder"  />
  <label for="bld">Builder</label>
  <br/>
  <input type="radio" name="dp" id="fm" value="Factory Method"  />
  <label for="fm">Factory Method</label>
  <p/>
  <input type="submit" value="View Pattern">
</form>
</body>
</html>
```

Figure 14-7 shows the UI.

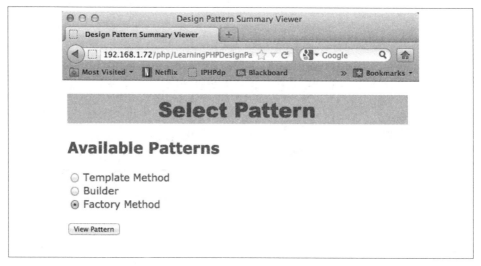

Figure 14-7. HTML UI for requesting web pages

Because reading the choices and making a selection on a mobile device was difficult using the general UI shown in Figure 14-7, a second UI was developed for mobile devices. Fortunately, a whole set of mobile device formats is available from jQuery Mobile (*http://jquerymobile.com*), and they were incorporated into a second UI for phone-size devices:

```html
<!DOCTYPE html>
<html>
<head>
<title>Mobile Viewer</title>
<meta name="viewport" content="width=device-width, initial-scale=1">
<link rel="stylesheet" href="http://code.jquery.com/mobile/1.2.0
                        /jquery.mobile-1.2.0.min.css" />
<script src="http://code.jquery.com/jquery-1.8.2.min.js"></script>
<script src="http://code.jquery.com/mobile/1.2.0/jquery.mobile-1.2.0.min.js">
            </script>
</head>
<body>
<div data-role="page">
  <div data-role="header">
    <h1>Design Patterns</h1>
  </div>
  <form action="SniffClient.php" method="post">
    <fieldset data-role="controlgroup">
      <legend> Select Pattern:</legend>
      <input type="radio" name="dp" id="tm" value="Template Method" />
      <label for="tm">Template Method</label>
      <input type="radio" name="dp" id="bld" value="Builder"  />
      <label for="bld">Builder</label>
      <input type="radio" name="dp" id="fm" value="Factory Method"  />
      <label for="fm">Factory Method</label>
    </fieldset>
    <input type="submit" data-theme="e" value="View Pattern">
  </form>
  <div data-role="footer"> PHP Patterns</div>
</div>
</body>
</html>
```

Figure 14-8 shows how the mobile UI appears on an iPhone.

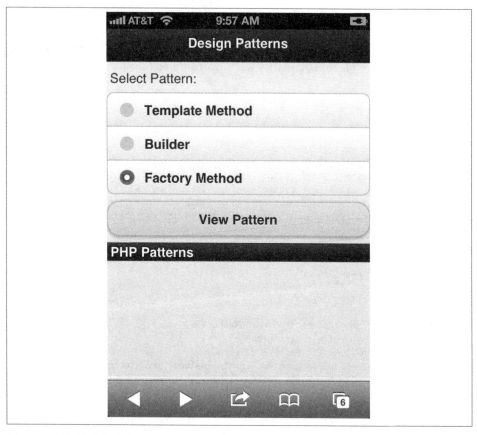

Figure 14-8. Mobile UI

Both UIs work the same. The user selects a pattern to view and then taps a button that generates the page. Unfortunately, the UI is not automatically selected as the viewing pages are.

The sniffer client

Because the request is optimized on the basis of the user's device, the first job of the client is to determine which device is in use. The SniffClient class selects from a small subset of mobile devices with a default value of a desktop device:

```php
<?php
//User agent as property of object
function __autoload($class_name)
{
    include $class_name . '.php';
}
class SniffClient
{
```

```php
private $userAgent;
private $mobile=false;
private $deviceObserver;
private $dpNow;
private $sub;

public function __construct()
{
    if (isset($_POST['dp'] ))
        $this->dpNow=$_POST['dp'];
    $this->sub=new ConcreteSubject();
    $this->userAgent=$_SERVER['HTTP_USER_AGENT'];
    if(stripos($this->userAgent,'iphone'))
    {
        $this->mobile=true;
        $this->deviceObserver=new ConcreteObserverPhone();
    }
    if(stripos($this->userAgent,'android'))
    {
        $this->mobile=true;
        $this->deviceObserver=new ConcreteObserverPhone();
    }
    if(stripos($this->userAgent,'blackberry'))
    {
        $this->mobile=true;
        $this->deviceObserver=new ConcreteObserverPhone();
    }
    if(stripos($this->userAgent,'ipad'))
    {
        $this->mobile=true;
        $this->deviceObserver=new ConcreteObserverTablet();
    }
    if(stripos($this->userAgent,'trident'))
    {
        $this->mobile=true;
        $this->deviceObserver=new ConcreteObserverTablet();
    }
    if(stripos($this->userAgent,'kindle fire'))
    {
        $this->mobile=true;
        $this->deviceObserver=new ConcreteObserverTablet();
    }
    if(stripos($this->userAgent,'silk'))
    {
        $this->mobile=true;
        $this->deviceObserver=new ConcreteObserverTablet();
    }

    if(!$this->mobile)
    {
        $this->deviceObserver=new ConcreteObserverDT();
    }
```

```
            $this->sub->attachObser($this->deviceObserver);
            $this->sub->setState($this->dpNow);
        }
    }

    $worker=new SniffClient();

    ?>
```

The client is simple and could be cast as a Chain of Responsibility pattern with new handlers added as needed. However, to show how an Observer pattern can be used with a simple CMS and device-sensitive functionality, this client demonstrates the important capabilities.

The Subject classes

The interface for this Observer implementation uses an abstract class but with concrete methods for attaching and detaching observers. Likewise, the notify() method is fully implemented and will be used by the ConcreteSubject class:

```php
<?php
//Subject.php
abstract class Subject
{
    protected $observers=array();

    public function attachObser(Observer $obser)
    {
        array_push($this->observers,$obser);
    }

    public function detachObser(Observer $obser)
    {
        $position=0;
        foreach($this->observers as $viewer)
        {
            ++$position;
            if($viewer==$obser)
            {
                array_splice($this->observers,($position),1);
            }
        }
    }

    protected function notify()
    {
        foreach($this->observers as $viewer)
        {
            $viewer->update($this);
        }
    }
```

```
        }
    ?>
```

The ConcreteSubject class in this application connects to the cms table to get the data required to meet the request from the user. The attach/detach methods are the same as used in prior examples, but the setState() method is quite different than in previous examples:

```php
<?php
//ConcreteSubject.php
class ConcreteSubject extends Subject
{
    private $hookup;
    private $tableMaster;
    private $designPattern;
    private $stateSet=array();

    public function setState($dpNow)
    {
        $this->designPattern=strtolower($dpNow);
        $this->tableMaster="cms";
        $this->hookup=UniversalConnect::doConnect();

        //Create Query Statement
        $sql = "SELECT * FROM $this->tableMaster WHERE dpheader=
                '$this->designPattern'";
        //Add appropriate data from MySQL table to $stateSet array
        if ($result = $this->hookup->query($sql))
        {
            while($row=$result->fetch_assoc())
            {
                    $this->stateSet[0]=$row["dpHeader"];
                    $this->stateSet[1]=$row["textBlock"];
                    $this->stateSet[2]=$row["imageURL"];
            }
            $result->close();
        }
    $this->hookup->close();
    //The update() method is part of notify()
    //implemented in Subject as concrete method.
    $this->notify();
    }

    public function getState()
    {
        return $this->stateSet;
    }
}
?>
```

All of the required data is placed into an array ($stateSet) and then made available through the getState() method to attached observers.

Multiple concrete observers

The Observer interface is unchanged from previous examples:

```php
<?php
//Observer.php
interface Observer
{
    function update(Subject $subject);
}
?>
```

The `update()` method expects a Subject instance as an argument, but otherwise no other methods are declared.

The implementation of the `Observer` interface is another story. Each of the concrete observers uses the same data from the subject, but they create very different pages.

The mobile phone observer. The greatest problem with generating pages for mobile phones is the size of the text and graphics. Using CSS and JavaScript, it is possible to create dynamically sized text and buttons that have a viable phone web page. However, by using jQuery Mobile, a lot of the work has been done. So the `ConcreteObserver` Phone class uses the prebuilt jQuery Mobile for phone formatting, as shown in the following:

```php
<?php
//ConcreteObserverPhone.php
class ConcreteObserverPhone implements Observer
{
    private $currentState=array();
    private $dpHeader;
    private $bodytext;
    private $imageURL;

    public function update(Subject $subject)
    {
        $this->currentState=$subject->getState();
        $this->dpHeader=$this->currentState[0];
        $this->bodytext=$this->currentState[1];
        $this->imageURL=$this->currentState[2];
        $this->doMobile();
    }

    private function doMobile()
    {
$showPage = <<<MOBILE
    <html>
        <head>
            <title>Mobile Page</title>
            <meta name="viewport" content="width=device-width, initial-scale=1">
            <link rel="stylesheet" href="http://code.jquery.com/mobile/1.2.0/
```

```
                                        jquery.mobile-1.2.0.min.css" />
                <script src="http://code.jquery.com/jquery-1.8.2.min.js"></script>
                <script src="http://code.jquery.com/mobile/1.2.0/
                           jquery.mobile-1.2.0.min.js"></script>
        </head>
    <body>

        <div data-role="page">
        <div data-role="header">
            <h1>$this->dpHeader</h1>
        </div>

        <div data-role="content">
        <p>$this->bodytext</p>
        <img src="mobile/$this->imageURL" alt="image urls" width="100%">
        </div>
        </div>

    </body>
    </html>
MOBILE;
    echo $showPage;
    }
}
?>
```

Figure 14-9 shows a page formatted for a mobile phone in an iPhone. As you can see, the text is sufficiently large to easily read without having to adjust the size.

A useful tool for formatting any HTML page within a PHP file uses the heredoc (here document) formatting. Basically, the code within a heredoc container accepts all formatting, including double and single quotation marks and PHP variables. It has the following format:

```
$stringVar = <<<CATCHER
<html>
  <body>
   <h1>Header</h1>
   Text that has dangerous "quotes" and outrageous ideas, even $variables.
  </body>
</html>
CATCHER;
echo $stringVar;
```

The heredoc <<< operator is used only at the beginning of the container. The $string Var is assigned the literals within the CATCHER container, making it very easy to dynamically generate code that contains a lot of text or code.

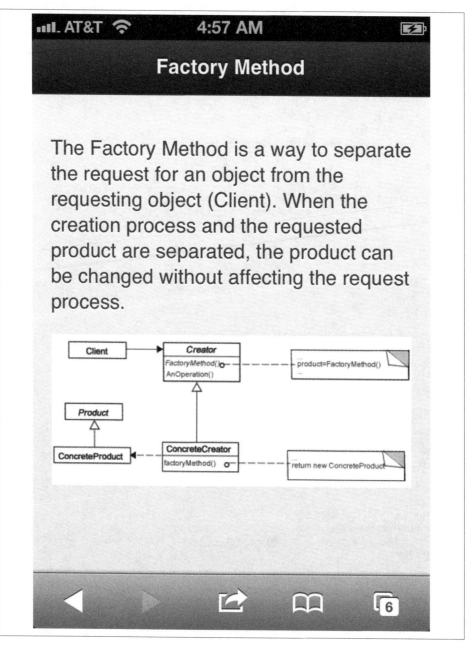

Figure 14-9. Page formatted using jQuery Mobile via PHP

Tablet observer. The `ConcreteObserverTablet` implementation of the Observer interface is similar to the `ConcreteObserverPhone` class except that it does not use jQuery Mobile. It has its own CSS with a two-column format:

```php
<?php
//ConcreteObserverTablet.php
class ConcreteObserverTablet implements Observer
{
    private $currentState=array();
    private $dpHeader;
    private $bodytext;
    private $imageURL;

    public function update(Subject $subject)
    {
        $this->currentState=$subject->getState();
        $this->dpHeader=$this->currentState[0];
        $this->bodytext=$this->currentState[1];
        $this->imageURL=$this->currentState[2];
        $this->doTablet();
    }

    private function doTablet()
    {
//Heredoc syntax
$showPage = <<<TABLET
    <!DOCTYPE html>
    <html>
        <head>
            <meta charset="UTF-8">
            <link rel="stylesheet" type="text/css" href="tablet.css">
            <title>Tablet Page</title>
        </head>
    <body>
    <article>
        <header>
            <h1>$this->dpHeader</h1>
        </header>

        <section>
            <img src="tablet/$this->imageURL" alt="image urls" >
            <p>$this->bodytext</p>

        </section>
        </article>
    </body>
    </html>
//End of Heredoc text must not have margin
TABLET;
    echo $showPage;
    }
```

```
    }
?>
```

Figure 14-10 shows a page viewed in an iPad.

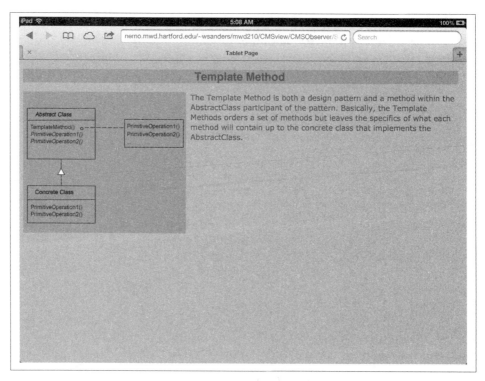

Figure 14-10. Tablet (horizontal) view of the Subject data

Both views share the same data but use a different CSS source.

Desktop view. At one time, the only view of a web page was from a desktop or laptop computer. However, it is now one view of many. The following code for the `Concre teObserverDT` is similar to the previous first two:

```php
<?php
//ConcreteObserverDT.php
class ConcreteObserverDT implements Observer
{
    private $currentState=array();
    private $dpHeader;
    private $bodytext;
    private $imageURL;

    public function update(Subject $subject)
    {
```

```php
            $this->currentState=$subject->getState();
            $this->dpHeader=$this->currentState[0];
            $this->bodytext=$this->currentState[1];
            $this->imageURL=$this->currentState[2];
            $this->doDesktop();
        }

        private function doDesktop()
        {
$showPage = <<<DESKTOP
    <!DOCTYPE html>
    <html>
        <head>
            <meta charset="UTF-8">
            <link rel="stylesheet" type="text/css" href="desktop.css">
            <title>Desk Top Page</title>
        </head>
    <body>
    <article>
        <header>
            <h1>$this->dpHeader</h1>
        </header>

        <section>
            <img src="desktop/$this->imageURL" alt="image urls" >
            <p>$this->bodytext</p>

        </section>
        </article>
    </body>
    </html>
DESKTOP;
        echo $showPage;
        }
}
?>
```

The desktop view is very similar to the tablet view, as can be seen in Figure 14-11.

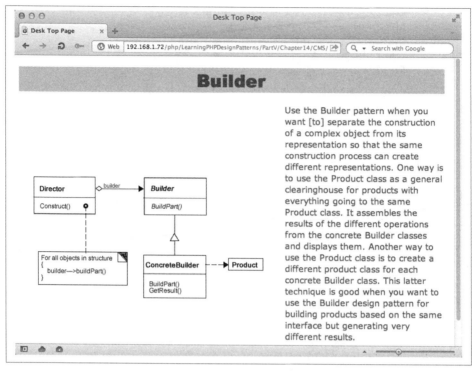

Figure 14-11. Desktop view provides ample padding for the image

The graphics for the three different device ranges are different as well. The desktop graphics are all configured in a 500 × 500 pixel frame; the table graphics all have a dark tan background; and the phone graphics are set for single-column viewing (reducing the need for added space, or gutters, between columns). However, all can be displayed from the single set of data provided by the Subject. Observers call different graphics with the same names stored in folders (directories) with uniquely named folders—*mobile*, *tablet*, and *desktop*.

Thinking OOP

One of the special features of the Observer design pattern in PHP lies in the built-in *Standard PHP Library* (SPL) interfaces designed specifically for the Observer pattern —SplSubject and SplObserver. In no small way, these library interfaces show unequivocal support for design patterns and OOP in the PHP community. At the same time, though, they do not insist that one must incorporate library supplied interfaces when developing an Observer pattern; you can use an abstract class instead of an interface for a Subject participant, as was done in the CMS example.

However, like a lot of the built-in features in PHP 5, many of them go unused or are used outside of an OOP framework or mindset. A lot of the interplay between HTML and PHP in the same file is often done outside of an OOP design, but as was seen using the heredoc operator and formatting, HTML can easily be incorporated into a PHP object.

An important lesson about the Observer pattern used in this last example is that it can be changed and improved. As noted, a Chain of Responsibility pattern could be used for the SniffClient to determine the type of device in use. OOP and design patterns were developed specifically for improving the development process. By thinking in terms of loosely coupled objects carrying out specific tasks and communicating with one another, the development process is much faster and easier to reuse. In the OOP learning process, design patterns are guides to how objects can be arranged to communicate with one another to solve different types of problems.

A further improvement to the CMS example involves adding buttons to the selection menus as new design patterns are added through the CMS. In the current form, it's easy to add new design patterns—a header, a graphic, and a write-up. Each new pattern does not generate a new radio button in the menu to make the selection. The menu has to be rewritten with each new addition. How would one go about adding modules to the current CMS to update the menus as well as the content web pages that the menu document links to? Think in terms of what objects to create and how to communicate with or alter existing objects. Loose coupling should make that task less onerous.

Intermediate and advanced programmers would not hesitate to use a loop structure in PHP to complete a programming task that requires recurrent operations. However, like a design pattern, a loop structure is nothing more than a general solution to a common programming task. Design patterns are the same thing: general solutions to programming tasks. Yes, they are more advanced, but so are more familiar structures such as a loop or a function in comparison to a strict sequence structure. Once you get used to OOP and design patterns, you may wonder how you programmed for so long without them, just as you see the inevitable necessity of loops to ease the task of programming.

Index

We'd like to hear your suggestions for improving our indexes. Send email to index@oreilly.com.

currency exchange example, 127–131

D

data entry
 CMS, 313
 data security and parameterized algorithms,
  256–261
data security, 251–269
 adding parameters to algorithm methods,
  254
 Client, 261
 concrete strategies, 263–269
 Context class, 262
 data entry modules, 256–261
 helper class, 251
 tables, 254
data types in code hinting, 45
date driven requests, 285
dating service example, 152–159
 Client, 158
 component interface, 153
 component methods, 155
 concrete components, 153
 concrete decorators, 155
decorations, HTML UI, 165
Decorator pattern, 141–165
 about, 141
 example, 143–149
  Client, 148
  component interface, 143
  concrete component, 145
  concrete decorators, 146
  interface, 144
 HTML UI, 159–165
  Client class passing HTML data, 163
  decorations, 165
  variable name to object instance, 164
 multiple components, 151–159
  concrete components, 152
  concrete decorators with multiple states
   and values, 152
  example, 152–159
 when to use, 142
 wrappers, 149
Design pattern, wrappers, 151
diagrams
 interaction diagrams, 73
 object diagrams, 72
 role of in OOP, 74

domain objects, defined, 41
dynamic object instantiation, 117
dynamic programming, 6

E

encapsulation, 29–34
 about, 29
 getters and setters, 33
 Prototype design pattern, 109
 visibility, 30–33
  private, 30
  protected, 31
  public, 32
error reporting, php.ini file, 11

F

Factory Method pattern, 79–98
 about, 79
 Chain of Responsibility pattern, 284–295
 class changes, 85–98
  adding new products and parameterized
   requests, 89
  changing the graphic product, 89
  changing the text product, 88
  Client and parameters, 94
  coordinating products, 87
  file diagram, 96
  graphic elements, 85
  helper classes, 94
  new factories, 91
  new products, 92
  one factory and multiple products, 90
  product changes, 96
 Client class, 61
 example, 81–85
 Template Method pattern, 178
 when to use, 80
family of algorithms, 242
file diagram, Factory Method pattern, 96
flow of control, 174
frameworks
 defined, 174
 versus design patterns, 57
fruit fly Prototype design pattern example, 104–
 108
functions, defined, 15

About the Author

Dr. William B. Sanders is a Professor of Multimedia Web Design and Development at the University of Hartford. He teaches courses in PHP, MySQL, C#, SQL, HTML5, CSS, and ActionScript 3.0, among other Internet languages. He co-authored *ActionScript 3.0 Design Patterns* (O'Reilly, 2007) and has been actively working with design patterns in PHP for several years. He has published 45 computer and computer-related books, written software ranging from Basic to assembly language to Flash Media Server, and he has served as a consultant and beta tester for different computer software companies including Macromedia and Adobe. He also is an Apple iOS devloper.

Colophon

The animal on the cover of *Learning PHP Design Patterns* is an Alaska plaice (*Pleuronectes quadrituberculatus*). The Alaska plaice is a saltwater fish that lives primarily in the Pacific Ocean, from the Gulf of Alaska in the east to the Chukchi Sea in the north and the Sea of Japan in the west. The plaice can be found up to 600 meters deep, down on the bottom of the continental shelf. The plaice is a flatfish, meaning it has an eyed side and a blind side, which faces the ocean floor. These particular flatfish can grow up to 24 inches long with five to seven small bony cones on its eyed side.

The plaice can live up to 30 years, thanks in part to the lack of interest from commercial fisheries. The majority of Alaska plaice that are harvested are a byproduct of commercial fisheries targeting other groundfish, such as yellowfin sole.

The cover image is from *Johnson's Natural History*. The cover font is Adobe ITC Garamond. The text font is Adobe Minion Pro; the heading font is Adobe Myriad Condensed; and the code font is Dalton Maag's Ubuntu Mono.

Have it your way.

O'Reilly eBooks

- Lifetime access to the book when you buy through oreilly.com

- Provided in up to four DRM-free file formats, for use on the devices of your choice: PDF, .epub, Kindle-compatible .mobi, and Android .apk

- Fully searchable, with copy-and-paste and print functionality

- Alerts when files are updated with corrections and additions

oreilly.com/ebooks/

Safari Books Online

- Access the contents and quickly search over 7000 books on technology, business, and certification guides

- Learn from expert video tutorials, and explore thousands of hours of video on technology and design topics

- Download whole books or chapters in PDF format, at no extra cost, to print or read on the go

- Get early access to books as they're being written

- Interact directly with authors of upcoming books

- Save up to 35% on O'Reilly print books

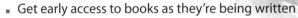

See the complete Safari Library at safari.oreilly.com

O'REILLY®

Spreading the knowledge of innovators.

oreilly.com

©2011 O'Reilly Media, Inc. O'Reilly logo is a registered trademark of O'Reilly Media, Inc. 00000